In this highly accessible and most welcome addition to the literature on public order policing, Michael Smith employs tremendous academic rigour and dexterity in producing a work of undoubted theoretical and practical significance. His case study approach to explaining and "championing" a fundamentally tolerant, inclusive and democratic "liaison" approach to protest policing is infused with a surefootedness and credibility becoming of a serving officer. What emerges in these pages is a truly enlightened and compelling blueprint for police tactics and strategy.

David Waddington, Emeritus Professor, Sheffield Hallam University

Michael Smith has produced an invaluable text which shows how dialogical forms of policing can be effectively used in the management – and facilitation – of protests. This book, based upon extensive fieldwork and interview material, will enormously advance understandings of the role of police liaison officer and will be invaluable for researchers, students and practitioners alike.

Peter Millward, Professor of Contemporary Sociology, Liverpool John Moores University

Dialogue is one of the most crucial elements of a healthy and human rights-respecting democracy. And so is security of that democracy through policing. If one takes over the other, democracy fades away. In his book Michael Smith gives a critical justice theoretical appreciation of dialogical forms of policing and presents a well-balanced empirical study of protest policing and the premises and promises of "dialogical policing." Smith includes highly relevant practical recommendations to raise awareness by those involved in protesting and policing of one another, from which dialogue and policing both can benefit.

Yarin Eski, Assistant Professor in Public Administration, Vrije Universiteit Amsterdam

Protest Policing and Human Rights

This book examines protest policing and the toolbox of options available to police commanders in response. The right to peacefully protest is intrinsic to democracy and embedded in British history and tradition. The police are responsible for managing public order and facilitating peaceful protest and this has not been without criticism. On occasions, the police have found themselves in opposition to protest groups and there have been incidents of disorder as a result. In response, the development of Police Liaison Teams in the UK has presented the police with a gateway for dialogue between themselves and those involved in protest.

Drawing on two contrasting case studies, the policing of the badger cull in South West England and an English Defence League (EDL) march in Liverpool, this book explores the experiences of police commanders, police liaison officers, protesters, counterdemonstrators, members of local businesses and other interested parties. It explores how a dialogical approach with all those engaged in or affected by a protest has assisted the police in balancing human rights and reducing conflict for all.

An accessible and compelling read, this book will appeal to students, scholars and practitioners of policing, politics, criminology, sociology, human rights and all those interested in how protests are policed.

Michael Smith is a police officer in Merseyside Police, UK.

Routledge Frontiers of Criminal Justice

Penal Responses to Serious Offending by Children
Principles, Practice and Global Perspectives
Nessa Lynch, Yannick van den Brink and Louise Forde

A Restorative Approach to Family Violence
Feminist Kin-Making
Joan Pennell

Interviewing of Suspects with Mental Health Conditions and Disorders in England and Wales
A Paradigm Shift
Laura Farrugia

Convictions Without Truth
The Incompatibility of Science and Law
Robert Schehr

The Evolving Protection of Prisoners' Rights in Europe
Gaëtan Cliquennois

Protest Policing and Human Rights
A Dialogical Approach
Michael Smith

The Politics of Prison Crowding
A Critical Analysis of the Italian Prison System
Simone Santorso

Disassembling Police Culture
Mike Rowe

For more information about this series, please visit: www.routledge.com/Routledge-Frontiers-of-Criminal-Justice/book-series/RFCJ

Protest Policing and Human Rights

A Dialogical Approach

Michael Smith

LONDON AND NEW YORK

Designed cover image: Cameron Smith

First published 2023
by Routledge
4 Park Square, Milton Park, Abingdon, Oxon OX14 4RN

and by Routledge
605 Third Avenue, New York, NY 10158

Routledge is an imprint of the Taylor & Francis Group, an informa business

© 2023 Michael Smith

The right of Michael Smith to be identified as author of this work has been asserted in accordance with sections 77 and 78 of the Copyright, Designs and Patents Act 1988.

All rights reserved. No part of this book may be reprinted or reproduced or utilised in any form or by any electronic, mechanical, or other means, now known or hereafter invented, including photocopying and recording, or in any information storage or retrieval system, without permission in writing from the publishers.

Trademark notice: Product or corporate names may be trademarks or registered trademarks, and are used only for identification and explanation without intent to infringe.

British Library Cataloguing-in-Publication Data
A catalogue record for this book is available from the British Library

Library of Congress Cataloging-in-Publication Data
Names: Smith, Michael, author.
Title: Protest policing and human rights: a dialogical approach/Michael Smith.
Description: Milton Park, Abingdon, Oxon; New York, NY: Routledge, 2023. |
Includes bibliographical references and index. |
Identifiers: LCCN 2022034335 | ISBN 9780367749675 (hardback) | ISBN 9780367749682 (paperback) | ISBN 9781003160533 (ebook)
Subjects: LCSH: Police administration–England. | Crowd control–England. | Protest movements–England. | Demonstrations–England. | Police-community relations–England. | Social control–England.
Classification: LCC HV8196.A3 S65 2023 | DDC 363.20941–dc23/eng/20220803
LC record available at https://lccn.loc.gov/2022034335

ISBN: 978-0-367-74967-5 (hbk)
ISBN: 978-0-367-74968-2 (pbk)
ISBN: 978-1-003-16053-3 (ebk)

DOI: 10.4324/9781003160533

Typeset in Bembo
by Deanta Global Publishing Services, Chennai, India

To Heidi, Callum, Dillon and Ethan.

Contents

List of figures		x
Acknowledgements		xi
1	Introduction to a dialogical approach	1
2	Policing, protest and balancing human rights	16
3	A theoretical framework for a dialogical approach	50
4	Conducting research: Insider or outsider?	74
5	Case study 1: The badger cull	101
6	Case study 2: The EDL march	154
7	The contribution and value of a dialogical approach	210
8	Conclusion and recommendations	240
	Index	255

Figures

5.1　The policing of the badger cull dialogical wheel　122
5.2　Bronze PLT command structure for the policing of the badger cull　134
6.1　The policing of the EDL march dialogical wheel　180
6.2　Bronze PLT command structure for the policing of the EDL march　187
8.1　The Dialogical Wheel template　246

Acknowledgements

Many thanks to ***Somerset Against the Badger Cull*** who have given permission for their photographs to be used throughout the book for editorial purposes only.

Chapter 1

Introduction to a dialogical approach

Introduction

Nobel Peace Prize Winner, Elie Wiesel, in his Nobel lecture, declared that "there may be times when we are powerless to prevent injustice, but there must never be a time when we fail to protest" (Wiesel, 1986). This book explores the right to protest, the policing of protest events and the contribution that a police dialogical approach has made to the balancing of competing human rights at protest events in the UK.

Everyone has the right to freedom of thought, expression and peaceful assembly in the UK, and these rights are protected in legislation by the Human Rights Act 1998. However, the challenge for the police has been to balance these rights of peaceful protest with the rights of those who want to enjoy privacy and their possessions. This role of arbitrator includes maintaining the Queen's Peace and upholding order through implementing public order legislation. On occasions, the policing of protest has witnessed outbreaks of disorder, where protesters[1] and police officers have come into conflict. UK history provides notable examples of such incidents, including the G20 London summit protests of April 2009 and a subsequent call for "a national overhaul of the policing of protests" (Lewis, Laville and Walker, 2009). Her Majesty's Inspectorate of Constabulary (HMIC), responsible for independently assessing police forces and policing "in the public interest" (HMIC, 2017) examined the police response to protests that ensued at the G20 London summit. HMIC concluded (2009b: 73) that "the police have been deficient in communicating with protesters" and recommended (2009b: 90) that "the police should seek to inform themselves about the culture and general conduct of particular protest crowds."

In response, strategies were developed to enable engagement and communication with protest groups, pre, during and post events (National Policing Improvement Agency, 2010). A key tactical option emerged with the development of dialogue officers as a tactical option, deployed as Police Liaison Teams (PLT) at protest events, identifiable by the wearing of distinctive light blue tabards and utilised to provide a "link between the police, protest organisers and protesters by focusing on negotiation, mediation, initiation, communication

DOI: 10.4324/9781003160533-1

and sensing" (College of Policing, 2018). Gorringe, Stott and Rosie (2012) and Waddington (2013) advocated the use of PLT as an instrumental police option in the avoidance of unnecessary use of force in moments of tension. Some critics have opposed the role since their first deployments, with claims that PLT are "suspiciously friendly" and in fact "spies in blue bibs" (NetPol, 2014).

This book will therefore examine the dialogical approach employed by the police in liaising with those engaged in protest prior to and during two contrasting events; protests against the badger cull in South West England in 2016 and an English Defence League march in Liverpool in 2017. Through the examination of data gathered from 48 semi-structured interviews conducted across both case studies, the book will consider how a dialogical approach was extended to engage all those affected by the protest events. Further, this book will examine the contribution that this dialogical approach made to the balancing of the human rights of all those whom the events impacted upon.

The book will examine the concept of peaceful *protest* and consider a *dialogical* approach to policing them. Both terms will be explored within the following chapters. However, for clarity at the outset within this book; the term *protest* will refer to all forms of public expression (Liberty, 2016), whether in the form of a march, static demonstration, press conference, public or private meeting, counterdemonstration or sit-in; and *dialogical* will include all the terms identified to describe dialogue undertaken between the police and interested parties, such as liaison, negotiation, communication and engagement (for example, Waddington, 2013; Tyler and Blader, 2003; Stott, West and Radburn, 2018).

A dialogical approach to policing protest events using designated liaison officers in the UK can be traced back to origins in Sweden (Stott, 2009; Waddington, 2013). This chapter will by way of introduction provide a historical examination of the development of PLT as a tactical option in the UK through documentary research, mapping historical origins in Sweden (Holgersson, 2010) and the introduction of a dialogical approach to the policing of protest events in the UK (HMIC, 2009a). The chapter will conclude by outlining the scope and framework for the research conducted into a dialogical approach to protest policing.

Dialogue policing in Sweden

The US-EU Summit of leaders of the United States and European Union took place in June 2001 in Gothenburg, Sweden. The summit attracted protests and demonstrations, including demonstrations against then US President George W. Bush, against Swedish membership in the European Union, and a demonstration "for another Europe" (Wahlström, 2011). Although most demonstrations passed peacefully and without incident, isolated incidents of disorder were reported on the eve of the summit, with reports of over 200 arrested as environmentalists and anti-globalisation activists "clash with Swedish riot police" (Webb, 2001).

As the US and European leaders held their summit, confrontations continued between demonstrators and the police, which resulted in two days of riots with numerous demonstrators and police officers injured, extensive damage caused and reports that one demonstrator had been shot. The actions of those engaged in violence were condemned, and British Prime Minister Tony Blair described it an "outrage" that peaceful demonstrations had turned into "thuggery" (Black and White, 2001). However, there were also allegations that the police had overreacted during the events, and "complaints of police heavy-handedness from the organisers of protests that were supposed to be peaceful" (Black and White, 2001). The initial support the police had received from the public and the media for their heroic restoration of order gave way to critical scrutiny of their actions (Wahlström, 2011), both during the summit and in their planning prior to the policing of the events.

Wahlström (2011) noted that there was a significant criticism of the Swedish police in that they failed to differentiate between the separate groups within the body of demonstrators and police each group proportionately. Hedkvist (2004: 5) observed that the police "tried to control the political resistance expressed by the many organizations, political parties and grassroots networks in the demonstrations." Instead of identifying individual groups within the whole protest, demonstrators were policed as a single group and all participants were prevented from marching, threatened with arrest and contained by the police (Dissent!, 2001). When the demonstrators responded with pressure on the police cordon, "the police made a quite blunt attack with horses and dogs that triggered a riot on the main avenue in Gothenburg" (Wahlström, 211: 23).

At the behest of the Swedish government, the Gothenburg Committee was formed to investigate the policing of the events of June 2001, and their report criticised the preparation, tactics and organisation of the policing of demonstrations and highlighted "serious deficiencies in crowd management training for the police as well as deficiencies in terms of know-how" (Holgersson, 2010: 15). The Gothenburg Committee highlighted a lack of police understanding and application of crowd psychology theories, such as Elaborated Social Identity Model (for example, Reicher, 1996) and the effects of police action on a group of demonstrators. Holgersson explained:

> If the police carry out a collective intervention against demonstrators, it creates an 'us versus them' situation which may lead to that a group which started out as heterogeneous will unite through the perception of the police as an assailant. This leads to a considerable risk that the conflict may escalate and that the police may be obliged to resort to increasingly robust methods. This may have the effect of increasing group solidarity still further in the group.
>
> (Holgersson, 2010: 50)

The Gothenburg Committee observed that the dialogue between the police and demonstration leaders was clearly deficient and concluded that the issues that arose would appear to be because of a "lack of communication with demonstrators on the part of the police" (Betänkande av Göteborgskommittén, 2002: 3). Wahlström (2011) noted that dialogue had only been implemented by the police at a late stage in the planning for protest. Adang (2011: 71) described the events that occurred in Gothenburg as "the dialogue that failed." Dialogue policing was at this time in its infancy and had not yet been established as a police tactic in Sweden, and Adang observed that the dialogue officers that were deployed established only a limited trust with demonstration group leaders.

The Committee therefore recommended that the police should develop dialogue as a working method to ensure "dialogue between the Swedish Police, political organisations and other opinion-shaping groups prior to major events" (Betänkande av Göteborgskommittén, 2002: 5) to break down mutual suspicion. The Committee recommended selecting specific police officers to be assigned to conduct dialogue, and that these officers should be suited to the task and adequately trained to build communication with protest groups. Ottina (2011) observed that this demonstrated a willingness by the Swedish government to acknowledge a role for protesters that highlighted their implicit values and recognised their power. In response, the Swedish National Police Board implemented a national model, which saw the implementation of a specific role in the Special Police Tactics Unit of "dialogue officer" with a Sweden-wide policing remit (Menzies, 2013). Holgersson (2010: 6) noted that the officers provided "a link between the police command and organizers of demonstrations and manifestations before, during and after an event." Holgersson further observed that the dialogue officers afforded police commanders a better understanding of different groups within the crowds, their cultural norms and legitimate intentions, and equipped the police to more readily facilitate peaceful protests, communicate intentions and proportionately intervene when crimes were committed.

Since its inception, the role of dialogue officer has become integral to the policing of protest in Sweden, and research has been conducted into the effectiveness of these designated and trained officers (for example, Holgersson, 2010; Wahlström, 2011; Baker, 2014). Holgersson (2010: 26) provided examples of incidents where dialogue officers had contributed to facilitating communication between commanders and demonstrators in Sweden and concluded that "it was possible to avert and minimise confrontations through the work of the dialogue police officers." In the context of protest policing in Sweden, a dialogical approach can therefore be viewed as one where two-way communication is encouraged between police and protesters, with an emphasis on relationship building to promote trust.

The development of police liaison in the UK

The Group of Twenty (G20), founded in 1999 and comprising 19 countries plus the European Union, is an international forum concerned with cooperation on financial and economic issues. A G20 leaders' summit has been held annually since the inaugural Washington summit in 2008. The second summit took place on 2 April 2009 in London, hosted by British Prime Minster Gordon Brown, and saw the attendance of over 20 heads of state to the city (G20, 2017). The summit also attracted widespread protests, many gatherings which were initially planned and organised online. Media reports over a week prior to the summit identified a wide range of groups who intended to demonstrate. These included marches from four London underground stations organised by G20 Meltdown; a protest by the London Anarchists; a Stop the War Coalition anti-war campaign focusing on Barack Obama's first presidential visit to Britain, a climate camp; and a march supported by the Trades Union Congress (Weaver, 2009).

On the eve of the summit, ten separate protests and marches took place at seven London sites. Most passed off peacefully, however violent confrontations were witnessed between protesters and the police at the Bank of England and at Bishopsgate. Outbreaks of serious violence included the storming of a London office of the Royal Bank of Scotland, missiles being launched by demonstrators and an attack on a branch of the HSBC bank. BBC News reported 63 arrests, police officers and protesters injured, the death of a man who had collapsed (later identified as Ian Tomlinson) and that mounted police and "riot officers using shields" had pushed demonstrators back (Brown, 2009). The police were reported to have used "containment" and then "controlled dispersal" to address the situation (Brown, 2009).

The Metropolitan Police Service (MPS) was given a limited time to plan the police operation to deliver a safe and secure environment for the G20 summit, and the tight timescale provided a challenge for such a large operation with so many world leaders in attendance (HMIC, 2009a). HMIC (2009a) reported that the MPS planned and responded effectively regarding security, notified protests and disorder. The policing of the protest was remarkably successful and, aside from a few high-profile incidents, passed without drama (Home Affairs Committee, 2009). However, the police management of protests in the City of London was the subject of criticism which assessed that those incidents that did occur had the potential to "seriously damage the public's faith in the police" (Home Affairs Committee, 2009: 2). Adang (2011) observed that the police were criticised for failures in communication and noted that there had been little engagement between the police and the various groups who wished to protest prior to the event. Adang observed that although a legal team from the climate camp had met with the police, this had occurred the day before the camp and the team were reluctant to provide the police with details of their intentions or numbers attending the protest event.

The policing of protest in the UK was at that time already under scrutiny. The Joint Committee on Human Rights, a cross parliamentary committee appointed by the House of Lords and the House of Commons to consider matters relating to human rights in the UK (UK Parliament, 2022b), had issued a call for evidence in April 2008, and published their final report on 23 March 2009, just over a week before the summit. The report concluded;

> We have found no systematic human rights abuses in the policing of protest but we have some concerns which can be addressed by legal and operational changes. Making these changes would further protect the rights of people who wish to protest in the UK.
> (Joint Committee on Human Rights, 2009: 5)

The report emphasised a need to include human rights inputs in police training and advocated an approach to protest policing of "no surprises" for the police, for protesters and for those the target of the protest. The report stated that the police should foster dialogue with protest groups and that protest groups "should also, where possible, engage with the police at an early stage in their planning, in order to facilitate peaceful protest" (Joint Committee on Human Rights, 2009: 5).

Subsequently, the House of Commons Home Affairs Committee, a cross party committee largely tasked with examining the policies and work of the Home Office and associated public bodies (UK Parliament, 2022a), reported on the policing of the G20. Their report, published in June 2009, provided recommendations for the future policing of protest events. The Committee accused police commanders of using language that served "to create a 'them and us' attitude" (Home Affairs Committee, 2009: 11) in relation to protest groups prior to the G20. The Committee concluded that the police should train specific officers in communicating with protester groups. The Committee stated that large protests should contain at least one officer trained and able to communicate with the groups, which would enable communications with the protesters "to take place on a consistent, codified basis, and increase the opportunities for large groups of protesters to be policed by consent" (Home Affairs Committee, 2009: 12). In response, at the request of the MPS Commissioner Sir Paul Stephenson, HMIC conducted a review of the policing methods used on the day and published Adapting to Protest in July 2009 (HMIC, 2009a). The report addressed fundamental issues in the police's approach to protests;

> During the review it has become clear that a number of police officers / police commanders have approached peaceful protest in terms of "is the protest lawful / unlawful?" A better approach is to consider how to facilitate the peaceful protest but then to look at the implications.
> (HMIC, 2009a: 6)

HMIC concluded that the current national training manuals were severely lacking in the police response to the whole range of protest activity, specifically on the containment and release of peaceful protesters. The report stated that a key part of police training must be "the ability to differentiate between 'disorderly' and 'peaceful' protesters" (HMIC, 2009a: 59) to assist decision-making both for individual officers' use of force, and the collective use of force as deployed by a commander during an event.

At the same time as publishing their first report, HMIC commissioned Dr Clifford Stott to provide an overview of literature on crowd psychology which impacts on the management of groups in a public order setting (HMIC, 2009b). Stott (2009) proposed a reform of public order training to reflect modern theories of crowd psychology based on the Elaborated Social Identity Model of crowd behaviour (ESIM). Stott argued that ESIM was the leading theory for understanding crowd behaviour and replaced classic theory (for example, Le Bon, 1895), which was still perceived as the theoretical basis formulating police commanders' rationale in the twenty-first century (Hoggett and Stott, 2010). Stott recommended (2009: 1) an increase in the police's "capability for 'dialogue' and communication with crowds and formally recognise these as primary tactical options for public order policing." Stott also advocated the Swedish police approach to dialogue policing and the positive results documented in reducing disorder.

HMIC published a second report in November 2009, posing the question (2009b: 5) "How best should the police as a service adapt to the modern day demands of public order policing whilst retaining the core values of the British model of policing?" HMIC advocated a new approach to policing crowds, stating (2009b: 86) that there was "considerable evidence of the practical benefits of a policing approach based upon principles of the Elaborated Social Identity Model." HMIC also identified police deficiency in engaging with protesters and recommended that the police should adopt a no surprises approach in their communication with protesters and consider implementing a dialogical model like that adopted by the Swedish police. Further, HMIC identified a "confusion" regarding the legal framework for protest policing and provided an immediate recommendation that the police should ensure that public order training "consistently incorporates relevant human rights principles and standards" (2009b: 63). HMIC observed that such training should not simply provide understanding of the Articles engaged at a protest event but should also educate commanders in the decision-making process required in balancing the rights of opposing groups.

The HMIC reports prompted a significant change in police public order training throughout the UK. Public order training was at that time governed in the UK by the National Policing Improvement Agency (NPIA), a non-departmental public body established to support police by providing expertise in such areas as information technology, information sharing and recruitment (Government UK, 2022). In response to HMIC recommendations, a three-day development course was written by the NPIA to provide an update for operationally competent police commanders. The training was bespoke for public order silver (tactical) and bronze (operational) commanders, ensuring that public order command nationally reflected "the uniquely British Model of Policing that places high value on tolerant policing and policing by consent: the strategic driver" (NPIA, 2010: 3). The course was mandated for all existing commanders and addressed areas such as crowd psychology, human rights and use of force. The course also required commanders to examine several different communication models advocated by HMIC in liaising with protest groups, and to consider applying such approaches in their commanding of protest pre, during and post protest events. Some of the approaches identified were based on experiences encountered from outside England and Wales (for example, in Sweden and Northern Ireland). Others found their origins within other areas of policing, such as the role of Family Liaison Officer (NPIA, 2010), a role where the officer interacted with the family during a major investigation, such as a murder enquiry, and provided close liaison with the police Senior Investigating Officer "to ensure families are treated appropriately, professionally and with respect for their needs" (NPIA, 2008).

The NPIA subsequently adapted the communication methods and initiated the development of the role of the dialogue officer, to be utilised in protest events in the UK and to fulfil the role of protest group liaison. The development saw the NPIA act as advisors to police commanders during the deployment of officers in light blue tabards as liaison officers at Operation Obelisk, the Liberal Democrat conference in Sheffield, in 2011 (Bowen, 2015). Although liaison officers in light blue tabards had been deployed at earlier events, such as with protest groups who had demonstrated at the Liberal Democrat conference in Liverpool in 2010 (Armitt, 2015), the role of the NPIA in Sheffield allowed consideration of the tactic at a national level. This prompted the Association of Chief Police Officers (ACPO) Tactical Tasking and Co-ordination Group (TTCG) to commission the NPIA to produce a bespoke course to train officers "who will be deployed as Protestor Liaison Officers (PLO) at public order or public safety events" (NPIA, 2012: 3).

The first PLO course was written by the NPIA under the direction of Chris Bowen, with advice from Stott regarding academic considerations and a pilot course was delivered at NPIA Bramshill in 2012 (Bowen, 2015). Further courses were delivered pre summer 2012 to train PLO in preparation for the policing of the Liberal Democrat party conference in Sussex, the Conservative party conference in Birmingham and the Diamond Jubilee and Olympics in London. ACPO TTCG also agreed that the coloured tabard to denote PLO officers would be light blue in colour (Bowen, 2015).

NPIA was dissolved in 2013, and the function of overseeing the National Police Public Order Training Curriculum lay with its successor, the College of Policing, launched in February 2013 as "the professional body for everyone who works for the police service in England and Wales" (College of Policing,

2015a). Following feedback, the College updated the training, reflecting the advantages that PLT had already brought to the policing of public order and public safety events (Roadnight, 2015). PLO were also renamed Police Liaison Teams (College of Policing, 2013). Roadnight (2015) explained that the change from "Protestor" to "Police" was made firstly to reflect the observation that many people traditionally labelled "protestors" did not favour that nomenclature. Secondly, it was recognised that on some occasions PLT could, and were, being deployed to events outside of protest, for example at raves and football matches. The change to "Team" was made to reflect the fact that officers should not deploy individually and were expected to work within a defined team structure. In this regard, it followed two other specialist tactical options of Forward Intelligence Teams and Evidence Gathering Teams (Roadnight, 2015). Seven police forces were licensed by the College of Policing to deliver the new PLT course (Blowe, 2013a).

In October 2013, PLT were included as a tactical option for public order commanders in the Public Order Section of Authorised Professional Practice, an open access web portal that provides "the official source of professional practice on policing" (College of Policing, 2016a). PLT are defined as police officers who provide a "link between the police, protest organisers and protesters by focusing on negotiation, mediation, initiation, communication and sensing" (College of Policing, 2018). Since their first deployments, the training and use of PLT at protest events has grown across the UK, and they have been "embedded as the primary tactic" for many in protest policing (Stott et al., 2015). PLT have been deployed at significant events such as the Barton Moss environmental protest in Greater Manchester (Lloyd, 2014), anti-fracking protests in Balcombe, West Sussex (Popham, 2013) and the policing of the NATO conference in South Wales (Deans, 2014). Since the research described in this book was completed, PLT have continued to be deployed in protest settings in the UK, for example at the Sarah Everard vigil on Clapham Common in March 2021 (HMICFRS, 2021), protests at the G7 in Cornwall (Stephens, 2021) and at the COP26 United Nations Climate Change Conference in Scotland (Police Scotland, 2021).

Although there has been evidence of the positive effect the use of PLT has had on facilitating peaceful protest (for example, Stott, Scothern and Gorringe, 2013), there has equally been criticism and opposition to PLT, particularly regarding their perceived role in the gathering of intelligence (NetPol, 2015). Those opposed have described PLT as being "suspiciously friendly in their pale blue bibs" (Blowe, 2013b), claimed that PLT were "not just there to make friends" but "play a 'pivotal role' in intelligence gathering" (Ecologist, 2014) or abused their role and intimidated protesters (Parkinson and Evans, 2012). In a report into the policing of the Barton Moss environmental protest, Lloyd (2014: 16) suggested that some protesters thought PLT "were there to gather intelligence rather than build rapport." NetPol, "the Network for Police monitoring" wrote several articles on their forum warning protesters to avoid PLT and suggested that their intentions were solely to seek intelligence (NetPol, 2015). The forum claimed that PLT were a rebranding of Forward Intelligence Teams (FIT). The College of Policing (2016b) stated that the police tactic of FIT was used in establishing "dialogue with such individuals or groups, thereby gathering information / intelligence" providing police commanders with "fast-time updates." However, NetPol strongly opposed the tactic "as we do not consider that protest should be considered criminal" (NetPol, 2017) and the use of FIT received much criticism on a website dedicated to contesting the validity of the tactic, Fitwatch, until the site was closed in 2010 (Apple, 2010). The College of Policing (2015b) defined police information as "all information obtained, recorded or processed for a policing purpose," and defined intelligence as "information which has been subject to a process of evaluation." The role of PLT as intelligence or information gatherers therefore would appear to be open to conjecture.

Despite the anecdotal evidence, there has been scant research into the use of PLT. A small cannon of research (Gorringe, Stott and Rosie, 2012; Waddington, 2013; Stott, Scothern and Gorringe, 2013) was undertaken prior to the inclusion of PLT as a national tactical option (College of Policing, 2013). Since the inclusion, PLT research has been limited to advocating a liaison-based approach to the policing of football (Hoggett and West, 2018; Stott, West and Radburn, 2018), a critique of the policing of anti-fracking demonstrations in Greater Manchester (Jackson, Gilmore and Monk, 2019) and the examination of police liaison at the Notting Hill Carnival (Kilgallon, 2020). In contrast to the use of dialogue officers in Sweden with a country-wide remit enabling a consistent approach and continual dialogue (Holgersson, 2010), the deployment of PLT in the UK remains on a local police force basis (Smith, 2015; College of Policing, 2018) with a gap in research into a UK-centric approach. Furthermore, existing research solely examines a dialogical approach between police and protesters (for example, Gorringe, Stott and Rosie, 2012; Waddington, 2013) football supporters (for example, Hoggett and West, 2018) and event organisers (Kilgallon, 2020). No research to date has examined the role that the police must undertake in balancing competing human rights of all those engaged in an event, including those owning and working businesses affected by protest events and people in the local community within which protests occur who wish to go about their daily affairs unaffected by the protests.

It is evident that there have been differences in approaches to engaging in dialogue with protesters and utilising liaison officers in different countries and within the UK, although such differences are nuanced (Smith, 2015). This book, therefore, provides further research into the approaches and examines a "dialogical" approach to policing protest events. The next chapter will evidence that numerous terms, such as liaison, negotiation, communication and dialogue are used, often interchangeably, to describe the interaction and will argue that significance is placed less on the term used and more on the extent into which dialogue is entered by participants (College of Policing, 2016a; Gilmore, Jackson and Monk, 2016). However, for clarity at the outset, recognising that the meaning of dialogue is not always consistent, this book will utilise "dialogical" to encompass all the terms identified and will focus less on the words used and more on the level of interaction.

A dialogical approach to protest policing

The research in this book will therefore seek to contribute to scant existing research by examining the liaison between PLT and protesters at two contrasting events and considering the contribution that such a dialogical approach has made to the policing of the events. Moreover, the research in this book will further extend research by examining a dialogical approach between the police and all interested parties engaged in the event. The research will argue that there is value for all those affected by a protest event to engage in dialogue with the police pre, during and post protest events; protesters and those intent on holding marches and processions; counterdemonstrators; the business the subject of or affected by the protest; other agencies and authorities; and the public within which the protest occurs. Furthermore, this study will make a unique contribution by examining the role of the police as arbiter in balancing competing human rights and will argue that the employing of a dialogical approach between the police and all interested parties assists in balancing competing human rights and promoting a procedurally fair approach to the policing of protest events.

To fill the lacuna identified, this book is divided into eight chapters. Chapter 2 will provide an analysis of the body of existing research documenting protest and police approaches, examining the legislative framework in which the police must operate, and Chapter 3 will examine a theoretical framework and a dialogical approach to policing protests. These chapters will allow an evaluation of the relevant literature and an exploration of the gap that this research will seek to fill. Chapter 4 will provide a self-ethnographical insight into the author's journey as both researcher and serving police officer and will explore the author's role as insider and outsider in conducting interviews and gathering empirical data. Chapters 5 and 6 will present key findings that emerged during the research conducted. Chapter 5 will detail findings from the first case study examining the policing of the badger cull in South West England in 2016, identifying interested parties and considering the dialogical approach employed. Chapter 6 will detail the second case study findings with an examination of the policing of an English Defence League (EDL) march in Liverpool in 2017 and will similarly consider dialogue engaged with interested parties pre, during and post the march. Chapter 7 will provide a discussion of key themes across both case studies and will evaluate the data to consider the contribution made by a dialogical approach to policing protest and balancing human rights. Finally, Chapter 8 will draw conclusions from the research conducted which will assist in informing local and national police policy and present considerations for all those engaged in or affected by the policing of future protest events. This chapter will present the *Dialogical Wheel* template as a generic model derived from the research which can be adapted and applied to any protest event.

Note

1 The use of the word "protester" was open to conjecture during the research conducted and is further discussed in later chapters. Where it appears in this research, the term "protester" is used as a collective noun to encompass all the individuals and groups identified in this research who were opposing, marching or demonstrating. It is recognised that participants in this research disassociated themselves from being labelled as such, preferring terms such as "protector," "hunt sab," "activist" or "demonstrator."

References

Adang, O. (2011) *Managing collective violence around public events: An international comparison.* Polite and Wetenschap. Amsterdam: Reed Business.

Apple, E. (2010) They've closed down the Fitwatch site, but we'll carry on resisting. *The Guardian* [online], 16 November 2010. Available at: http://www.theguardian.com/commentisfree

Armitt, C. (2015) *Interview by author.* Liverpool. 24 March 2015.

Baker, D. (2014) Police and protester dialog: Safeguarding the peace or ritualistic sham? *International Journal of Comparative and Applied Criminal Justice,* 38(1), 83–104.

Betänkande av Göteborgkommittén (2002) *Göteborg 2001: Summary in English* [pdf] Justitiedepartementet Betänkande av Göteborgkommittén. Available at: http://www.regeringen.se/contentassets

Black, I. and White M. (2001) Sweden asks: Who set off riots? 'Thuggery' of protests against EU-US talks condemned. *The Guardian* [online], 16 June 2001 Available at: http://www.theguardian.com/world/2001/jun/16/

Blowe, K. (2013a) *Guidance on Police Liaison Officers* [online] Available at: https://www.whatdotheyknow.com/request/guidance_on_police_liaison_offic

Blowe, K. (2013b) *Spies in Blue Bibs* [online] Available at: http://www.blowe.org.uk/2013/10/spies-in-blue-bibs.html

Bowen, C. (2015) *PLO and PLT in NPIA* [email] 14 June 2015. Message to author from christopher. bowen@westyorkshire.pnn.police.uk

Brown, B. (2009) Police clash with G20 protestors. *BBC News* [online] 1 April 2009. Available at: http://news.bbc.co.uk/1/hi/in_depth/business

College of Policing (2016a) *Authorised Professional Practice* [online] Available at: https://www.app.college.police.uk/

College of Policing (2015a) *College of Policing: About us* [online] Available at: http://www.college.police.uk/About/Pages/

College of Policing (2016b) *Forward intelligence team* [online] Available at: https://www.app.college.police.uk/app-content/public-order/planning-and-deployment/tactical-options/#forward-intelligence-team

College of Policing (2015b) *Information management* [online] Available at: https://www.app.college.police.uk/app-content/information-management

College of Policing (2013) *National Police Public Order Training Curriculum: Police Liaison Team: Trainers Guide*. Wyboston, Bedfordshire: College of Policing.

College of Policing (2018) *Police liaison teams* [online] Available at: https://www.app.college.police.uk/app-content/public-order/planning-and-deployment/

Deans, D. (2014) Nato Summit 2014: Police officers and armed patrols swarm into Cardiff city centre 31 August 2014. *Wales Online* [online], 31 August 2014 Available at: http://www.walesonline.co.uk/news/wales-news/nato-summit-2014-police-officers

Dissent! (2001) *A recipe for repression: The Gothenburg riots of 2001* [online] Available at: http://www.daysofdissent.org.uk/gothenburg.htm

Ecologist (2014) Smiling spies: Police Liaison Officers exposed. *The Ecologist* [online] 18 June 2014. Available at: http://www.theecologist.org/News

G20 (2017) *G20 FAQs: Questions and answers on the G20* [online] Available at: https://www.g20.org/Webs/G20/EN/G20/FAQs

Gilmore, J., Jackson, W. and Monk, H. (2016) *Keep moving! Report on the policing of the Barton Moss community protection camp: November 2013 –April 2014*. Centre for the Study of Crime, Criminalisation and Social Exclusion, Liverpool John Moores University: Centre for Urban Research, University of York.

Gorringe, H., Stott, C and Rosie, M. (2012) Dialogue police, decision-making, and the management of public order during protest crowd events. *Journal of Investigative Psychology and Offender Profiling*, 9, 111–125.

Government UK (2022) *National Policing Improvement Agency* [online] Available at: https://www.gov.uk/government/organisations/national-policing-improvement-agency

Hedkvist, T. (2004) Regulating resistance: The ideological control of the protests in Gothenburg 2001. *Communication in English*, 41–60. Malmö Högskola.

Her Majesty's Inspectorate of Constabulary (2017) *About Us: Inspecting policing in the public interest* [online] Available at: http://www.justiceinspectorates.gov.uk/hmic

Her Majesty's Inspectorate of Constabulary. (2009a) *Adapting to protest* [pdf]. London: HMIC. Available at: http://www.justiceinspectorates.gov.uk/hmic

Her Majesty's Inspectorate of Constabulary. (2009b) *Adapting to protest: Nurturing the British model of policing* [pdf] London: HMIC. Available at: http://www.justiceinspectorates.gov.uk/hmic/media

Her Majesty's Inspectorate of Constabulary and Fire and Rescue Services (2021) *The Sarah Everard vigil: An inspection of the Metropolitan Police Service's policing of a vigil held in commemoration of Sarah Everard on Clapham Common on Saturday 13 March 2021* [online]. Available at: https://www.justiceinspectorates.gov.uk/hmicfrs/publication-html/inspection-metropolitan-police-services-policing-of-vigil-commemorating-sarah-everard-clapham-common/

Holgersson, S. (2010) Dialogue Police: *Experiences, observations and opportunities* [pdf]. Stockholm: Swedish National Police Board. Available at: https://polisen.se/Global

Hoggett, J. and Stott, C. (2010) Crowd psychology, public order police training and the policing of football crowds. *Policing: An International Journal of Police Strategies and Management*, 33(2), 218–235.

Hoggett, J. and West, O. (2018) Police Liaison Officers at football: Challenging orthodoxy through communication and engagement *Policing: A Journal of Policy and Practice*, 14(4), 945–961.

Home Affairs Committee (2009) *Policing of the G20 Protests*. [pdf] London: House of Commons. Available at: http://www.publications.parliament.uk

Jackson, W., Gilmore, J. and Monk, H. (2019) Policing unacceptable protest in England and Wales: A case study of the policing of anti-fracking protests. *Critical Social Policy*, 39(1), 23–43.

Joint Committee on Human Rights (2009) *Demonstrating respect for rights? A human rights approach to policing protest*. [pdf] London: House of Lords, House of Commons. Available at: http://www.publications.parliament.uk/pa/

Kilgallon, A. (2020) Police interaction and Notting Hill Carnival. *Policing and Society*, 30(1), 28–46.

Le Bon, G. (1895) *The Crowd: A study of the popular mind*. London: Unwin.

Lewis, P., Laville, S. and Walker, P. (2009) Police handling of protest 'needs national overhaul'. *The Guardian* [online], 7 July 2009. Available at: https://www.theguardian.com/politics/2009/

Liberty (2016) *Article 11 right to protest and freedom of association* [online]. Available at: https://www.liberty-human-rights.org.uk/human-rights/what-are-human-rights/human-rights-act

Lloyd, T. (2014) *The Barton Moss environmental protest*. Greater Manchester: Police and Crime Commissioner.

Menzies, C. (2013) *Police liaison with protest groups*. Aberdeen: The Scottish Institute for Policing Research Practitioner Fellowship. Robert Gordon University.

National Policing Improvement Agency (2008) *Family Liaison Officer Guidance 2008*. Wyboston, Bedfordshire: National Policing Improvement Agency.

National Policing Improvement Agency (2010) *Trainer's guide: Public Order Bronze / Silver Interim Course*. Wyboston, Bedfordshire: National Policing Improvement Agency.

National Policing Improvement Agency (2012) *Trainer's guide: Protestor Liaison Officers*. Wyboston, Bedfordshire: National Policing Improvement Agency.

NetPol (2017) *About* [online] Available at: https://netpol.org/about/

NetPol (2015) *Latest news from NetPol*. May 2015 [online] Available at: https://netpol.org/posts/

NetPol (2014) *Police Liaison Officers* [online] Available at: https://netpol.org/police-liaison-officers/

Ottina, A. (2011) *Government response to political activism: Conflict between the public and the state, Genoa 2001*. M.A. thesis, Centre for Peace and Conflict Studies. University of Sydney, Australia. Available at: https://ses.library.usyd.edu.au/handle/2123/7864

Parkinson, J. and Evans, R. (2012) Sussex police criticised for harassment during protestor liaison *The Guardian* [online], 4 September 2012. Available at: http://www.theguardian.com/uk/2012/sep/04

Police Scotland (2021) *What's Happening: Events: COP26: Protest* [online] Available at: https://www.scotland.police.uk/what-s-happening/events/cop26-home/protest/

Popham, P. (2013) The battle of Balcombe: West Sussex town is new front line in fracking debate *Independent* [online], 25 August 2013. Available at: http://www.independent.co.uk/news/uk/home-news

Reicher, S. (1996) The Battle of Westminster: Developing the social identity model of crowd behaviour in order to explain the initiation and development of collective conflict. *European Journal of Social Psychology*, 26, 115–34.

Roadnight, J. (2015) *From PLO to PLT – the development of Police Liaison Teams in the College of Policing* [email] 6 July 2015. Message to author from julian.roadnight@college.pnn.police.uk

Smith, M. (2015) *The use of Police Liaison Teams in the policing of events: A review of practice*. Ryton: College of Policing. Available at: https://library.college.police.uk/docs/college-of-policing/Use-of-police-liaison-teams-2015

Stephens, H. (2021) *Civil service local: The G7 comes to Cornwall* [online] Available at: https://civilservicelocal.blog.gov.uk/2021/06/18/the-g7-comes-to-cornwall/

Stott, C. (2009) Crowd Psychology & Public Order Policing: An Overview of Scientific Theory and Evidence. *Submission to the HMIC Policing of Public Protest Review Team*. University of Liverpool.

Stott, C., Scothern, M., and Gorringe, H. (2013) Advances in Liaison based public order policing in England: Human rights and negotiating the management of protest? *Policing*, 7(2), 212–226.

Stott, C., West, O., Cawkwell, R., Lunn, D., Hughes, D. and Kemp, B. (2015) *Public Order and Public Safety (POPS) Policing* [online] University of Leeds. Available at: http://www.law.leeds.ac.uk/research/projects

Stott, C., West, O. and Radburn, M. (2018) Policing football 'risk'? A participant action research case study of a liaison-based approach to 'public order'. *Policing and Society*, 28(1), 1–16.

Tyler, T. and Blader, S. (2003) The group engagement model: Procedural justice, social identity, and cooperative behavior. *Personality and Social Psychology Review*, 7(4), 349–361.

UK Parliament (2022a) *Committees: Home affairs committee* [online] Available at: https://committees.parliament.uk/committee/83/home-affairs-committee/

UK Parliament (2022b) *Committees: Human rights joint committee* [online] Available at: https://committees.parliament.uk/committee/93/human-rights-joint-committee/role/

Waddington, D. (2013) A 'kinder blue': Analysing the police management of the Sheffield anti-'Lib Dem' protest of March 2011. *Policing and Society*, 23(1), 46–64.

Wahlström, M (2011) The making of protest and protest policing: Negotiation, knowledge, space, and narrative. *Göteborg studies in sociology* No 47 [pdf]. Department of Sociology, University of Gothenburg.

Weaver, M. (2009) A guide to G20 protests in London. *The Guardian* [online], 23 March 2009. Available at: http://www.theguardian.com/business/blog/2009

Webb, J. (2001) Environmentalists clash with Swedish riot police. *BBC News* [online], 14 June 2001. Available at: http://news.bbc.co.uk/1/hi/world

Wiesel, E (1986) *Nobel lecture: Hope, despair and memory* [online], 11 December 1986 Available at: https://www.nobelprize.org/prizes/peace/1986/wiesel/lecture/

Chapter 2

Policing, protest and balancing human rights

Introduction

Protest is "a defining feature of a working democracy" (Villiers, 1997: 20), providing a means for public expression and is one of the foundations of a democratic society (Liberty, 2016). The power of peaceful protests is such that it has confronted and defeated "the military might of authoritarian regimes" (Waddington, 1994b: 1). The role of the police within this setting is as guardians of social stability and order (Jackson and Bradford, 2009).

This chapter will analyse the body of evidence documenting protest and police approaches, examine the change in police strategy from escalated force, through a negotiated management style (McCarthy and McPhail, 1998; Waddington, 1994b), through strategic incapacitation (Gillham, 2011) towards strategic facilitation (Waddington, 2011; Gorringe et al., 2012) and beyond. Having established an academic grounding from which to view the policing of protest, consideration will then turn to the legislative framework within which the police must operate. Mansley (2014: 10) surmised that "the art of protest policing lies in maintain the balance between liberty and order," a balance rooted in human rights legislation which impact significantly on the policing of protest events. The chapter will explore the origins and implications of the Human Rights Act 1998 (Fenwick, 2009) and examine how peaceful protest (Mead, 2010) is framed in legislation. Examination will be made of case law and its impact on the decision-making of police commanders in balancing competing Articles contained within the Act (Rosie and Gorringe, 2009). Finally, the chapter will begin to examine the communication between police and protesters during events.

Policing and protest

Within the extensive body of research into protest, there exist varying definitions of what constitutes protest, and where protest might be considered as social action rather than public disorder. Turner (1969) examined indicators which predisposed the public to view collective disruption and violence as social protest and not acts of crime. Turner concluded that for such an

DOI: 10.4324/9781003160533-2

occurrence, the protest first needed credibility and to be seen as just. Turner then observed that defining an event as social protest by those who are the target of the disturbance, in an attempt of conciliation, prevented recourse to serious conflict. When a disturbance was defined as a protest by a third party, Turner concluded that this provided an opportunity for protest groups to coalesce. Finally, providing the definition of protest provided the authorities with a bargaining relationship with those engaged in the event. Therefore, there is a role for those outside of protest groups, such as the police and those against whom protests are targeted, in defining collected action as protests legitimised by the masses.

In a letter to fellow clergymen, the incarcerated Dr Martin Luther King Jr wrote: "One has not only a legal but moral responsibility to obey just laws. Conversely, one has a moral responsibility to disobey unjust laws" (King, 1963). History provides examples of such legislation which has not only been challenged but in some cases amended due to its opposition. As recently as 2014, the wording of Section 5 of the Public Order Act 1986 was amended to no longer include words, behaviour or displays which are simply "insulting" (Crown Prosecution Service, 2019). The amendment followed a very public campaign under the banner of Reform Section 5 who brought together "people from all walks of life; from the religious to the secular and from right across the political spectrum" (Reform Section 5, 2013) to challenge legislation. In early 2022, four defendants were acquitted by a jury at Bristol crown court of causing criminal damage to a statue of Edward Colston, having maintained that "the presence of the statue was a hate crime and it was therefore not an offence to remove it" (Mathers, 2022). Such examples provide further consideration, therefore, as to whether protests involving disobedience to the law are still civil and even peaceful. Villiers (1997) argued that the motives of such protesters are significantly different to other lawbreakers who do so for personal gain (such as the thief), for the thrill (the vandal) or because they do not accept the legitimacy of the state (the terrorist). Instead, protesters' actions are to highlight their cause, and they do so fully accepting any consequences that their actions may bring.

Alternatively, King and Brearley (1996), further explored by Baxter (2001), defined protest in terms of types and suggested three typologies: political; industrial; and single-issue conflict. King (2006) further extended the research to a fourfold typology: political; industrial; festival; and urban, although observed that these excluded protests relating to sporting events. King observed a recognition by the police that policing based on such typology was "increasingly out of step with much contemporary protest." Ratliff and Hall (2014) proposed six categories of protester activity: literal symbolic, aesthetic and sensory; movement in space; solemnity and the sacred; civil disobedience; institutional and conventional activity; and collective violence and threats. Ratliff and Hall (2014: 268) concluded across all categories that the actions of protesters, while sometimes confrontational, were overwhelmingly nonviolent, and that majority of all protester activity at protest events involved "literally symbolic, aesthetic, and sensory qualities."

Protests however do not exist in a void, but within the community, whatever that community might be for a given event. The police themselves are also active within communities in a way that brings them in direct contact with protest crowds (Redekop and Paré, 2010), and have a duty to police protest events within the communities for whom they have responsibility. Within this role, Villiers (1997) suggested that there are two police responses: one as problem solvers, experts in managing conflict achieved by negotiation and finding a common ground; the other is that of law enforcement and may necessitate the use of force. della Porta and Reiter (1998: 1) defined the policing of protest as "the police handling of protest events – a more neutral description for what protesters usually refer to as 'repression' and the state as 'law and order.'" Willis (2001: 15) described the policing of protest as "being largely characterised either by coercion or by compromise." D, Waddington (1992) concluded that the police role was to strike a balance between liberty and order in liberal democratic societies, whilst P. Waddington (1994b: 14) further claimed that "for the police, protest represents a threat to public order."

della Porta and Reiter (1998: 25) suggested how the police distinguished between "good" and "bad" demonstrators was based on their conception of "legitimate" protest, as well as on their expectations of the demonstrators' behaviour. della Porta and Reiter further described a set of variables relevant to define different styles of protest policing (for example, brutal versus soft referring to the degree of force used; diffused versus selective referring to the number of repressed groups; illegal versus legal referring to police respect of the law; reactive versus preventive referring to the timing of police intervention). Such variables indicated the policing style, and della Porta and Reiter (1998: 3) observed that "police who repress a large number of protest groups, prohibit a wide range of protest activities, and intervene with a high degree of force are employing a diffused, repressive, and 'brutal' protest policing style."

The definition of protest and the role of the police as law enforcers and arbitrators is therefore subjective. To further explore the role of the police in policing protests, the next section examines existing literature and seeks to identify trends in approaches to the policing of protest. The examination will commence at the early 1980s, when a change in legislation saw a new approach to policing develop.

Escalated force

The early 1980s was marked with a series of disorder incidents across the UK, including the England riots of 1981 in Brixton, Handsworth, Chapeltown and Toxteth, and conflict between the police and the striking miners in 1984. Indeed, Joyce (1992) described the 1980s as the "decade of disorder" and observed, notwithstanding the need to unpack what 'disorder' might mean, that a regular response was a series of actions between police and protest groups that pre-empted the use of what has been termed "escalated force." HMIC (2009a: 40) defined escalated force as "the increasing use of force to control large crowds." McPhail, Schweingruber and McCarthy (1998) provided a more nuanced definition, referring to a police approach to protests where the police used force to disperse those who were engaged in demonstrations, even when those demonstrating were doing so to exercise their right of peaceful assembly. Mansley (2014) asserted that the theoretical framework of the police doctrine of escalated force was routed in the classic theory of crowd psychology popularised by Le Bon (1895).

The Scarman (1982) report into the 1981 riots recommended a change of policing methods to make the police more accessible to the community. This, together with a review of the Public Order Act 1936, legislation that adversely affected the ability of individuals to engage in protest (Joyce and Wain, 2014) and the response to the 1980 Green Paper (Hansard, 1985) eventually saw a change in legislation and the emergence of the Public Order Act 1986, which came in to power in April 1987. Aided by the legislative changes, particularly the requirements of Section 11 of the Act for organisers to provide the police with written notification of an intended protest march (Public Order Act, 1986), police and protesters now began to engage, signifying a move away from escalated force (Joyce, 2009) and led to "organisers having to negotiate with the police" (Joyce and Wain, 2014: 262). This move in the UK reflected a change in the policing approach to protest across Western democracies to a new epoch of policing by negotiated management (McCarthy and McPhail, 1998).

Negotiated management

The 1990s saw a marked change globally in the policing of protest, as an escalated force approach was replaced by a "negotiated management" process. This approach saw the police negotiate with those wishing to demonstrate before the event to allow peaceful assembly and protest with minimal recourse to resort to conflict with the police (McPhail, Schweingruber and McCarthy, 1998). HMIC (2009b: 40) defined the approach as "a police tactic emphasising co-operation and communication between police and protesters," and observed that "the intent is to 'de-escalate' sensitive situations and reduce the likelihood of violence."

McPhail, Schweingruber and McCarthy (1998) proposed that police authorities utilised a system of standards to manage protests within public areas, which they entitled the Public Order Management System (POMS). McPhail, Schweingruber and McCarthy suggested that the police implemented three significant principles in policing protest: negotiation with all those affected by the protest; a planning process for the police or relevant authority; and an encouragement for those organising the protest to also plan for the event.

Implementing such a system allowed the police to predict as far as possible the outcomes of a protest event and build communication links should the event not proceed as predicted. POMS examined the police response to demonstrators' rights to peacefully assemble. McPhail, Schweingruber and McCarthy observed that the police either ignored or disregarded these rights under an escalated force approach but considered the rights of primary concern to the police in engaging a negotiated management approach. McPhail, Schweingruber and McCarthy also observed that a tolerance for disruption within the community, not witnessed previously, was now prevalent under a negotiated management style of policing, where the police accepted a level of disruption as an inevitable by-product the efforts of those protesting to enact social change. The move from escalated force to negotiated management saw the emergence of an approach based on communication and led to an approach where police use of force was a last resort. Although research was predominantly US-based, McPhail, Schweingruber and McCarthy concluded that the key characteristics of POMS were present within the protest policing systems of England.

A negotiated management approach also became apparent in protest policing in the UK in the 1990s. In researching the Metropolitan Police, Waddington (1994b: 69) observed that "the principal method of securing compliance was through negotiation with the organizer of the protest." della Porta and Reiter (1998: 6) concurred and observed that the police approach in the UK changed whereby lawbreaking, implicit in several forms of protest, tended to be tolerated by the police and breaking the law was "usually considered as less important than peacekeeping."

However, Waddington saw police negotiation as an extension of the police's desire to maintain control and considered the process a bureaucratic result of the police inducing protesters to comply with their strategic intentions. When the police did negotiate, Waddington (1994b) elucidated, they were "spuriously" friendly "winning over" those intent on engaging in protest. Waddington concluded that this was not a balanced two-way equal power negotiation process, rather the balance of power lay firmly with the police. The negotiations were "less a process of 'give and take' and more that of the organizer giving and the police taking" (1994b: 101). Joyce and Wain (2014: 262) concurred, observing that the focus was on "organisers having to negotiate with the police." Further, Waddington (1994a: 373) described the police strategy as a "carrot and stick" approach, encouraging the leadership of the militant groups by "a mixture of coercion and accommodation, to comply with police wishes." Waddington argued that this process, implemented during the policing of the anti-poll tax campaign, witnessed the police providing "overt assistance" and concessions to those organising the protests to get them on side. However, Waddington observed that the police's accommodating stance was coupled with the imposing of legislative powers under the Public Order Act (1986) to ensure that where there was threat of disorder, it was contained due to the conditions imposed, thus marginalising those perceived by the police as intent on causing trouble.

In further exploring the approach of negotiated management in the UK, Waddington (1998) observed that senior officers adopted a tactic of not arresting protesters and this formal policy was communicated to the rank-and-file officers through briefings to ensure that everyone understood the police strategy. However, Waddington postulated (1998: 123) that "a more significant problem lies in ensuring that constables and sergeants understand and accept what is expected of them." Waddington surmised that protesters entered negotiation with the police pre-event and actively sought police assistance with demonstrations as without it their protest or march was more difficult for them to manage. However, Waddington argued that when negotiating with those organising demonstration, the stance of the police was "one of proffering help and advice – 'How can we help you?' – 'help you', that is, to 'do it our way'" (1998: 121). Waddington observed an outward show of good relationship being fostered between police commanders and organisers on the day of the event. However, Waddington asserted that the police were subtly attempting to ensure that they maintained as much control as possible over the protest.

P. Waddington further questioned the extent to which the police bought into the negotiation process, observing that the police deployed numerous police resources in reserve and would revert to an escalated force approach if necessary. Waddington also noted occasions where a negotiated management approach was not implemented, including at key London locations, such as Downing Street, the Palace of Westminster and the American Embassy, outside where there was strict control of any protest. Waddington observed (1998: 126) that any attempt at protesting at a royal occasion was "vigorously prevented." Waddington also provided an example where a peace protester who tried to play a pennywhistle during the two-minute silence of a Remembrance Service was quickly arrested and taken away by the police without any attempt at negotiation. Waddington concluded that there was a desire for the police to avoid confrontation with those organising protest events by engaging in negotiation and accommodation.

King and D. Waddington (2005) posited that for a negotiated management approach to work, there was a prerequisite for the group of protesters to have a hierarchical order and structure that rendered the presence of leaders; representative of the group with whom the police may negotiate. King and Waddington noted a trend in the "proliferating anti-globalization / anti-capitalist protests of recent years" (2005: 263), where the protesters consisted of leaderless, non-hierarchical groups, which assisted in confounding police attempts to utilise a negotiated management approach to control public order situations. Gorringe et al. (2012) noted that the approach placed an alternative pre-eminence on the police to collaborate with protesters, even if such cooperation required the police to accept a low level of disruption to the public and to overlook symbolic actions which may technically constitute minor offences but were peaceful in nature. Villiers (1997: 20) concurred, stating that "protest activity may be lively, forceful, and even confrontational, while remaining acceptable according to the mores and standards of the time." Similarly, in his research into public order policing in the UK, Willis (2001: 15) noted a new feature in the police approach, which was "rather less public–police confrontation and rather more accommodation" and that "policing today has become less adversarial and more rights-based." Furthermore, Gorringe and Rosie (2008) suggested that the danger with a negotiated management approach was that those engaged in "genuine" protests were only able to express themselves in a way that was safe, consensual and permitted by the police. Gorringe and Rosie concluded (2008: 200) that "protesters, thus, play a vital role in testing the limits of 'negotiation', rendering power visible and raising searching questions about the spaces available for democratic debate and contestation."

The 1990s certainly saw a reduction in the number of major public disorder occurrences in the UK (Solomon et al., 2007). The specific contribution that a change from an escalated force to negotiated management approach made to such a reduction is unqualified. However, the literature does suggest that a change in police approach and a focus on dialogue was significant in the move from that of escalated force. Additionally, there are other contributing factors that may have been influential. Reiner (1998) noted that this change also coincided with a change in protest events, with the rise in the 1990s of "single-issue protests," for example, against the Newbury bypass, poll tax demonstrations and the emergence of Reclaim the Streets, which replaced 1980s disorder. However, at the dawn of a new millennium, della Porta, Peterson and Reiter (2006) identified another noticeable shift in protest policing across Western democracies at the policing of transnational summits from the norm that had become one of negotiation. della Porta, Peterson and Reiter questioned (2006: 5) whether this was the emergence of "a new repressive protest policing style" rather than a re-emergence of escalated force. This approach to the policing of transnational protests became known as one of strategic incapacitation.

Strategic incapacitation

Noakes and Gillham (2006) also observed a shift in police response to protest at the start of the new millennium and identified the emergence of "transgressive protesters" which signified a move in policing style to an approach of strategic incapacitation. Noakes and Gillham defined "transgressive protesters" as those the police perceived as "bad" protesters, as opposed to "good" protesters who engaged in negotiation. In researching mass demonstrations in the US, Noakes and Gillham observed a police perception that transgressive protesters had begun exploiting elements of a negotiated management approach and surmised (206: 103) that because "transgressive protesters would not negotiate their tactics and plans ahead of time, police had to manage greater uncertainty." Furthermore, transgressive protesters engaged in direct action that sought to disrupt the very protests that the police were seeking to facilitate. Therefore, the police were unable to rely on communicating with demonstrators and had to adopt an approach that was removed from that of negotiated management approach.

Noakes and Gillham did not see this as a return to escalated force, rather a "new penology" where the police used new tactics to disrupt and disperse demonstrations when negotiation with protesters was not possible. Tactics included: restricting access to certain large areas near to primary protest locations; creating protest-free zones; a zero tolerance for transgressive protesters where legislation was aggressively enforced; a strategy of using force, including less lethal options such as tear gas, pepper spray and rubber bullets, to specifically target transgressive protesters; and the use of surveillance tactics to incapacitate demonstrators. This new approach was a step away from a negotiated management style where force was used as a last resort. However, Noakes and Gillham (2006: 111) argued that this was not a return to escalated force but "a third response to political protests, which we refer to as the strategic incapacitation style of policing protests." Noakes and Gillham observed the approach implemented where the police selectively incapacitated those protesters, particularly the group leaders, who were seen to pose the greatest danger to an event or location. The police approach was to remove selected transgressive protesters and incapacitate them temporarily, such as by containment or arrest, thereby creating obstacles to their participation in demonstrations.

Gillham and Noakes (2007: 353) argued that the police move to an approach of incapacitation had largely passed under the radar of public criticism "partly because the tactics employed by some transgressive activists are not seen as legitimate by the mainstream media and public." Gillham and Noakes contended that the challenge of policing transgressive protesters highlighted the limitations of a negotiated management approach. However, Gillham and Noakes provided the caveat that a strategic incapacitation approach did not result in the police abandoning negotiated management for those protesters who were willing to negotiate with the police.

At the same time, della Porta, Peterson and Reiter (2006: 1) opined that "protest increasingly tended to target international institutions" and this heralded the emergence of a new policing approach. della Porta and Reiter (2006: 13) argued that the police adopted three identifiable strategies in the policing of protest events; "coercive strategies" whereby the police control protests by deploying tactics that involve the use of physical force; "persuasive strategies" where control is gained through entering into discourse with organisers of demonstrations; and "information strategies" where control is gained through an information gathering approach where potential troublemakers are targeted in order to attempt to prevent disorder. In their research into the policing of the G8 international summit in Genoa, della Porta and Reiter documented the police approach following the strategies summarised. della Porta and Reiter noted persuasive strategies implemented whereby "red zones" were erected to barrier off a large area to prevent access to anyone intent on violent protest. This approach was supported by over one hundred thousand border checks. In utilising persuasive strategies, della Porta and Reiter noted that the Italian police "did not favour the element of negotiation, even though police leadership repeatedly claimed attempts to establish a relationship and open lines of communication with protest movements" (2006: 17). Any attempts at negotiating were only implemented late in the day. Information strategies centred on the collection of indiscriminative data and misinformation provided by the police. della Porta and Reiter concluded (2006: 19) that the most apparent policing approach in Genoa was the use of "brutal coercive strategies" littered with excessive use of police force, and a clear departure from a negotiated management approach.

Gorringe and Rosie's (2008) examination of the police of protests at the G8 summit in Gleneagles, Scotland in 2005 provided a study into the strategy the police were implementing in the UK in approaching policing of protests at international summits. Gorringe and Rosie argued that the negotiated management approach could not be absorbed in its entirety into UK policing. However, Gorringe and Rosie posited (208: 187) that this approach "works best when both sides are committed to negotiation and that police stereotyping or protester intransigence can lead to the escalation of any given event." Gorringe and Rosie observed the interaction between police and protesters and noted that where the police adopted an approach in line with negotiated management, there was minimal disorder and disruption. However, the parameters of such an approach were clearly set by the police in Scotland and where the parameters were exceeded, such as an attempted breach of a fence by the protesters, or a sit-down protest nearby, Gorringe and Rosie observed a departure from negation in favour of police intervention, regardless of the actual intentions of the protesters. Gorringe and Rosie (2008: 194) also detected a different police response determined by the group's identity and noted that "where Christians were ushered to the gates, G8 Alternatives were allowed, reluctantly, to march and 'anarchists' were subject to more 'robust' policing."

Werren (2014) attributed the shift in policing style to an increased use of information gathering and surveillance to assess risk. Werren suggested that a strategic incapacitation style reflected a police desire to maintain control in unpredictable situations and that this can conflict with the aims of those organising the protest "who often see an element of surprise and unpredictability as essential requirements for a successful and noticeable protest" (2014: 22). De Lint (2005) also noted a change in the policing of protest in Canada and referred to the style as a "hybrid police form." De Lint argued that the policing style was marked by the merging of a community-based approach with an intelligence-led focus and concluded that it was "not simply becoming more 'soft hat' or 'hard hat': it is both" (2005: 196).

Contrastingly, Vitale (2005) suggested an alternative progression from a negotiated management approach. Vitale's study into the policing strategies employed by the New York Police Department (NYPD) at large demonstrations provided evidence of a new style of protest policing which Vitale entitled "command and control." Vitale observed police attempts to micro-manage the demonstrations thus attempting to prevent outbreaks of disorder and disruption to the local community. Vitale noted that this approach was significantly different to previous strategies, as the NYPD sought to set clear and strict guidelines for those engaged in demonstrations to limit their recourse to disorder. Vitale noted that negotiation with organisers was significantly limited. However, Vitale argued that this approach did not mark a return to escalated force, as the NYPD sought to plan and prepare to such an extent that limited the use of force. Vitale observed that where force was used, this was in a managed process that sought to regain control over those engaged in the demonstrations. Vitale asserted that the command and control approach was based on the NYPD infatuation at that time in promoting the philosophy of maintaining the quality of life of those living in New York City, based on the "broken windows" theory (Kelling and Coles, 1996). This theory advocated a zero-tolerance approach to minor crimes to promote an atmosphere of law and order, thus preventing more serious offences. Vitale concluded that where the approach had been successful in earlier demonstrations in New York, there was a vulnerability when the police faced either very large crowds or demonstrators who were intent on defying the police and resisting their controlling approach. In such incidents, Vitale witnessed the return to the use of high levels of force. Therefore, Vitale surmised that a command and control approach was a diversion from what had begun to work in the policing of protest and recommended (2005: 302) that the "police should re-examine the usefulness of the negotiated management approach to protest policing."

Button, John and Brearley (2002) also observed a change of approach when examining UK protest policing. However, rather than focusing on the police response, Button, John and Brearley argued that a contributing factor was a new trend emerging with those engaged in protests. Button, John and Brearley examined environmental activism protesting the construction of the Newbury bypass and Manchester airport extensions and the emergence of the activist group Reclaim the Streets, and uncovered new, innovative tactics which they argued "amount to a 'professionalisation' of protest" (2002: 17). Button, John and Brearley announced an emergence of "full-time protesters," who were well trained in different tactics of protesting, and an adherence to unwritten but clear codes of conduct. Button, John and Brearley argued that some activists were engaged in several different campaigns, where they were joined by those who were only able to campaign in their spare time, united together to protest against a common cause. Button, John and Brearley observed that the protest groups did not present a hierarchical order or clear leadership structure and concluded that the police faced significant challenges in policing environmental protests and developing effective strategies to control what were very different protest tactics to what had been experienced in previous years.

Additionally, Button and John (2002) introduced the concept of "plural policing" in response to protest events in the UK. In examining the policing of environmental protests in England and Wales, Button and John (2002: 111) noted that the police were only one of several organisations engaged in the social process of conducting protest and identified a "complex range of agencies" involved in the policing of environmental protest, including private agencies, bailiffs, the Health and Safety Executive and the police. Button and John observed that the police commanders had received specific training in public order, whereas other agencies had received no training. Button and John argued a need for transparency in professionalising the role, which should include defined national training.

Mansley (2014) also concluded in his research of this period that the protest policing style had changed. However, Mansley suggested that this was a move towards hard policing (della Porta and Reiter, 1998), which Mansley summarised as a deviation from negotiated management and a return to a police paramilitary structure in dealing with public disorder as experienced in the 1980s (Jefferson, 1990). Mansley attributed this shift to a combination of better police public order equipment, the use of additional legislation, such as counter-terrorism laws, with increasing regularity, and the development of hard but non-lethal tactics, such as containment. The significance in this movement to a harder policing style, Mansley summarised (2014: 129), was that this style was "positively correlated with police violence."

The events of the late 2000s and subsequent HMIC reports (2009a; b) brought the policing of protest to the fore in the UK and the police approach was scrutinised under a national microscope. Immediate recommendations stated that the police should seek to improve dialogue with both protest groups and the public through the media, prior to events (HMIC, 2009a), and dramatic changes to the training of police commanders were implemented throughout the UK (NPIA, 2010). In addressing HMIC recommendations, Gravelle and Rogers (2011) introduced what they describe as a "smarter way" for the police in engaging protesters and adopting a "no surprise" communication philosophy. Gravelle and Rogers noted that the concept of the public as "customer" was comparatively new to the world of policing, and although this brought with it some reservations internally in the nuance of language utilised for those with whom the police interacted, it signified an increasing desire for the police to increase public confidence and engage with their communities. Gravelle and Rogers suggested (2011: 8) that with such a drive for increased professionalism "correctly implementing 'Corporate Social Responsibility' as a definitive basis for public order policing could offer a real and robust option" as the police sought to re-engage with society and reaffirm the desire to police by consent.

Gravelle and Rogers noted the growth of the concept of Corporate Social Responsibility (CSR) in both private and public sectors, where organisations made decisions based on ethical values, compliance with legislation and cognisant of maintaining respect for people, communities and the environment (Dahlsrud, 2008). Gravelle and Rogers conjectured that by applying a CSR approach to policing of protests, the police would emphasise their wider moral duty to the local community that stretched past the narrow view limiting their obligation to policing disorder and preventing and detecting crime. Gravelle and Rogers argued that when specifically applied to transgressive protesters, a CSR approach would place those protesting into a model of neighbourhood policing supported by a process of consultation and would break down barriers and stimulate community re-engagement rather than the enforcement approach typically applied by the police.

Enticing though the theory may be, Gravelle and Rogers provide no empirical research in support that would champion such an approach in the policing of protest. However, their observations do herald a marked change in approach to the policing of protest post Adapting to Protest (HMIC 2009a; b), and the emergence of a different approach, referred to as towards "strategic facilitation" (Waddington, 2011; Gorringe et al., 2012).

Strategic facilitation

As the new millennium entered its second decade, there was a marked shift in UK police approaches to demonstrations and policing protests, due to the changes in training and strategy highlighted in the "Introduction" chapter of this book. This change of direction saw a move from strategic incapacitation to what Waddington (2011) and Gorringe et al. (2012) termed "strategic facilitation." Gorringe et al. welcomed the changes in attitude as police commanders translated theory into practical application and came to terms with a focus on facilitating peaceful protest (NPIA, 2010). In its infancy, Gorringe et al. observed different police approaches to manage the facilitation, such as the use of plainclothed police officers, introducing themselves as "facilitators" during the "Smash NATO" demonstrations in Scotland in 2009. Gorringe et al. note that the police selected trained negotiators to undertake the role, chosen for their excellent "people skills," and argued that this demonstrated that the police saw significant value in facilitating protest and had an appetite to implement innovative tactics. Gorringe et al. noted that those engaged as facilitators were sincere and committed to engage but questioned their influence on police commanders and whether the main police strategy was to facilitate or to incapacitate those wishing to protest. Gorringe et al. accepted that the approach was in its infancy and argued that they had observed a new policing approach to protest, concluding;

> We may have just witnessed the start of a transition to what we might reasonably refer to as a "strategic facilitation" approach. This hardly represents a revolution in police methods for handling public disorder, but it seems that the next stage in its evolution is unsteadily under way.
>
> (Gorringe et al., 2012: 129)

The emergence of a strategic facilitation as a new approach to the policing of protest has been abetted by the introduction of Police Liaison Team (PLT) officers to provide a communication link between protesters and police commanders (College of Policing, 2018). The next chapter will explore the limited research which examines the use and effectivity of this approach as a tactical option.

Different approaches to policing protests

Existing literature has described the different approaches to the policing of protest, from escalated force through negotiated management to strategic incapacitation and facilitation, as a sequenced historical development (for example, Vitale, 2005; Gillham, 2011; Waddington, 2011) with new social control strategies replacing earlier approaches and the failure of one approach being replaced by the next. However, within the literature, questions have been raised as to whether the shifts in approaches were more nuanced (Stott, Scothern and Gorringe, 2013) and whether the changing models of policing (Waddington, 2011) heralded new models or a return to previous approaches (Noakes and Gillham, 2006). Despite the sequential nature described, research into the policing of protest continues to map the ebbs and flows of current police procedures and processes, and "organizational memory" (Walsh and Ungson, 1991) continues to affect the methodology used throughout the Western world in facilitating protests. The emergence of movements such as Black Lives Matter in the United States signalled a growth in demonstrations where the police were themselves the subject of the grievance as well as the authority responsible for policing resulting protest events (Reinka and Leach, 2017; Williamson, Trump and Einstein, 2018). Such occurrences have also emerged in the UK in recent years, heightened during the Covid-19 pandemic, where the policing of Black Lives Matter protests have provided opposition over the police approach to protest under new coronavirus legislation (Harris et al., 2021). A proposed Police, Crime, Sentencing and Courts Bill (UK Parliament, 2022), which will provide the police with increased powers to impose restrictions on protests, drew further protests across the UK where the police were again arbitrators and yet a primary focus of the "kill the bill" demonstrations (Davies and Gayle, 2022).

Despite the recent emphasis on a policing approach of strategic facilitation, others suggest a different transition ongoing in global protest prompting a more militaristic police response. Wood (2014: 3) asserted that the policing of protest in "democratic, capitalist countries is now both more militarized and more dependent on intelligence gathering and pre-emptive control" than was the case previously. Although research concentrated on protests in cities in the United States and Canada, Wood claimed this trend has also been observed in Europe. Similarly, Myers-Montgomery (2016) observed a militarised police approach in the US and suggested that the traditional police approach using dogs, batons and water cannon was now long gone and replaced with the use of armoured vehicles and sniper rifles. This militaristic standpoint meant that protests which had been peaceful until the police attended had the potential to denigrate into serious disorder between protesters and police due to the police armoury. Myers-Montgomery concluded (2016: 278) that "when police mistake city streets for a warzone and the community for enemies, we encounter the social problem we have today." Such an approach might be described as more akin to an escalated force approach rather than a new method of policing protest.

In drawing parallels closer to home, it is significant that UK police commanders do not have such US armoury available at their disposal. Indeed, the tactical use of water cannon, replaced with a more militaristic approach in the US, has never been an option for UK police outside of Northern Ireland, with then Home Secatry Theresa May refusing to authorise their use by any police force in England and Wales (Travis, 2015). However, Gilmore, Jackson and Monk (2016) questioned whether the policing of protest in the UK has increasingly moved towards an authoritarian style. Conducted research into the policing of anti-"fracking" protests in Greater Manchester, Gilmore, Jackson and Monk raised questions about "the nature of democratic accountability and public order policing in England and Wales," and argued (2016: 4) that there was substantiated evidence that the policing operation that they observed "was violent, disproportionate to the size and peaceful nature of the protest and carried out with impunity." Further, Gilmore, Jackson and Monk questioned the extent and gravitas to which the police facilitated peaceful protest;

> Negotiation appeared to be set as a precondition for acceptable protest; in this sense it appeared that "peaceful" protest was only that which is negotiated with, and sanctioned by, police. For many protesters this was an unacceptable constraint placed on their disruptive, yet peaceful, action. The clear lack of trust between protesters and police prevented effective dialogue and this appeared only to become worse as the police operation became notably more physical, and the number of arrests increased, as the protest developed.
>
> (Gilmore, Jackson and Monk, 2016: 20)

Therefore, despite the body of research that maps the policing of protest as a sequenced historical response, this chapter has evidenced that a variety of approaches have been implemented at different times during this period applicable to the circumstances. Therefore, it is argued that the different approaches to the policing of protests are not a historical trend, rather they provide a tool kit of possible responses available to police commanders. Police commanders have utilised the approaches most applicable to achieve their strategies in policing the protests, depending on the information and intelligence available to them. The implementation by police commanders of different approaches will be explored in subsequent chapters.

Political influences on the policing of protest

Throughout the varying incarnations of police approaches, political influences and pressures have been identified as factors impacting on the police approach to protests. Wood (2014) examined protests in the US and Canada and noted that although different police departments used similar approaches, their implementation varied greatly depending on the local political context. Wood noted an increased perception of police legitimacy intermingled with public fear in New York post the terrorist attacks of September 2001 and argued (2014: 79) that this allowed the NYPD to "control protester activity more intensively that the police in other cities studied." Noakes and Gillham (2006) observed there was a greater probability that the police would use force when protest was made at international events or where the event was attended by significant political figures. Similarly, researching anti-globalisation protests at the 2001 Summit of Americas in Quebec City, King and Waddington argued (2005: 278) that "irresistible international pressure" made it "politically imperative" that the police would even "die in a ditch" if required, in order to protect the integrity of the summit and key political dignitaries in attendance.

Such political influence was also identified in Western Europe by della Porta and Reiter (2006) in police organisations that were "still-militarized." della Porta and Reiter argued (2006: 27) that the police public order response to protests at G8 in Genoa was heavily influenced by political influences at "both the supranational and the national levels." della Porta and Reiter concluded (2006: 17) that the "government obviously retains a great potential influence on protest policing."

Waddington (1998) also identified political pressure as an impact factor in policing protest in the UK. Waddington highlighted events such as royal occasions and at key strategic locations where the police would divert from negotiation and resort to an escalated force approach, utilising numbers of police officers kept in reserve. Waddington argued (1998: 127) that this move was as a result of pressures from those "who occupy institutionalized positions of power" such as the government, Parliament, the monarchy and foreign ambassadors. Mansley (2014: 139) argued that the police were the embodiment of the state at political demonstrations in the UK and the policing style was "a telling indicator of the government's priorities." Mobbs (2009) was more damning of the state in his observations:

> If we look at the change in the policing of protest in Britain over the last decade it's clear that the state is seeking to stamp down on any action that seeks change "outside of the usual channels". This limits protest to the scope of "regular" representative processes, such as letter writing, talking to your MP, or signing petitions – *in short, those things which don't create significant changes in the public debate because they happen outside the media and the public's gaze.*
>
> (Mobbs, 2009: 19)

The power of the state in protest events and the role of the police in facilitating protests provided further consideration. Such power may be contested by the very protests enacted. Coleman (2004: 30) argued a need to rethink the state and state power and observed that the state "is not a static body in time and space." Further, Coleman et al. (2009) challenged the assumption that it was not possible to stand outside the ideology of the state and yet still engage in political policy. Coleman et al. argued (2009: 16) that there were several "counter-hegemonic groups that stand firmly and unapologetically in opposition to the state's criminal justice agenda but still remain engaged with government in consultations, lobbying and policy work." Johnson (1999) noted that the state did not have a monopoly on policing and observed that policing must be seen as a social function and not solely the domain of the police as a specific body. Although sparsely examined in this chapter, it is acknowledged that conflict theory (for example, Bartos and Wehr, 2002; Oberschall, 2010) provides further consideration when examining political pressures. Bartos and Wehr (2002: 7) opined that conflict theory and its application could be "as useful for those dissatisfied with the status quo as for those who wish to keep things as they are." Bartos and Wehr argued that, at times, conflict management was the most effective manner to affect change of power, whereas at others it was better to escalate conflict and contest power. Contrastingly, Weitzer (1995: 283) argued that conflict theorists had "exaggerated the degree to which conflict theory explains policing and police-community relations in relatively integrated, democratic societies lacking civil strife." In examining policing in Northern Ireland, Weitzer concluded (1995: 4) that conflict theory was better suited to "explaining policing where state repression and/or social inequality is extreme."

The role of the police as actors of the state continues to be debated and there is conjecture to the degree to which the police are impartial in policing protest. Goold (2016: 232) argued that the police are "typically the most visible agents of state power," although recognised that they exist to serve the public and "derive their authority from a deep societal commitment to democracy" which far outreaches the power of any political authority or government. The changes of legislation during Covid-19 lockdowns in the UK, which effectively provided the police with extensive powers in restricting public gatherings (McKerrell, 2021), provided further fuel to the debate. Proposed legislative changes provided the police with increased powers in imposing restrictions on peaceful procession and assembly (Liberty, 2022). Mead (2021: 108) propounded that the extent to which people can express their discontent "is going to move up the political agenda" and that "having lain in the hinterlands for several decades, the pandemic has tipped it over the edge."

The examination of the police approach to protest events and protesters will undoubtedly continue to be examined, particularly in an age of intense public and media scrutiny (Soares et al., 2018). Rosie and Gorringe (2009: 1) argued that the media had instigated and ignored "the very 'abuses' they are now so eager to condemn." Greer and McLaughlin (2010: 1050) noted the rise of the "citizen journalist" in a world of readily available social media who have instigated a "collective realignment" of the established press, and a marked "transition from 'protester violence' to 'police violence.'" Kilgallon (2020) also noted the dangers of social media polarising opinions of protest and recognised the difficulties of presenting the perspectives of all parties. Kilgallon (2020: 844) cautioned that observing public order policing in England and Wales "from YouTube videos and the perspective of protesters" provided a "very one dimensional image of the event, often focusing on the extra-ordinary instead of the mundane."

Protest events do not occur in a vacuum and the police have finite resources with which to police demonstrations; as Waddington (1998: 118) observed, the policing of protest events "is simply one of the many policing tasks with which local police deal." Moreover, there are other interested parties, in addition to those protesting, whose human rights are engaged during such events. The police must balance the competing rights of all those affected by protest, not just those seeking to protest. The role of the police in balancing competing human rights will be examined in the next section.

Protest and balancing human rights

> The unenviable task for the police service is to balance both the rights of those lawfully demonstrating against the rights of all other individuals within society.
>
> (Gravelle and Rogers, 2011: 6)

Whereas much has been written on the policing of protest, there is scant mention within such a large body of literature of the balancing act that such a process necessitates. Indeed, where a "balance" is recognised, this invariably focuses exclusively on the police–protester relationship and relates to a balance between liberty and order (Reiner, 1998; Mansley, 2014). Accordingly, it has been described as the "balance between powers of the state and rights of citizens" (de Lint, 2005: 181); the "balance between maintaining public order and protecting civil and political liberties" (Peterson, 2006: 61) and the "balance between the competing requirements of facilitating protest and controlling disorder" (Werren, 2014: 23). Further, della Porta, Peterson and Reiter (2006: 3) argued that controlling protests required a difficult balance between the protection of law and order and the defence not just of the freedom of the individual, but also of "citizens' rights to political participation, and thus the very essence of the democratic system."

The balance between liberty and order necessitates facilitating "peaceful protest" (HMIC 2009a; b). Rosie and Gorringe (2009: 8) questioned this terminology, suggesting it gave the police "the discretion to determine who is and is not a 'peaceful protester,'" based on police preconceptions of legitimate causes, and argued that there was a danger that "all protesters can be (and often are) presented as potentially violent." Jackson, Gilmore and Monk concurred (2019: 17) and argued that the police perception of acceptable and unacceptable protest was not based on the threat of violence "but on the target or goal of a protest and a desire to be disruptive." Mills (2015) criticised the use of civil legislation in seeking court injunctions to "control" protests and argued that this was an attempt to restrict the human rights of individuals wishing to protest. Further, Mobbs (2009: 20) observed that although there will always be disagreement about protest boundaries, there was "an obvious disparity between the stated 'rights of the individual' to free expression and association and the way in which the public's exercise of those rights are policed."

However, there are other relationships aside from that of police–protester which impact upon on the decision-making process regarding facilitating peaceful protest. Waddington (1998: 124) noted that "the police are duty-bound to balance the interests of everyone: protesters, motorists, bystanders, traders." Grace (2018: 5) described the difficult position for the police of "attempting to facilitate legitimate political protest whilst protecting the public from harm arising from unlawful or violent protest." Wood (2014: 16) described the challenge of policing protest as "networks of struggles" with external players such as activists, the general public, politicians and non-governmental organisations. In researching environmental protests, Button and John (2002: 119) identified numerous relationships in the policing of protest and observed that the relationship between the under-sheriff and the police commander was "of particular interest." Mansley (2014: 10) further noted that there was a requirement for the police to "protect both the democratic rights of those wishing to engage in the democratic process by protesting, and the 'peace', rights and property of those wishing to continue their lawful business." Dahlsrud (2008: 6) described the balance of often conflicting concerns as "a challenging task." Vitale (2005) surmised;

> As police departments review the varieties of strategies available to them in dealing with large and small-scale demonstrations they must attempt to balance the desire of residents and businesses to avoid disruption with the rights of demonstrators to express their views. The nature of that balancing point and how it is achieved is a constantly shifting equation.
>
> (Vitale, 2005: 302)

The challenge of balancing human rights led to an examination by Her Majesty's Inspectorate of Constabulary and Fire and Rescue Services (HMICFRS) of the police effectivity in dealing with protests, and the mandate that "a fair balance should be struck between individual rights and the general interests of the community" as "the police do not strike the right balance on every occasion" (HMICFRS, 2021). This review of protest policing suggested that this balance "may tip too readily in favour of protesters when – as is often the case – the police do not accurately assess the level of disruption caused, or likely to be caused, by a protest" (HMICFRS, 2021) and led to a proposed Police, Crime, Sentencing and Courts Bill 2021. The Bill was a response to address "certain tactics used by some protesters" which had "caused a disproportionate impact" on those seeking to go about daily business, disrupting public transport networks, draining public funds and resulting in 172 Metropolitan Police Service officers being "assaulted by a violent minority during the BLM protests" in the summer of 2020" (Home Office, 2022). The Bill also received much criticism, with those opposing the legislation describing it as "anti-protest law" to silence protesters and claiming that "it is cancel culture on a statutory footing, directed against the left" (Dunt, 2021). Opposition to the Bill also galvanised numerous "kill the bill" protests throughout the UK, where demonstrators condemned the proposed legislative change as "an attack on the right to protest" (Davies and Gayle, 2022). The Police, Crime, Sentencing and Courts Act was given royal assent in April 2022 (UK Parliament, 2022).

December 2021 heralded a further proposed change of legislation when the government announced their plans to reform the Human Rights Act and replace it with a Bill of Rights (Ministry of Justice, 2021b). The government stated that it would "continue this country's long tradition of protecting people's rights and freedoms" (Ministry of Justice, 2021a: 28) and that the proposals for a Bill of Rights were intended to restore the role of the Supreme Court in interpreting UK human rights law rather than being dictated by the European Court of Human Rights (ECHR) in Strasbourg. The Bill of Rights was intended to maintain the status quo in the UK of creating and maintaining a fair, free and tolerant society rather than conflict the ECHR Convention.

Despite a potential change in legislation, the government proposals for a Bill of Rights maintained the approach set out at Section 6(1) of the Human Rights Act 1998 making it unlawful for a public authority to act in a manner which is incompatible with rights. The government also clarified that "The rights as set out in Schedule 1 to the Human Rights Act will remain. We regard the Convention as offering a common-sense list of rights" (Ministry of Justice, 2021a: 56). Of the Bill of Rights, deputy prime minister Dominic Raab stated that

> The thrust is going to be making sure that when we balance rights, whether it's the right to free speech and the right to privacy or other rights, we make sure that the greatest overriding importance and weight is attached to free speech.

The proposed Bill would still maintain safeguards on free speech to prevent the incitement of violence or promotion of terrorism (Forrest, 2022).

However, whether the Bill is enacted into legislation or not, the balancing of rights is even more than that of balancing between the right to protest and the disruption of daily business. On occasions, the police must also balance the right to protest with the right to counterprotest as well as consider the impact on the community and transport networks. Therefore, the police must facilitate peaceful protests within the legislative framework within which they operate, cognisant of the nuances of a changing legal landscape and within the framework of the day. This requires the police balancing human rights as set out in Schedule 1 of the Human Rights Act 1998, a balancing act that will not change should a new Bill of Rights be brought into legislation (Ministry of Justice, 2021a). The courts will always legislate retrospectively on decisions made in protest situations where human rights have been engaged, whether that be in Strasbourg or at the Supreme Court. However, this does not prevent police commanders needing to make decision on the day in balancing competing rights. The next section outlines the Articles and the rights and freedoms as set out in Schedule 1 of the Human Rights Act and examines the legal structure within which the police must facilitate peaceful protest and balance human rights.

Human rights legislation

The Universal Declaration of Human Rights was adopted by the United Nations General Assembly on 10 December 1948 as a result of the experience of the Second World War (United Nations, 2015). The declaration of commitment to upholding dignity and justice was subsequently translated into law in the form of the European Convention on Human Rights, which was drafted by the nations of the Council of Europe (including the UK) in Strasbourg in 1949 and came into force on 3 September 1953 (European Convention on Human Rights, 2015).

However, it was not until 1998 that the Articles of the convention entered UK legislation via the Human Rights Act 1998, which came into effect in October 2000, and meant that human rights cases could now be taken to a UK court rather than to Strasbourg (Ministry of Justice, 2006). The Act had significant implications for all public authorities, including the police, as Section 6 made it "unlawful for a public authority to act in a way which is incompatible with a Convention right." A "public authority" was widely defined to include a court; a tribunal which exercises functions in relation to legal proceedings; and "any person certain of whose functions are functions of a public nature" (Ewing, 1999: 89). Willis (2001: 16) observed that the act would "have the effect of accelerating the drift towards a rights culture" and that policing would now become the guarantor of freedom of expression.

The Human Rights Act further places two types of human rights obligation on to public authorities: negative and positive. A positive obligation requires the authority undertake specific preventive or protective actions to secure human rights, whereas a negative obligation places a restriction on the actions undertaken by the authority. The UK Parliament website assisted in contextualising the obligations thus:

> An example of a negative obligation would include not placing unnecessary obstacles in the way of individuals wishing to protest. An example of

a positive obligation would include facilitating counter protests or protests in the same geographical location. Positive obligations can require the state to take steps to protect individuals from the actions of other private parties (such as companies against whom people may wish to protest, or targets of protests against protesters).

(Parliament, 2009)

The Act defines three categories of rights; absolute, limited and qualified rights (categories and rights which would be maintained in the proposed Bill of Rights). Absolute rights, for example the right to protection from torture and inhuman and degrading treatment (Article 3), can never be withheld or taken away by the state. Limited rights, for example the right to liberty (Article 5), may only be limited under explicit and finite circumstances (Ministry of Justice, 2015). However, of consideration for police commanders has been their decision-making where there is an engagement of qualified rights, "rights which require a balance between the rights of the individual and the needs of the wider community or state interest" (Ministry of Justice, 2006: 3). Qualified rights include:

- The right to freedom of thought, conscience and religion (Article 9)
- The right to freedom of expression (Article 10)
- The right to freedom of peaceful assembly and to freedom of association with others (Article 11)

(Ministry of Justice, 2015)

Articles 9, 10 and 11 form the basis of the rights of individual to participate in "peaceful protest" (College of Policing, 2013). Article 11 protects the right to protest peacefully but precludes participation in violent protests. It also places both negative and positive duties on the police; the police must not prevent, hinder or restrict peaceful assembly, nor impose restrictions that are unreasonable; however, in certain circumstances, the police have a duty "to take reasonable steps to protect those who want to exercise their rights peacefully" (College of Policing, 2016). However, there are competing qualified rights to those to peacefully protest, including:

- The right to respect for his private and family life, his home and his correspondence (Article 8)
- Every natural or legal person is entitled to the peaceful enjoyment of his possessions (Article 1 of Protocol 1)

(Ministry of Justice, 2015)

Interference with qualified rights is permissible only if there is a clear legal basis for the interference and the restriction fulfils "a pressing social need and must be proportionate to that need" (Ministry of Justice, 2006: 57) as set out in the

Articles. Further, all rights are to be read together with Article 17 which legislates that nothing in the Act may be interpreted as implying by anyone as the right to engage in "any activity or perform any act aimed at the destruction of any of the rights and freedoms" of the Human Rights Act 1998. Liberty (2011) paraphrased Article 17 in their guide that "none of the rights give anyone a right to engage in any activity that aims to destroy other people's rights and freedoms or limit them in ways not set out in the Convention."

The challenge for the police has therefore been managing protest situations that require "a fair balancing of competing rights" (Donald, Gordon and Leach, 2012: 78), for example in balancing the right to respect for privacy with the right to freedom of expression. Recognising the shortcomings identified by the HMIC, the police developed and incorporated comprehensive training inputs into human rights, in conjunction with Ms Jane Gordon, human rights legal advisor (HMIC, 2009b). The inputs were included in updated public order command training courses and subsequently PLT courses (NPIA, 2010; College of Policing, 2013) to ensure that the rights were "understood in practical and operational terms by individuals on the front line of public service delivery and applied to day-to-day service activities" (Gordon, 2010: 619). In applying human rights considerations in operational settings, a police commander must therefore consider whether their decision "engages a convention right" and if so, whether the decision "restrict or limit any of the rights it engages" (Department for Constitutional Affairs, 2006: 53). In seeking to reform the Human Rights Act, the government acknowledged the challenges of balancing competing rights and stated that they wished to "provide more guidance to the courts on how to balance qualified and limited rights" (Ministry of Justice, 2021a: 81). However, the proposed reform very much concentrated on the "legitimate aim of balancing the rights of individuals with the wider public interest" (Ministry of Justice, 2021a: 105) which was a response to the actions of some protesters having a disproportionate impact on daily life (Home Office, 2022). The challenge remains for the police commander to balance the rights of a group wishing to peacefully protest, not just with a wider public interest but also with the rights of another group to counterdemonstrate. This challenge will be considered in greater detail in Chapters 5, 6 and 7 of this book through the examination of two case studies. However, the following example is provided here to assist in understanding the practical and operational implications of identifying and balancing competing qualified rights.

In 2012, SodaStream opened the UK's first EcoStream store in Brighton, a store which "pumps household products such as laundry detergents, beauty products and cooking ingredients into reusable containers" (Keenan, 2012). However, the store immediately attracted protests from pro-Palestine campaigners who claimed that the store's "eco-image disguises the fact that it has set up its factory on land confiscated from Palestinians" (Brighton and Hove Palestine Solidarity Campaign, 2014). There then followed two years of regular street protests by pro-Palestine campaigners outside the store in central Brighton, and this attracted pro-Israel campaigners who attended to voice their own contrary views. The protests and counterdemonstrations continued on a weekly basis until the closure of the store in 2014. Benedictus (2013) summarised the complexities of the protest:

> The shoppers on Western Road have been able to witness an ethical-consuming protest against an ethical-consuming shop – and latterly a protest against that protest too, from pro-Israel activists.
>
> (Benedictus, 2013)

In identifying the qualified human rights engaged during these protests, consideration might be given to the rights of the pro-Palestine campaigners (Articles 9, 10 and 11), the rights of the pro-Israel campaigners (Articles 9, 10 and 11), the store owners and staff (Article 8 and Article 1 of Protocol 1), and the shoppers and local residents (Article 8 and Article 1 of Protocol 1). As all the Articles are qualified rights, a balance must be struck with competing rights. Further, all rights must be read in light of Article 17. There is a positive obligation for the police to facilitate both protest and counterprotest in the same geographical location. The decision and rationale in striking a balance between the competing rights of all ultimately lies with a police commander. The results of this decision may determine the location and duration of each protest, and the perception of the validity of the decision may have a considerable impact on the demeanour and action of all parties involved in the protests.

Balancing qualified rights

Whilst providing clear direction and recommendations for the policing of protest post the London G20 demonstrations, HMIC recognised the "policing dilemma" that existed in balancing the rights of protesters and other citizens. The report clearly defined the police role:

> Presently, the police are required to act as arbiter, balancing the rights of protesters against the rights of the wider public, the business community and local residents. In dealing with this dilemma, the police must take a common-sense approach.
>
> (HMIC, 2009a: 5)

Starmer (1999: 169) described the balancing of qualified rights as the "need to find a fair balance between the protection of individual rights and the interests of the community at large." Gilmore (2013: 209) questioned the role of the police "as neutral arbitrators" and argued that "the official discourse obscures the fundamental power imbalance between the police and protest groups: they do not stand before the law as equals." Nevertheless, UK legislation such as the

Public Order Act 1986 placed requirements on the police in making legislative decisions and Neyroud and Beckley (2001: 60) argued that the Human Rights Act has implication for the police "as both the guarantor of those rights and, as it seeks to enforce the law and balance the rights of victims, offenders and community, the agency most directly exposed to their effect." Mead (2010: 146) further observed that the right to peaceful protest "needs properly to be tempered by and balanced against legitimate security concerns and the need to avoid damaging disruption to the day's business."

In considering human rights, the police commander must balance the rights of individuals comprised in Article 11(1) of the Act, the right to freedom of peaceful assembly, against what Mead (2010: 36) described as "the general (perhaps more nebulous?) community interest" comprised in Article 11(2) of the Act, namely that no restrictions shall be placed on the exercise of the right to peacefully assemble "other than such as are prescribed by law and are necessary in a democratic society in the interests of national security or public safety" (Human Rights Act, 1998). Neyroud and Beckley (2001) provided a case study to illustrate the tactical discretion in application;

> An extreme political grouping applies to march through the main town of the police area. Their presence seems likely to provoke violent counter-demonstrations and fear in the community. The police commander has to decide whether to permit the march or seek to ban it. In doing so he/she must balance the rights of the marchers and the local community and set the right tactics to achieve that balance.
> (Neyroud and Beckley, 2001: 84)

Furthermore, the police commander must consider case law in applying a human rights approach and if restricting the right to peaceful protest (Parliament, 2009) and be cognisant of the rulings made by the European Court of Human Rights in scrutinising whether actions or decisions were relevant and sufficient in the circumstances (Mead, 2010). Thus, *Appleby and Others v The United Kingdom [2001] ECHR 6* informed decisions regarding the positive obligations owed under Articles 10 and 11 to protect the right of the peaceful protest while at the same time balancing with those of property owners. In contrast, *Regina (Brehony) v Chief Constable of Manchester Police [2005] QBD 23* impacted upon decisions made regarding restricting conditions placed on a counterdemonstration in close proximity to the protest outside a shop in Manchester. However, *Plattform Ärzte Für das Leben v Austria [1988] EHRR 204* highlighted a breach of Article 11 where the police did not prevent the actions of those engaged in a counter-demonstration. *Percy v Director of Public Prosecutions [2001] ADMN 21* outlined the balancing act between on one side facilitating freedom of expression and on the other corporate rights regarding Article 1 of Protocol 1 and of members of the public under Articles 3 and 8. *R (on the application of Laporte) v Chief Constable of Gloucestershire Constabulary [2006] UKHL 55* provided consideration of Articles 10 and 11 pertaining to the immediacy of the apprehended breach of the peace. *Redmond-Bate v Director of Public Prosecutions [1999] ADMN 23* had further bearing regarding the direction from which the breach of the peace came, Lord Justice Sedley ruling that Article 10 included freedom of speech that included "not only the inoffensive but the irritating, the contentious, the eccentric, the heretical, the unwelcome and the provocative, provided it does not tend to provoke violence" (Swarbrick, 2016). Further, *R (McClure & Moos) v Commissioner of Police of the Metropolis*

[2011] EWHC 957 provided consideration regarding the police tactic of containing protesters and ensuring that there was a reasonably apprehended breach of the peace sufficient to justify such action. Additionally, *R (on the application of Hicks and Others) v Commissioner of Police of the Metropolis [2017] UKSC 9* contained implications under Article 5 regarding pre-emptive arrests, which deemed it lawful for the police "to detain persons to prevent a breach of the peace and to release them once the risk had disappeared without bringing them before a competent court" (Riddell, 2017).

It is in this legislative landscape with the backdrop of such case law that the police must make their decisions in an often-changing protest environment. However, as Clapham (2014: 1) noted, the paradox for the police commander is that "the application of human rights law in court is almost always contested, with both parties to a dispute demanding that human rights law be applied in their favour." Contrastingly, Gilmore, who highlighted "dangers in relying on human rights law as a panacea for progressive reforms in public order policing" (2013: 211) also recognised the limitations of applying "abstract legal principles" in seeking to highlight "the repressive function of law and policing practices and the fragility of official interpretations of human rights" (2013: 63). Further Neyroud and Beckley (2001) observed;

> It is also important to recognise that police officers have both responsibilities and rights – to be protected, to private and family life and to freedom of expression and assembly to name but three – and the balance between them and the rights of other citizens provides an additional complexity to the dilemmas of police managers.
>
> (Neyroud and Beckley, 2001: 87)

If it is accepted, as Bronitt and Stenning (2011: 320) argued, that "police work by its very nature is discretionary in the sense that it involves the exercise of choice or judgement," then not only are the decisions made by police commanders key in the balancing of the competing human rights of those engaged in a protest event, the communication of the rationale behind such decisions may prove vital in facilitating the right of all. For as Bourne (2011: 190) noted, "The right to peaceful protest is thus intrinsically and necessarily communicative." The next section of this chapter will further explore a communicative approach to policing protest events.

Communication between police and protesters

D. Waddington (2007: 59) argued that "The greater the police emphasis on police negotiation and communication with the crowd, the lesser are the chances of violence escalating." However, different communication strategies have been witnessed when policing protest events. McPhail, Schweingruber and McCarthy (1998) observed that communication between the police and protesters was minimal under an escalated force approach. della Porta and Reiter (1998) noted that the degree to which the police communicated with demonstrators defined their styles of protest policing from a confrontational to a consensual approach. P. Waddington (1998) suggested that a negotiated management approach placed a requirement for organisers of protesters to engage with the police. Alternatively, Joyce and Wain (2014: 262) purported that "liaison between the police and protesters is not necessarily confrontational," and argued that organisers realised they required police cooperation in areas such as traffic management and would therefore voluntarily agree to police suggestions. Joyce and Wain concluded that opposition was more likely to come from those that do not accept the authority of the state and thus refuse to comply with legislative requirements. De Lint (2005: 194) argued that "communications are the best way to improve public order practice." Baker (2014) further observed:

> Dialog with protesters, by fostering communication, negotiated agreements and conflict mediation provides some degree of legitimacy and order to large-scale protest and the opportunity for peaceful dissent.
> (Baker, 2014: 100)

Wahlström and Oskarsson's study into political protest in Gothenburg and Copenhagen (2006) mapped their findings against three stages of negotiation between police and protesters: entering into communication; coming to agreement; and the outcomes of such evaluation and its value to those engaged in the process. They argued that if any value was to be gained from engaging in dialogue, it was essential that the police understood that their actions may both calm the situation and provoke protest, even when these protests were peaceful. Wahlström and Oskarsson concluded that by breaking down mutual distrust and going beyond previous negative experiences, all involved parties in the protest would be satisfied, resulting in a minimal recourse to violence. Wahlström and Oskarsson observed that although most demonstrators saw value in engaging in dialogue with the police, some expressed serious doubts. This lack of trust was attributed to a belief that the police were only engaging to attempt to manipulate protesters and gain information, and an expectation that the police would break their promises. This was exacerbated by a police desire to communicate with demonstration leaders, which was in direct conflict with the non-hierarchical order within the protesting community consisting of several autonomous groups. However, Wahlström and Oskarsson observed several occasions when the demonstrators and the police still tried to maintain lines of communication, despite the mistrust.

Atak and della Porta (2016) argued that police perceptions were negatively biased in labelling protesters irrational, dangerous and illegitimate, and such cynicism constrained a dialogical approach to policing protest groups. Redekop and Paré (2010) advocated an approach where the police respected protesters as principled dissenters and in turn protesters respected the police as non-repressive public order agents. Redekop and Paré (2010: 17) proposed a relational system where the interests of the police and protesters were "mutually affected," and analysed the relationship that a protest crowd had with the police, as well as with the target of the protest, bystanders, media, counterprotest crowd and society. della Porta and Reiter (1998: 21) argued that police–protester dialogue was an ongoing process, not restricted to the dynamics of a single encounter, but that "individual incidents may have long-term repercussions on police attitudes toward protest."

In their research into the policing of anti-"fracking" protest, Jackson, Gilmore and Monk (2019: 11) observed that the protesters were not included as "one of the parties with 'mutual interests' in the delivery of the Gold strategy" and therefore not afforded the same access to policing as were the local authority, land owners or the energy company itself. Peterson argued (2006: 63) that "police knowledge of protest cultures and particular activist organizations and networks is fundamental for good public order policing." Peterson concluded that this knowledge was most effectively accumulated over a period through the police having direct contact with those organising protest events, allowing the police to plan most effectively for the event. della Porta and Atak (2015) observed that the police also consisted of multiple players who interacted internally and externally to shape protest dynamics.

Trust, relationship building and understanding of the intentions of protesters have therefore been identified as key considerations for the police (for example, Gillham and Noakes, 2007; Redekop and Paré, 2010; Jackson, Gilmore and Monk, 2019). In addressing such considerations, De Lint (2005: 195) observed that the flow of communication was "dependent on some transparency of intention" and this worked most effectively through visible liaison. Wood (2014: 158) argued that although there may be variations from police force to police force and within the ranks therein, "overall, police culture contributes to a general suspicion about both protesters, and their activities." Further Waddington (2007) postulated that liaison officers should be local officers who are likely to have cognisance of "cultural sensibilities" and concerned with the implications of their actions on the long-term relationship between the police and the local community. Communication between police and protesters and the use of PLT as a conduit between both parties will be further explored in the next chapter.

Conclusion

Research into the policing of protest is plentiful, and this chapter has mapped different approaches implemented over recent decades and across a range of events in different continents, from an escalated force though negotiated management and strategic incapacitation to the emergence of an approach centred on strategic facilitation. This chapter has further examined the competing pressures of political influences and balancing competing human rights that encumber police commanders in decision-making. It has been argued that the different approaches identified are not sequenced historical developments but provide a range of strategic options that police commanders are able to deploy in policing protest events. The use of this strategic policing tool kit will be further explored in further chapters.

Despite the extensive research into protest policing, this chapter has identified that there is limited contemporary research that examines protest events within the UK. Furthermore, all existing literature examines the police–protester relationship. As will be further explored in the next chapter, protesters and the police are two of several groups of social actors that are affected by protest events. The research offered in this book will add to the body of research by providing a contemporary insight into the policing of protest events in the UK. Further, it will fill the lacuna in existing literature by examining the role and identity of a range of groups and interested parties affected by a protest event and considering their interaction with the police prior to and during the event.

References

Atak, K. and della Porta, D. (2016) Popular uprisings in Turkey: Police culpability and constraints on dialogue-oriented policing in Gezi Park and beyond. *European Journal of Criminology*, 13(5), 610–625.

Baker, D. (2014) Police and protester dialog: Safeguarding the peace or ritualistic sham? *International Journal of Comparative and Applied Criminal Justice*, 38(1), 83–104.

Bartos, O. and Wehr, P. (2002) *Using conflict theory*. Cambridge: Cambridge University Press.

Baxter, N. (2001) *Policing the line: The development of a theoretical model for the policing of conflict*. Dartmouth: Ashgate.

Benedictus, L (2013) SodaStream: The Israeli-run shop dividing Brighton. *The Guardian* [online], 29 September 2013. Available at: http://www.theguardian.com/uk-news/shortcuts

Bourne, K. (2011) Commanding and controlling protest crowds. *Critical Horizons*, 12(2), 189–210.

Brighton and Hove Palestine Solidarity Campaign (2014) *EcoStream store closes following two years of street protests* [online], 1 July 2014. Available at: http://www.brightonpalestinecampaign.org/local-news-reports/

Bronitt S. and Stenning P. (2011) Understanding discretion in modern policing. *Criminal Law Journal*, 35, 319–332.

Button, M. and John, T. (2002) 'Plural policing' in action: A review of the policing of environmental protests in England and Wales. *Policing and Society*, 12(2), 111–121.

Button, M., John, T and Brearley, N. (2002) New challenges in public order policing: The professionalisation of environmental protest and the emergence of the militant environmental activist. *International Journal of the Sociology of Law*, 30, 17–32.

Clapham, A. (2014) *Human rights: A very short introduction*. Oxford: Oxford University Press.

Coleman, R. (2004) *Reclaim the streets: Surveillance, social control and the city*. Cullompton, Devon: Willan Publishing.

Coleman, R., Sim, J., Tombs, S. and Whyte, D. (2009) *State, power, crime*. London: Sage Publications.

College of Policing (2013) *National Police Public Order Training Curriculum: Police Liaison Team trainers guide*. Wyboston: College of Policing.

College of Policing (2016) *Authorised Professional Practice* [online] Available at: https://www.app.college.police.uk/

College of Policing (2018) *Police liaison teams* [online] Available at: https://www.app.college.police.uk/app-content/public-order/planning-and-deployment/

Crown Prosecution Service (2019) *Public order offences incorporating the charging standard* [online] Available at: https://www.cps.gov.uk/legal-guidance/public-order-offences-incorporating-charging-standard

Dahlsrud, A. (2008) How corporate social responsibility is defined: An analysis of 37 definitions. *Corporate Social Responsibility and Environmental Management*, 15, 1–13.

Davies, C. and Gayle, D. (2022) 'Kill the bill' protests: New legislation is proportionate, says Buckland. *The Guardian* [online] 17 January 2022. Available at: https://www.theguardian.com/law/2022/jan/17/kill-the-bill-protests-new-legislation-proportionate-robert-buckland

de Lint, W. (2005) Public order policing: A tough act to follow? *International Journal of the Sociology of Law*, 33, 179–199.

della Porta, D. and Atak, K. (2015) The police, in Duyvendak, J. and Jasper, J. eds., *Breaking down the state: Protestors engage*. Amsterdam: Amsterdam University Press.

della Porta, D., Peterson, A. and Reiter, H. (2006) *The policing of transnational protest*. Aldershot: Ashgate.

della Porta, D. and Reiter, H. (1998) *Policing protest: The control of mass demonstrations in Western democracies*. Minneapolis: University of Minnesota Press.

della Porta D., and Reiter, H. (2006) The policing of global protest: The G8 at Genoa and its aftermath, in della Porta, D., Peterson, A. and Reiter, H. eds., *The policing of transnational protest*, 13–41. Aldershot: Ashgate.

Department for Constitutional Affairs (2006) *Human rights: Human lives*. London: Crown Copyright.

Donald, A., Gordon, J. and Leach, P. (2012) *The UK and the European Court of Human Rights*. London: Equality and Human Rights Commission.

Dunt, I. (2021) *Silencing Black Lives Matter: Priti Patel's anti-protest Law* [online] Available at: https://www.politics.co.uk/comment/2021/03/11/silencing-black-lives-matter-priti-patels-anti-protest-law

European Convention on Human Rights (2015) *The European Convention* [online] Available at: http://www.echr.coe.int/Pages/home

Ewing, K. (1999) The Human Rights Act and parliamentary democracy. *The Modern Law Review*, 62(1), 79–99.

Fenwick, H. (2009) Marginalising human rights: Breach of the peace, 'kettling', the Human Rights Act and public protest. *Public Law*, 2009(4), 737–765.

Forrest, A. (2022) Raab vows to protect free speech from 'wokery' with plan to scrap Human Rights Act. *Independent* [online] 27 March 2022. Available at: https://www.independent.co.uk/news/uk/politics/woke-free-speech-raab-human-rights

Gillham, P. (2011) Securitizing America: Strategic incapacitation and the policing of protest since the 11 September 2001 terrorist attacks. *Sociology Compass*, 5(7), 636–652.

Gillham, P. and Noakes, J. (2007) "More than a march in a circle": Transgressive protests and the limits of negotiated management. *Mobilization*, 12(4), 341–357.

Gilmore, J. (2013) *'This is not a riot!' Regulation of public protest and the impact of the Human Rights Act 1998*, Ph.D. thesis. The University of Manchester.

Gilmore, J., Jackson, W. and Monk, H. (2016) *Keep moving! Report on the policing of the Barton Moss community protection camp: November 2013 –April 2014*. Centre for the Study of Crime, Criminalisation and Social Exclusion, Liverpool John Moores University: Centre for Urban Research, University of York.

Goold, B. (2016) Policing and human rights, in Bradford, B., Jauregui, B., Loader, I. and Steinberg, J. eds. *The Sage handbook of global policing*. London: Sage Publications.

Gordon, J. (2010) A developing Human Rights culture in the UK? Case studies of policing, in *European Human Rights Law Review*, 609–620. London: Thomson Reuters (Legal) Limited and Contributors.

Gorringe, H and Rosie, M (2008) It's a long way to Auchterarder! 'Negotiated management' and mismanagement in the policing of G8 protests. *British Journal of Sociology*, 59(2), 187–205.

Gorringe, H., Rosie, M., Waddington, D. and Kominou, M. (2012) Facilitating ineffective protest? The policing of the 2009 Edinburgh NATO protests. *Policing and Society*, 22(2), 115–132.

Grace, J. (2018) A balance of rights and protections in public order policing: A case study on Rotherham. *European Journal of Current Legal Issues*, 24 (1–25).

Gravelle, J. and Rogers, C. (2011) Engaging protesters: A smarter way for policing demonstrations. *The Police Journal*, 84, 5–12.

Greer, C. and McLaughlin, E. (2010) We predict a riot? Public order policing, new media environments and the rise of the citizen journalist. *British Journal of Criminology*, 50(6), 1041–1059.

Hansard (1985) *Public order legislation: Review*. House of Lords debate. 16 May 1985, 463, 1276–85 [online] Available at: http://hansard.millbanksystems.com/lords/1985/may/16/public-order-legislation-review

Harris, S., Joseph-Salisbury, R., Williams, P. and White, L. (2021) Notes on policing, racism and the Covid-19 pandemic in the UK. *Institute of Race Relations*, 63(3), 92–102.

Her Majesty's Inspectorate of Constabulary. (2009a) *Adapting to protest*. London: HMIC.

Her Majesty's Inspectorate of Constabulary (2009b) *Adapting to protest: Nurturing the British model of policing*. London: HMIC.

Her Majesty's Inspectorate of Constabulary and Fire and Rescue Services (2021) *Getting the balance right? An inspection of how effectively the police deal with protests*. London: HMICFRS.

Home Office (2022) *Police, Crime, Sentencing and Courts Bill 2021: Protest powers factsheet*. London: Crown Copyright.

Jackson, J. and Bradford, B. (2009) Crime, policing and social order: On the expressive nature of public confidence in policing. *British Journal of Sociology*, 60(3), 493–521.

Jackson, W., Gilmore, J. and Monk, H. (2019) Policing unacceptable protest in England and Wales: A case study of the policing of anti-fracking protests. *Critical Social Policy*, 39(1), 23–43.

Jefferson, T. (1990) *The case against paramilitary policing*. Philadelphia: Open University Press.

Johnson, L. (1999) Private policing in context. *European Journal on Criminal Policy and Research*, 7(2), 175–196.

Joyce, P. (1992) Decade of disorder. *Policing*, 8(3), 232–248.

Joyce, P. (2009) The policing of protest. *Policing Today*, 15(3), 30–33.

Joyce, P. and Wain, N. (2014) *Palgrave dictionary of public order policing, protest and political violence*. London: Palgrave Macmillan.

Keenan, J (2012) Unbottling the debate over Brighton's Ecostream store. The Argus [online], 23 October 2012. Available at: http://www.theargus.co.uk

Kelling, G. and Coles, C. (1996) *Fixing broken windows: Restoring order and reducing crime in our communities*. New York: Free Press.

Kilgallon, A. (2020) Policing in dispute: Academia versus activism. *Policing*, 14(4), 843–845.

King, M.L. (1963) *Letter from a Birmingham Jail, April 16, 1963*. Natural Law, Natural Rights, and American Constitutionalism. Available at: http://www.nlnrac.org/american/american-civil-rights-movements/

King, M. (2006) From reactive policing to crowd management? Policing anti-globalization in Canada. *Jurisprudencija*, 1(79), 40–58. Available at: https://repository.mruni.eu/bitstream/handle

King, M. and Brearley, N. (1996) *Public order policing: Contemporary perspectives on strategy and tactics*. Leicester: Perpetuity Press.

King, M. and Waddington, D. (2005) Flashpoints revisited: A critical application to the policing of anti-globalization. *Protest, Policing and Society*, 15(3), 255–282.

Le Bon, G. (1895) *The crowd: A study of the popular mind*. London: Unwin.

Liberty (2011) *A Journalist's guide to the Human Rights Act*. London: Liberty (National Council for Civil Liberties).

Liberty (2022) *The Policing Bill: What you Need to Know* [online] Available at: https://www.libertyhumanrights.org.uk/issue/the-policing-bill-what-you-need-to-know/

Liberty (2016) *Article 11 right to protest and freedom of association* [online] Available at: https://www.liberty-human-rights.org.uk/human-rights/what-are-human-rights/human-rights-act

Mansley, D (2014) *Collective Violence, Democracy and Protest Policing*. London and New York: Routledge.

Mathers, M. (2022) Attorney general says Colston verdict is 'confusing' and considers referring case to Court of Appeal. *Independent* [online], 7 January 2022. Available at: https://www.independent.co.uk/politics/colston-statue-bristol-case-appeal-b1988630.html

McCarthy, J. and McPhail, C. (1998) The Institutionalization of Protest in the United States, in Meyer, D. and Tarrow, S. eds., *The Social Movement Society: Contentious Politics for a New Century*, 83–110. New York: Rowman and Littlefield.

McKerrell, N (2021) Scottish public protest at a time of Covid-19. *Edinburgh Law Review*, 25, 105–111.

McPhail, C., Schweingruber, D. and McCarthy, J. (1998) Policing protest in the United States: 1960–1995 in della Porta, D. and Reiter, R. eds., *Policing protest: The control of mass demonstrations in western democracies*, 49–69. Minneapolis: University of Minnesota Press.

Mead, D. (2021) Policing protest in a pandemic. *King's Law Journal*, 32(1), 96–108.

Mead, D. (2010) *The new law of peaceful protest: Rights and regulation in the human rights act era.* Oxford: Hart.

Mills, G. (2015) 'Injunctivitis': A blurring of the policing of protest or a vision of the way ahead? *International Journal of Police Science and Management*, 17(2), 128–133.

Ministry of Justice (2015) *Human Rights Act* [online] London. Crown copyright. Available at: http://www.legislation.gov.uk/ukpga/1998

Ministry of Justice (2021a) *Human Rights Act reform: A modern bill of Rights: A consultation to reform the Human Rights Act 1998.* London: Crown Copyright. Available at: https://www.gov.uk/government/consultations/human-rights-act-reform-a-modern-bill-of-rights

Ministry of Justice (2021b) *Press release: Plan to reform Human Rights Act* [online] Available at: https://www.gov.uk/government/news/plan-to-reform-human-rights-act

Ministry of Justice (2006) *Making sense of Human Rights* [pdf] Ministry of Justice, Crown copyright. Available at: http://www.justice.gov.uk/downloads

Mobbs, P. (2009) *NETCU, WECTU and NPOIU: Britain's secretive police force – politicising the policing of public expression in an era of economic change* [pdf]. The Free Range Electrohippies Project. Available at: http://www.fraw.org.uk/fraw_admin

Myers-Montgomery, J. (2016) Militarized police and unpermitted protest: Implementing policy that civilizes the police. *Cultural Studies ↔ Critical Methodologies*, 16(3), 278–286.

National Policing Improvement Agency (2010) *Trainer's Guide: Public Order Bronze / Silver Interim Course.* Wyboston, Bedfordshire: National Policing Improvement Agency.

Noakes, J. and Gillham, P. (2006) Aspects of the 'New Penology' in the police response to major political protests in the United States, 1999–2000, in della Porta, D., Peterson, A. and Reiter, H. eds., *The policing of transnational protest*, 97–115. Aldershot: Ashgate.

Neyroud, P. and Beckley, A. (2001) *Policing, ethics and human rights.* Cullompton: Willan Publishing.

Oberschall, A. (2010) Conflict theory, in Leicht, K. and Jenkins, c. eds. *Handbook of politics: State and society in global perspective*, 177–193. New York: Springer.

Parliament (2009) *Demonstrating respect for rights? A human rights approach to policing protest* [online]. Available at: https://publications.parliament.uk/pa/jt200809/jtselect/jtrights

Peterson, A. (2006) Policing contentious politics at transnational summits: Darth Vader or the keystone cops? in della Porta, D., Peterson, A. and Reiter, H. eds., *The policing of transnational protest*, 33–74. Aldershot: Ashgate.

Public Order Act (1986) Chapter 86 [online] London: HMSO 1986. Available at: http://www.legislation.gov.uk/ukpga/1986/64

Ratliff, T. and Hall, L. (2104) Practicing the art of dissent: Toward a typology of protest activity in the United States. *Humanity and Society*, 38(3), 268–294.

Redekop, V. and Paré, S. (2010) *Beyond control: A mutual respect approach to protest crowd-police relations.* London: Bloomsbury.

Reform Section 5 (2013) *Victory!* [online] Available at: http://reformsection5.org.uk/2012/12/victory-in-the-house-of-lords/

Reiner, R. (1998) Policing, protest, and disorder in Britain, in della Porta, D. and Reiter, R. eds., *Policing Protest: The Control of Mass Demonstrations in Western Democracies*, 35–48. Minneapolis: University of Minnesota Press.

Reinka, M and Leach, C. (2017) Race and reaction: Divergent views of police violence and protest against. *Journal of Social Issues*, 73(4), 768–788.

Riddell, J. (2017) *R (Hicks) v Commissioner of Police for the Metropolis* [online] Available at: https://www.weightmans.com/insights/r-hicks-v-commissioner-of-police-for-the-metropolis

Rosie, M. and Gorringe, H. (2009) What a difference a death makes: Protest, policing and the press at the G20. *Sociological Research Online*, 14(5:4), 1–12.

Scarman, L. (1982). *The Scarman report: The Brixton disorders 10–12 April 1981: Report of an inquiry*. Harmondsworth: Penguin.

Soares, M., Barbosa, M., Matos, R., and Mendes, S. (2018) Public protest and police violence: Moral disengagement and its role in police repression of public demonstrations in Portugal. *Journal of Peace Psychology*, 24(1), 27–35.

Solomon, E., Eades, C., Garside, R. and Rutherford, M. (2007) *Ten years of criminal justice under Labour: An independent audit*. London: Centre for Crime and Justice Studies.

Starmer, K. (1999) *European human rights law: The Human Rights Act 1998 and the European Convention on Human Rights*. London: Legal Action Group.

Stott, C., Scothern, M., and Gorringe, H. (2013) Advances in Liaison based public order policing in England: Human rights and negotiating the management of protest? *Policing*, 7(2), 212–226.

Swarbrick, D. (2016) *Redmond-Bate v Director of Public Prosecutions; ADMN 23 Jul 1999* [online] Available at: http://swarb.co.uk/redmond-bate-v-director-of-public-prosecutions-admn-23-jul-1999.

Travis, A. (2015) Theresa May rejects Boris Johnson's request to use water cannon. *The Guardian* [online], 15 July 2015 Available at: https://www.theguardian.com/uk-news/2015/jul/15

Turner, R. (1969) The Public Perception of Protest. *American Sociological Review*, 34(6), 815–831.

UK Parliament (2022) *Parliamentary Bills: Police, Crime, Sentencing and Courts Bill* [online] Available at: https://bills.parliament.uk/bills/2839

United Nations (2015) *Universal Declaration of Human Rights: History of the document* [online] Available at: https://www.un.org/en/about-us/udhr/history-of-the-declaration

Villiers, P. (1997) Protest policing. *Police Review*, 8 August 1997, 20–21.

Vitale, A. (2005) From negotiated management to command and control: How the New York Police Department polices protests. *Policing and Society*, 15(3), 283–304.

Waddington, D. (1992) *Contemporary issues in public disorder: A comparative and historical approach*. London: Routledge

Waddington, D. (2011) Policing contemporary political protest: From strategic incapacitation to strategic facilitation? [online] Available at: http://www.shu.ac.uk/research/cresr/sites/shu.ac.uk/files/

Waddington, D. (2007) *Policing public disorder: Theory and practice*. Cullompton: Willan Publishing.

Waddington, P. (1994a) Coercion and accommodation: Policing public order after the Public Order Act. *The British Journal of Sociology*, 45(3), 367–385.

Waddington, P. (1994b) *Liberty and order: Public order policing in a capital city*. London: U.C.L. Press.

Waddington, P. (1998) Controlling protest in contemporary historical and comparative perspective, in della Porta, D. and Reiter, R. eds., *Policing protest: The control of mass demonstrations in Western Democracies*, 117–142. Minneapolis: University of Minnesota Press.

Wahlström, M. and Oskarsson, M. (2006) Negotiating political protest in Gothenburg and Copenhagen in della Porta, D., Peterson, A. and Reiter, H. eds., *The policing of transnational protest*, 117–144. Aldershot: Ashgate.

Walsh, J. and Ungson, G. (1991) Organizational memory. *The Academy of Management Review*, 16(1), 57–91.

Weitzer, R. (1995) *Policing under fire: Ethnic conflict and police-community relations in Northern Ireland*. Albany: State University of New York Press.

Werren, C. (2014) Intelligence gathering and the need for control: Managing risk in public order policing. *Criminal Justice Matters*, 96(1), 22–23.

Williamson, V., Trump, K. and Einstein, K. (2018) Black Lives Matter: Evidence that police-caused deaths predict protest activity. *Perspectives on Politics*, 16(2), 400–415.

Willis, A. (2001) Public order policing in the UK: A fading star? *Police Practice*, 2(1–2), 15–26. Leicester. Overseas Publishers Association.

Wood, L. (2014) *Crisis and control: The militarization of protest policing*. London: Pluto Press.

Chapter 3

A theoretical framework for a dialogical approach

Introduction

The previous chapter explored policing and protests and established that a police approach based on communication and dialogue created a sound footing for pursuing a negotiated management approach (Waddington, 1994; della Porta and Reiter, 1998) and accelerating a move towards strategic facilitation (Waddington, 2011; Gorringe et al., 2012). Within UK policing, contemporary crowd psychology under the banner of the ESIM (for example, Reicher, 1996), has provided a theoretical basis for examining communication between police and protesters. The model formed the theoretical grounding for the development of PLT (Stott, 2009; HMIC, 2009b; NPIA, 2010) and has been integrated into police training (College of Policing, 2013), doctrine (College of Policing, 2016) and deployment (Gorringe, Stott and Rosie, 2012). Alternatively, Waddington (2013) argued that the Flashpoints Model of Public Disorder provided a more comprehensive context in which to analyse the success of a liaison-based police approach. This chapter will critically examine both theoretical approaches to the policing of protest.

Further, the previous chapter established that trust (della Porta and Reiter, 1998; Gillham and Noakes, 2007; Gilmore, Jackson and Monk, 2016) and legitimacy (Wahlström and Oskarsson, 2006; Atak and della Porta, 2016) are key components of a dialogical approach. Such components also constitute an integral part of procedural justice theory (for example, Lind and Tyler, 1988; Bradford, 2014) and this theory is here offered as a complimentary theoretical approach in examining protest policing. Therefore, this chapter will explore a procedurally just approach and consider whether it may be both epistemologically compatible and blended with ESIM and/or Flashpoints to yield critical insights into understanding dialogical forms of policing protests. Further examination will then be made as to how police commanders may deploy different approaches to the policing of protest events within this theoretical framework. Final examination of the sparse research that has been conducted into the use of Police Liaison Teams (PLT) will conclude the chapter.

DOI: 10.4324/9781003160533-3

A theoretical framework

Elaborated Social Identity Model

Classic theory (for example, Le Bon, 1895) remained the leading theory of crowd psychology throughout the 20th century and was still perceived as the driving force behind the rationale of police commanders in policing protest crowds in the 21st century (Hoggett and Stott, 2010a; b). Rosie and Gorringe (2009: 3) argued that the police perception of crowds was significantly influenced by the established press, who reinforced classic theory through sensationalised stories of the "madding crowd," which may have resulted in police forces viewing protesters "as liable to turn into a mob." Stott and Drury (2016) observed that classical theory continued to be salient in popular culture, despite being lacking in support and outmoded. Further, Hoggett and Stott (2010a: 224) observed police commanders making decisions on crowd policing during their command training that were based on a classic crowd psychology belief that "a certain group intent on disorder were the primary factor governing the behaviour of the rest of the crowd." Hoggett and Stott (2010b: 223) postulated that this might lead to "police practices that inadvertently escalate public disorder." Stott (2009: 6) argued that classical theory "lacks any sustainable empirical support" and was outdated and recommended (2009: 3) that training in crowd psychology should be updated "to reflect contemporary theory and evidence." Stott (2009: 2) contended that ESIM was "now the leading scientific theory of crowd psychology" and that it provided a "theoretical basis for accurately explaining and predicting the nature of crowd behaviour, particularly as this relates to the emergence of collective 'disorder.'"

There is a considerable body of contemporary social science research that contradicts classic theory (for example, Reicher, 1996; Drury and Reicher, 2000; Drury, Reicher and Stott, 2003; Stott et al., 2008). The research has culminated in the development of ESIM which places greater emphasis on describing crowd events as "characteristically intergroup encounters" (Drury and Reicher, 2000: 581) and perceives the action of a crowd as socially meaningful, rather than irrational as Le Bon (1895) argued. The model emphasises a necessity to analyse crowd events as developing interactions between groups, where the understandings of one group "forms the actions which constrain the actions of the other" (Drury and Reicher, 2000: 579).

The origin of ESIM is found in social identity theory, a "social psychological analysis of the role of self-conception in group membership, group processes and inter group relations" (Hogg, 2006: 111). The theory was first developed in the UK by Tajfel (1978) and intertwined with self-categorisation theory to formulate a social identity approach (van Knippenberg, 2000). As the area of research grew, research was spawned in different academic fields and within social psychology, and led to Reicher (1984) developing a Social

Identity Model (SIM). Reicher conducted research into the St Paul's riots and proposed that the behaviour of an individual was affected in some part by their social self-definition. Reicher (1984: 19) argued that "not only is crowd behaviour moulded by social identity but conversely, crowd behaviour may mould social identity." Reicher proposed that individuals experienced a sense of pride for the first time because of their collective action in rioting against the police.

Reicher (1996) further expanded the model through research into the policing of student demonstrations in London and argued that legitimacy was a key component in the perception of both police and students. Reicher noted different narratives between groups and suggested that this ultimately affected the interaction between them, which escalated into conflict and resulted in the police using force to disperse crowds. Reicher argued that understanding legitimacy therefore provided an indication both of whether a crowd might enter conflict, and of the circumstances where crowd members who might see conflict as a legitimate action might not automatically confront the police. This extension of SIM matured to produce the ESIM, based on the observation that "crowd events are typically intergroup encounters and therefore the position of any one party must be understood in relation to the ongoing intergroup dynamic" (Drury and Reicher, 1999: 385).

The ESIM entailed three elements: "Concepts," "conditions" and "dynamics." Stott, Hutchinson and Drury (2001) described the "concept" as the context in which any one group acted as formed by the identity-based actions of other groups. Drury, Stott and Farsides (2003) based the "conditions" on the understanding that crowd conflict entailed an interaction between asymmetrical groups, between a crowd and an out-group, typically the police. Drury, Stott and Farsides argued that an in-group action against the police (as an out-group) might therefore be legitimised by the group where they perceive the out-group's actions to be illegitimate. Finally, "dynamics" considered inter- and intra-group dynamics. Stott, Hutchinson and Drury (2001) observed that when an out-group (such as the police) assumed that a crowd was homogenous and policed it as a single entity, this affected the dynamics of those within it. For example, when the police perceived a group as radicals, individuals within the group began to see themselves as radicals too. Drury and Reicher (2009) concurred:

> People's sense of their social position (social identity) changes to the extent that, in acting on their identity (participating in a crowd event), they are repositioned as a consequence of the understandings and reactions of an out-group (treated as oppositionalists by the police), and this repositioning leads both to a new sense of identity and new forms of action (oppositional violence).
>
> (Drury and Reicher, 2009: 713)

Stott (2009) proposed that by employing an ESIM approach, police public order commanders advanced towards a negotiated management style of policing and a police strategy where police intentions were to facilitate lawful behaviour, thereby promoting self-policing in the crowd and improving police–community relationships (HMIC, 2009b). Drury, Reicher and Stott (2003) argued that, conversely, when police actions were perceived to be illegitimate, such as using containment tactics restricting whole crowd movement or dispersal tactics preventing everyone from protesting, this can cause the crowd to coalesce. In such cases, active opposition to the police becomes a legitimate response for the crowd.

Stott and Drury (2016: 11) observed that by applying ESIM in understanding crowds, police commanders began to address the "pressing need to interpret those crowd actions as a meaningful and symbolic reaction to the subjective and material realities of the participants' social context." HMIC (2009b) hailed the approach as practical and beneficial to policing protest and suggested that the approach increased the capability of the police to communicate with members of the crowd. HMIC recommended (2009b: 20) that before events, the police should "seek to inform themselves about the culture and general conduct of particular protest crowds." In planning the policing of an event, commanders should gather information about each of the protest groups to understand their intentions. During the event, the police should engage with the crowd on the ground to further gather information about their intentions and concerns, and to understand their demeanour (HMIC, 2009b).

ESIM thus became the theoretical framework for the police command of protest events (NPIA, 2010) and provided the academic basis that became the strategic driver for the inception of PLT (College of Policing, 2013). Despite this, there has been criticism of the limitations of ESIM. Kilgallon (2020a: 844) argued that although ESIM recognises the importance of not viewing crowds as homogenous groups, "the model quickly fails to recognize that the police are made up of multiple groups or teams." Further, Waddington (2013) argued that ESIM failed to consider the political context in which disorder at an event took place and did not examine occurrences and the communication processes that had preceded such an incident. Waddington concluded that theories based on single factors do not adequately explain this complex social process and therefore the appropriate theoretical approach should be inclusive of the whole range of variables that are relevant to this social interaction. Furthermore, although acknowledging that ESIM had become central to current police doctrine, Waddington cautioned against its limitations and recommended (2013: 46) the application of "a more contextualised approach," arguing instead that the Flashpoints Model of Public Disorder (for example, Waddington, Jones and Critcher, 1989; King and Waddington, 2005; Waddington, 2013) provided a more comprehensive understanding of the success of a liaison-based police approach to protest than the ESIM, and afforded a wider context in which to analyse events.

Flashpoints Model of Public Disorder

Waddington, Jones and Critcher (1989) examined the policing of demonstrations, pickets and community disorders in Sheffield and produced a model of public disorder identifying areas they argued were critical in determining order and disorder. Waddington, Jones and Critcher's model was centred on a "flashpoint," defined as a "dramatic break in a pattern of interaction which might itself help to explain why and where disorder broke out" (1989: 21) and provided six levels by which to analyse an event and assess the potential for a protest to evolve into disorder.

At a "structural" level, Waddington, Jones and Critcher identified the different groups engaged in the event and divergence in ideologies between groups. They argued that key was the perception a group had of their relationship to the state, and to the police, who were considered to represent the state in a protest event. At a "political / ideological" level, Waddington, Jones and Critcher analysed the political standing of a group and how this may influence their propensity to use violence as a means of achieving their aims. A "cultural" analysis considered the understanding of the group as to where they sat in the social world. Waddington, Jones and Critcher argued (1989: 162) that these factors had a bearing on the potential for disorder as they "shape how dissenters and police view themselves and each other, and thus the most appropriate forms of their interaction." At "contextual" level, Waddington, Jones and Critcher analysed the police–protester relationship and considered historical grievances between the groups which may impact on police impartiality. Waddington, Jones and Critcher argued that the media's stance and their sensualisation of events might significantly increase or decrease the potential for disorder which in turn influenced the possibility of engagement between groups and the police.

Analysis at a "situational" level examined the control that those involved in an event had over the situation. Waddington, Jones and Critcher examined dialogue between police and protest organisers and concluded that where the organisers not only provide a commitment to refrain from violence but to also influence their group to respond in the same vein, this increased the likelihood that the police would respond accordingly. Finally, at an "interactional" level, Waddington, Jones and Critcher examined the interaction between police and protesters and argued that when disorder occurred, the primary concern was not who the initiator was, but why disorder had started, and this depended on what had occurred prior to the event. Therefore, this "flashpoint" incident was an indicator of an underlying issue centred on the perception of each group of the others. Disorder was still perceived as a form of interaction between the groups, however, and was resultant of a breakdown in all other methods of communication.

Waddington, Jones and Critcher argued that the model provided a method of analysis that could be applied consistently to a variety of situations:

political demonstrations; industrial pickets; and community disorder. Further, Waddington, Jones and Critcher identified the importance of establishing an understanding of the political and social standing of other groups, their structure and the context in which they functioned, achieved through interaction, to prevent a breakdown in dialogue, manifested by a flashpoint.

The Flashpoints Model received critical appraisal. P. Waddington (1994: 159) opined that the model was "neither analytically useful nor empirically testable," arguing that there may be numerous incidents that contribute to the outbreak of disorder rather than attributing this to one flashpoint incident. Waddington further argued that there was a distinct temporal division between the trigger incident and the onset of serious disorder. della Porta and Reiter (1998) and P. Waddington (1998) were critical of the "contextual" level concerning the location of events and the space and time within which they occur. More recently, Gorringe and Rosie (2008: 197) suggested that the model required updating "to better account for contemporary protest."

The Flashpoints Model has been re-examined and reapplied to supplementary pieces of research since its initial publication (for example, Gorringe et al., 2012; King and Waddington, 2005; Waddington, 2007). King and Waddington (2005: 261) revisited the model and acknowledged a need to "show greater sensitivity to the temporal and dynamic development of any riotous event," recognising that there may be concurrent events that contributed to the outbreak of disorder. Waddington (2007: 59) further observed that the model was built on an assumption that breakdowns in relationships between the police and the public may be repaired when the police initiate "well-timed pacificatory gestures," fundamentally because such actions signify a willingness by the police to "accommodate the goals and values of the crowd." However, Moran and Waddington (2015: 59) argued that the model allowed a "fully rounded appreciation of the underlying political motives and meanings" of serous disorder and the trigger incidents that served as catalyst. Moran and Waddington concluded (2015: 71) that the Flashpoints Model provided a "robust conceptual framework within which the anatomy of collective disorder can be dissected and understood." Therefore, the model provides a sound theoretical framework within which protest policing and the potential for protests to escalate into disorder may be examined.

Waddington (2013) argued that the Flashpoints Model provided a more contextual approach than ESIM. However, it is argued here that the two are not in opposition, and both offer insight to all those engaged in protest. Indeed, Newburn (2016: 140) utilised the Flashpoints Model, in his study of why riots *don't* happen, and argued that what was most significant in assessing this question was an examination of what occurred at the interactional level, and that greater clarity may be provided if analysis is made utilising some elements of SIM "in concert with the flashpoints approach" to provide "the basis for understanding the nature of police–crowd and police–community interaction."

Newburn aside, the application of the Flashpoints Model has been somewhat limited to researching the engagement between police and protester groups, and research has paid little cognisance to the interactional level on which the *police* need to operate; negotiating with other groups and organisations who may also be stakeholders in the same protest event. There are numerous points of contact and overlaps between both models. For example, an examination of the diverse groups and divergence in ideologies at structural and cultural levels (Flashpoints Model) would allow identification of in-groups and out-groups (ESIM). Further, the control that groups had as a situational level and the ability of organisers to influence group members in refraining from disorder (Flashpoints Model) echoes the presence of self-policing identified in protest groups (ESIM). Most significant for this book which considers a dialogical approach to protest, an examination at an interactional level of the police–protester interaction (Flashpoints Model) reflects the observation that events are characteristically intergroup encounters (ESIM) and that legitimacy is key to understanding a breakdown in communication. This book therefore seeks to extend the existing research and argues that ESIM and the Flashpoints Model both provide a sound theoretical background from which to examine protest policing and furthermore are mutually compatible. Additionally, the next section will examine procedural justice theory and consider whether all three may be combined as a sound theoretical framework in which to consider a dialogical approach to protest policing.

Procedural justice theory

Over recent years, a growing body of literature has emerged (for example, Myhill and Quinton, 2011; Bradford et al., 2014; Quinton et al., 2015) arguing that the police should encourage an approach consistent with procedural justice theory to build trust and confidence in the police within the communities they serve. Myhill and Quinton (2011: 13) observed that the police cannot function without the support of the public and opined that for the police to do so, it was "crucial that the principles of procedural justice are applied consistently to all individuals and groups." Further, a procedural justice approach was detailed as one of the seven "neighbourhood policing guidelines" which the College of Policing advocated as essential for chief officers for effective neighbourhood policing;

> Guideline 4: Promoting the right culture. Chief officers should ... take steps to ensure that all police contact with colleagues, partners and the public seeks to build trust and is consistent with procedural justice requiring fair decision-making and respectful treatment.
>
> (College of Policing, 2017)

This chapter argues that the theory of procedural justice (for example, Lind and Tyler, 1988; Bradford, 2014) also provides an alternative medium through which a dialogical approach may be examined. Furthermore, it is argued that procedural justice theory is compatible with and complimentary to both ESIM and the Flashpoints Model and that all three theories may be blended to provide a theoretical framework underpinning a dialogical approach to the policing of protest.

Procedural justice theory examines relationships and social experiences and evaluates them not on the results or outcomes, but on how the social interaction is undertaken and the degree to which this process is perceived as fair and just. Procedural justice is concerned with making and implementing decisions according to fair processes (Maiese, 2004), and contends that "process judgements are important determinants of attitudes and behaviour" (Lind and Tyler, 1988: 2). Research suggests that legitimacy in criminal justice decisions made by authorities in effectuating legislation is not dictated by the fairness of the decisions made or sanctions imposed, rather the fairness of the procedures implemented (Paternoster et al., 1997; Tyler and Lind, 1992). Paternoster et al. (1997) posited that treating individuals arrested for domestic assaults in a procedurally fair and impartial manner even when they were facing adverse outcomes reduced the propensity for them to reoffend. Sunshine and Tyler (2003) noted that when authorities such as the police used fair procedures to implement legislation and make decisions, the authorities were considered to be acting in a legitimate manner, which in turn fostered public cooperation. Conversely, Sunshine and Tyler observed (2003: 514) that "unfairness in the exercise of authority will lead to alienation, defiance, and noncooperation."

Tyler (2006) argued that procedural justice theory significantly assisted in understanding legitimacy. Tyler observed that over recent decades, legal authorities had predominantly gained compliance by using or threatening to use sanctions through the legal justice system. Therefore, Tyler noted, social order had been maintained mainly through the threat of punishment as a deterrence strategy for those that did not comply. However, Tyler argued that the alternative to having deterrence policies was legitimacy, which impacted upon compliancy with the law. Therefore, compliancy was not based on the resulting punishments but the legitimacy of the procedures in seeking legal justice. Tyler (2006: 270) concluded that the motivation behind people cooperating with legal authorities, such as the police, was "rooted in social relationships and ethical judgments, and does not primarily flow from the desire to avoid punishments or gain rewards." Thus, people were more likely to accept police decisions and adhere to legislation where the procedures utilised by the police to uphold the law were perceived to be just and fair. Bradford, Jackson and Milani (2021: 642) described legitimacy as the "justification of power" and "a felt moral duty to obey" which they argued has become "central to the way we understand policing."

Hough et al. (2010) promulgated that criminology spent too much time examining why people broke laws and not enough time considering why people complied with the law. Hough et al. examined the way people were treated by legal institutions, relationships built, their trust in the justice systems, the legitimacy and authority that the institution can command as a consequence of this trust and the resulting obedience that the public gave to the institution when procedures were perceived as legitimate. Tyler and Lind (1992: 163) asserted that a person's relationship with legal authorities was affected by their assessment of procedural fairness and neutrality, which they argued was "the crucial factors that lead to voluntary compliance with the directives of authority."

Tyler (2006) further observed that a resulting by-product of legitimacy through procedural justice was the building of relationships between authorities and the public. Tyler noted that when relationships were based on a fair process rather than the threat of punishment, the public voluntarily deferred to the authorities which governed them, seeing this as a part of their obligation to their leaders. Lind and Tyler (1988) asserted that a significant part of this relationship building was allowing the public to express their viewpoints and arguments to those in authority. Bottoms and Tankebe (2012: 169) argued that a "dialogic approach" allowed those in power to justify their claims to legitimacy with the public. Martin and Bradford (2019: 566) extended the dialogic approach and observed that "legitimation processes always rely at least in part on other actors, organizations and institutions" and therefore the police need the "support and assistance of other powerholders." Deutsch (2006: 48) observed that implementing fair procedures provided "voice" and "considerate treatment" for those involved in the processes, providing good information for authorities in their decision-making. Watson and Angell (2007) concurred and expanded;

> Key components of a procedural justice framework include participation (having a voice), which involves having the opportunity to present one's own side of the dispute and be heard by the decision maker; dignity, which includes being treated with respect and politeness and having one's rights acknowledged; and trust that the authority is concerned with one's welfare.
>
> (Watson and Angell, 2007: 787)

Tyler and Blader (2003) further examined the interpersonal aspects of procedural justice through a group engagement model. Tyler and Blader argued that groups benefitted when individuals absorbed themselves within, and this shaped the group's level of cooperation. Procedural justice, Tyler and Blader further suggested, impacted upon group engagement; the more that individuals felt that group decisions were based on a fair process, the more they were likely to have a sense of group identification. This was particularly evident when individuals were members of groups who had negative stereotyping attached to their identity. Tyler and Blader concluded (2003: 358) that procedural justice "appears to allay people's concerns that group membership will result in negative consequences for the self; it provides them with a sense of identity security."

Research into a procedural justice approach applied to policing has produced consistent conclusions. Van Damme and Pauwels (2016) argued that the public expected the police to treat civilians with respect, neutrality and integrity, provide explanations for their actions when asked and listen to the public. Sunshine and Tyler (2003) argued that when the police procedures were seen as legitimate, most of the public self-regulated most of the time. Further, this process resulted in the public aiding the police when the police needed to deal with more problematic individuals, and even supporting the police when a more robust approach was required. Tyler and Blader (2003) observed an inference amongst individuals in groups, particularly those that had negative stigmas attached to them, that the police were reaffirming their status when they treated them cordially and with respect, rather than reinforcing stereotypes.

In their study of policing in Australia, Hinds and Murphy (2007) further argued that the public were more likely to perceive police actions as legitimate when believed to being policed in a procedurally just manner. The research found that a procedural justice approach increased public satisfaction with the police and fostered better police–community partnerships. Hind and Murphy concluded that the police had the opportunity to augment public satisfaction, relationships with partners and legitimacy by being proactive in revising and changing existing practices to follow procedural justice principles. Such a pre-emptive approach was also advocated by Watson and Angell (2007: 787) who noted that a procedural justice approach had most impact early in police encounters and concluded that "how officers initially approach someone is extremely important."

Bradford (2014) examined procedural justice theory in the context of British policing, through a survey of young black and minority ethnic men from four London boroughs. Bradford noted that treating individuals in a group fairly promoted a feeling of inclusion and worth within that group. Further, Bradford observed that when a group outsider, such as a police officer, treated individuals with respect, this enhanced the individual's assessments of their own group and strengthened their identity within it, which subsequently influenced how positively they assessed the fairness of the police processes implemented. Bradford concluded (2014:35) that "perceptions of police fairness, social identity and legitimacy can all have effects on propensities to cooperate with officers." Bradford, Murphy and Jackson (2014) argued that, conversely, a sense that the police were acting in an unfair manner weakened an individual's identity with the group and diminished police legitimacy. Stott, Hoggett and Pearson (2012) similarly examined social identity and group dynamics in their ethnographic study of fans of Cardiff City Football Club and advocated an approach that was consistent with the theoretical principles of both procedural justice and ESIM. Stott, Hoggett and Pearson concluded that a process that promoted perceived legitimacy rather than the presence of a deterrent most effectively reduced conflict at domestic football matches.

Lydon (2020) examined the response of protesters in events to being treated fairly and with respect by the police in protests in the UK and considered whether this garnered legitimacy and encouraged compliance. Lydon (2020: 8) observed that "many participants described positive or benign encounters with police at protest events yet reported little or no support for the police."

Wells (2008) identified the significance of social engagement in implementing a procedural justice approach. Wells studied the use of fixed speed cameras to "monitor and punish" speeding motorists. Wells explored whether the indiscriminate use of fixed speed cameras might offer a consistent and therefore procedurally just enforcement, however contradictorily observed that motorists found the process grossly unfair. Instead, Wells argued that the removal of social engagement with a traffic officer also removed the police officer's decision-making processes and reasoned judgement based on individual circumstances. Wells concluded (2008: 815) that "the notions of 'common sense', 'discretion' and 'respect' are considered vital to a 'just' experience."

It is therefore argued that procedural justice theory provides a sound theoretical framework for examining a dialogical approach to policing protest events. By applying the theory, it is argued that there is less significance in the decisions made by police commanders regarding protest events and more that fair processes are implemented in reaching them. In reaching such decisions, all those engaged in a protest event should be afforded opportunity to present their side to the police, the decision-makers, whilst being treated with dignity, common sense, discretion and respect, in an overarching framework where they can trust that the police are concerned about their welfare (Watson and Angell, 2007; Wells, 2008).

In applying the theory to protest events, the police should therefore ensure that officers are available to hear the voice (Deutsch, 2006; Watson and Angell, 2007) of all those engaged in protest event to maintain legitimacy through the procedures implemented. There should be an early engagement by police officers (Watson and Angell, 2007) and a fostering of relationships (Hinds and Murphy, 2007) to reinforce group identities (Tyler and Blader, 2003). Hough et al. (2010: 210) noted that "to treat people with fairness and respect, police officers need genuinely to value fair treatment and genuinely to respect those who they police." Furthermore, such officers should be able to identify the groups within groups, engaging particularly with individuals who are members of "certain stigmatized demographic groups" with negative stereotyping applied to them (Tyler and Blader, 2003: 358).

This chapter argues that many key concepts integral to procedural justice theory are found in both ESIM and the Flashpoints Model and that all three offer an insight into a dialogical approach. Myhill and Quinton (2011: 2) noted that "the most important factor motivating people to cooperate and not break the law was the legitimacy of the police." The concept of legitimacy so pertinent to procedural justice has in this research been identified as integral to an examination at an interactional level of police–protester interaction (Flashpoints Model) and key to understanding a breakdown in communication (ESIM). Further, all approaches consider the influence of organisers (Flashpoints Model) and subsequently how groups facilitate self-policing (ESIM) fostering public cooperation due to a fair process implement by the police (procedural justice). Additionally, all three approaches consider groups not as homogenous rather as groups within groups (ESIM) with diverse ideologies at structural and cultural levels (Flashpoints Model) where police decisions based on a fair process promote a sense of group identity (procedural justice).

This chapter proposes therefore that procedural justice theory is epistemologically compatible with both ESIM and the Flashpoints Model and that all three can be blended to provide a theoretical basis for examining a dialogical approach to policing protest. The next section will use this theoretical framework to examine the different approaches to protest policing previously identified and provide insight into different option available to police decision-makers in protest situations.

Different approaches to policing protest within the theoretical framework

The last chapter provided an overview of different approaches to the policing of protest and this chapter has explored a theoretical framework for examining a dialogical approach to the policing of protest. It has been argued that the different policing approaches are not sequenced historically rather strategic options open to police commanders. This section will explore the different approaches to protest in light of the theoretical framework and consider how police decision-makers may chose different approaches to protest situations and the implications of such approaches.

Reicher (1996) argued, in developing the ESIM, that legitimacy was a key component of understanding recourse to disorder in the policing of protests and provided examples of where police actions, such as stopping students getting to parliament, were perceived by protesters as illegitimate. It can be argued that such an approach is one of strategic incapacitation and, where the actions of some students led to conflict with the police, one of escalated force. However, as identified in the previous chapter, the police decision-makers must also apply an approach that is cognisant of political pressures (for example, Noakes and Gillham, 2006; Mansley, 2014). Drury and Reicher (2009) argued that people's sense of social identity changed as a reaction to out-groups. A prominent feature of ESIM is understanding protest groups not as a homogeneous body but rather groups within groups (for example, Stott, 2009). Therefore, it is argued that by applying an ESIM method as advocated (HMIC, 2009b; College of Policing, 2018) and understanding both the changes in people's social identity and understanding and identifying the numerous groups within groups in a protest, police commanders may choose to select different approaches to police the diverse elements of a protest. For example, commanders may elect to deploy a strategic facilitation approach with the majority of the protest groups. However, commanders may choose to use a strategic incapacitation approach with an identified small minority where there is information and intelligence that they are set on causing disorder.

Similarly, analysing a protest event utilising the Flashpoints Model allows police commanders to assess the political standing of a group and their potential to cause disorder, viewing such disorder as still a form of interaction resultant of a breakdown in all other methods (Waddington, Jones and Critcher, 1989). Once assessed, commanders may then select the most appropriate police approach, depending on the circumstances. For example, an approach of strategic facilitation may be selected allowing the police to demonstrate their willingness to accommodate the crowd's goals and values (Waddington, 2007). However, where there is a breakdown in communication that leads to a flashpoint, a reversion to an escalated force approach may be selected by police commanders with those intent on violence (King and Waddington, 2005).

This book has argued that the police commander has a tool kit of strategic policing approaches from which they may select appropriate responses to protest events. However, it has been evidenced that there is a danger that the police approach can be perceived as illegitimate by the crowd (Drury, Reicher and Stott, 2003). Further, as has been established through examining procedural justice theory, less concern would be given by protest groups to the decision made, rather, legitimacy would depend on the perceived fairness of the approaches implemented (Paternoster et al., 1997; Tyler and Lind, 1992). Where the approach made is deemed unfair, there is a potential that this would invoke a response of defiance and noncooperation (Sunshine and Tyler, 2003). Where, for example, a police commander decides to utilise a different police approach to a small protest group where there is specific intelligence that the group are intent on serious disruption or damage, there is a danger of a perception by the majority of an illegitimate policing response. It may be that the majority are not cognisant of specific information which informs the commander's decision-making and subsequently may coalesce with the minority. By applying an approach based on procedural justice theory, the commander may seek to engage with the majority and explain the legitimate reasons behind their decision-making (Bradford, 2014) promulgating an approach based on respect, a just experience (Wells, 2008) and a voice for all (Deutsch, 2006). Therefore, an approach based on procedural justice would aid in ensuring that police decisions in selecting approaches are fair, treating people respectfully and promoting cooperation (Maiese, 2004; Wells, 2008; Bradford, 2014). In selecting different policing approaches, it is key therefore that the decision why such an approach has been implemented is communicated to those engaged in protest.

This chapter therefore argues that the different approaches to policing protest as identified in the previous chapter remain strategic options in the tool kit of the police commander. Commanders may choose approaches with diverse groups within groups identified depending on the responses required. However, in doing so, commanders must utilise a procedurally just approach by ensuring that their decisions and rationale are communicated. This dialogical approach will promote legitimacy and will allow the voice of those engaging in protest to be both heard and valued in the decision-making process.

In recent times, the police have utilised PLT to engage with different groups, as the "link between the police and groups before, during and after events to establish and maintain dialogue" (College of Policing, 2018). Later chapters in this book will examine the role in more depth against the theoretical framework, through the examination of two case studies, and will consider how PLT contribute to an understanding of the identity of different groups (ESIM) and their political and social standing (Flashpoints) and beget a police approach based on procedural justice theory. The following section will explore the sparse body of research into the use of PLT to further analyse the role in facilitating dialogue in protest events.

The use of Police Liaison Teams

The Liberal Democrats party spring conference was held in Sheffield in March 2011. The host force, South Yorkshire Police (SYP), was responsible for the planning and delivery of a policing operation which would cost an estimated £2,000,000 to manage the expected attendance of protest crowds of between 5,000 and 10,000 participants (Wainwright, 2011). In a response to the HMIC's Adapting to Protest recommendations (HMIC, 2009a; HMIC, b), SYP deployed PLT (known at that time as Protest Liaison Officers) in blue tabards to communicate and build relationships with protesters (Bowen, 2015). Two independent pieces of research into the use of these officers were undertaken during the conference (Gorringe, Stott and Rosie, 2012; Waddington, 2013). A third piece of academic research was undertaken into the deployment of PLT at six protest events in London and Sussex in 2012 after the first liaison officers had been trained earlier that year (Stott, Scothern and Gorringe, 2013).

Gorringe, Stott and Rosie (2012) conducted an empirical study of the policing operation surrounding the Liberal Democrat conference, utilising the ESIM as a theoretical framework. Gorringe, Stott and Rosie observed (2012: 113) that there was pressing need "for empirically grounded and theoretically informed research" to provide such governance that might subsequently impact on police policy, as the use of PLT was at that time not a national tactic. Gorringe, Stott and Rosie observed that PLT were utilised pre-event in the plan of avoiding unnecessary use of force options, which allowed an opportunity to maximise the crowd's perceptions of the legitimacy of police action. This process was initiated by the building of relationships between the

PLT and event organisers to understand their objectives and intentions, and this informed the police commander's policing plan for the event. PLT officers were selected because of communication skills rather than public order experience.

Self-regulation was identified within the crowd and Gorringe, Stott and Rosie argued (2012: 119) that this "was understood by the police as a direct outcome of PLT activity and the resultant lack of alternate intervention." Gorringe, Stott and Rosie also observed incidents of self-policing which they argued were due to the legitimacy provided by the interaction with PLT. Gorringe, Stott and Rosie advocated the use of PLT, and argued that their contribution was due to both decisions in the planning stage that the primary police tactic for the event would be liaison, and to the use of PLT within the crowd during the event which allowed commanders to gain a sense of how the crowd felt and the impact that police actions might have on them. Gorringe, Stott and Rosie noted (2012: 111) that the impact that PLT had on crowd dynamics "allowed for an improved capacity for proactive public order management, encouraged 'self-regulation' in the crowd, and avoided the unnecessary police use of force at moments of tension."

Similarly, Waddington (2013: 62) also examined the PLT approach to policing the protests in Sheffield and concluded that liaison officers "successfully explore a basis on which to accommodate each party's goals and interests." Waddington recognised that ESIM had become central to police doctrine but cautioned against its limitations and instead argued (2013: 46) that it was helpful "to apply a more contextualised approach" and advocated the use of the Flashpoints Model provided a wider context theoretical framework in which to analyse the use of PLT and a liaison-based approach. Waddington noted that the PLT were identifiable by the wearing of a blue tabard over conventional police uniform and provided a communication link between protest groups and the police that had not readily been previously witnessed when officers were deployed in conventional yellow jackets. Waddington recorded the response of one participant who remarked that the officers in tabards which were described as "kinda blue" in colour were "ironically a kinder blue than their colleagues were" (2013: 46). Waddington argued that the approach prompted the protest organiser to observe (2013: 46) that the PLT "seemed to be genuinely prepared to support us, to enable us to do the type of things we wanted to do and prevent any problems with the 'real' police."

Waddington structured analysis into the framework of the Flashpoints Model, identifying structural and political / ideological pressures that were significant as a backdrop to the conference being held in the SYP area. Institutional and organisational factors pertaining to both SYP post the Hillsborough stadium disaster and to the Student Union post significant London protests also provided a contextual background to the protests. At the situational and interactional levels, Waddington observed that the use of PLT provided legitimacy to the deployment of specific police tactics, such as the erecting of a steel fence around key locations, and the deployment of PLT prevented potential flashpoints by clarifying the intentions of protest groups and averting conflict.

Waddington strongly advocated the use of PLT during the protest events, arguing (2013: 63) that their use and the relationships they created with the crowd resulted in there being "little chance of inducing the type of hostility and opposition that would have greeted their more conventionally deployed police colleagues." Waddington (2016) revisited this research in response to Baker's (2014: 99) suggestion that "police–protester dialog can constitute a ritualistic game" with both sides intent on extracting information from the other. Waddington reflected that the use of PLT in Sheffield allowed the police to maintain open lines of communication with protesters, and this greatly assisted police commanders to dynamically assess the risks, preventing recourse to more severe police interventions. Waddington concluded (2016: 31) that the use of PLT engendered "a novel, safer and more enlightened form of protest policing, and constitute a genuine and sincere attempt by the police to facilitate the 'right to protest.'"

Stott, Scothern and Gorringe (2013) provided a second source of data in which to analyse the deployment of PLT, exploring the effectiveness of PLT at six protest events in London and Sussex, and argued that PLT were most effective when deployed at an early stage to engage with protesters and establish relationships, resulting in PLT being welcomed within protest crowds. Stott, Scothern and Gorringe (2013: 7) noted that the PLT officers in blue tabards were accepted within protest communities as protesters "distinguish between the 'blue' and 'yellow' coated police." They argued that deploying PLT assisted in reducing conflict during events where protest policing was, after dialogue, undertaken solely by PLT. However, it was also noted that protesters reacted negatively to the deployment of PLT when the officers were perceived as an intelligence-gathering source, where their presence was deemed as illegitimate. Further, it was noted that PLT not only faced the challenge of building relationship with protesters, but more significantly faced conflict from their own colleagues in performing the role. Stott, Scothern and Gorringe concluded (2013: 11) that the ability of PLT to be inside rather than outside crowds without their presence creating tension "appears to have increased police capacity to mediate and manage the emergent 'problems' they were confronted with, particularly when those protests involved 'direct action' groups."

The research conducted provided initial empirical insight into the development of PLT as a new police tactic. Despite differences in methodology and theoretical framework, each approach concluded by advocating the use of PLT in protest events and acknowledge that little research had been undertaken at present into their use in the UK. In fact, all three studies were undertaken whilst there were only three police forces trained in the use of liaison officers (Bowen, 2015) and prior to the creation of the current College of Policing PLT course (College of Policing, 2013). Gorringe, Stott and Rosie (2012) observed that their research was formative in informing police training, and Roadnight (2015) observed that all three pieces of research provided context for the development of a national PLT training course. However, this scant research was made prior to the inclusion of PLT as a national tactical option for public order commanders in Authorise Professional Practice at the end of 2013.

Since their inclusion as a tactical option in UK police practice, PLT have become the primary tactic for policing protest events (Stott et al., 2015). Hoggett and West (2018: 957) extended the use of PLT and suggested that they could play an important part in policing football matches in providing information to aid command decision-making, develop rapport and facilitate legitimacy. Additionally, Stott, West and Radburn (2018: 18) suggested that through a "process of dialogue and positive influence," PLT had the "capacity to promote 'self-regulation'" within a small crowd of away football fans.

However, Jackson, Gilmore and Monk (2019: 12) were critical of the dialogue processes in policing anti-"fracking" protests in Greater Manchester and proffered that despite having attempted to negotiate with the police, the protesters perceived that "the response of police suggested that a commitment to meaningful dialogue was not reciprocated." Jackson, Gilmore and Monk (2018: 13) observed that the PLT were "perceived to be primarily involved in gathering intelligence," which exacerbated the lack of trust between protesters and the police, and also "reinforced suspicions" of many of the protesters about the role of PLT. They concluded (2018: 17) that despite a change in UK policy post-2009 to facilitate peaceful protest and despite "assurances to the contrary in the academic literature," police commitment to facilitation and dialogue was not universal, and what constituted legitimate protest was still contested.

Therefore, the dialogical process has not been without suspicion or criticism. A statement released by the movement Extinction Rebellion (XR) highlighted the tensions, stating that XR would not "be pre-liaising actions with police for any of the London based actions that will be part of the Impossible Rebellion" as the police "have chosen not to recognise their duty to facilitate peaceful protest, rendering pre-liaison meetings superfluous" (Extinction Rebellion, 2021). However, Kilgallon's research into the use of PLT at Notting Hill Carnival evidenced how PLT and revellers collaborated to ensure a positive experience. Kilgallon observed that the PLT interaction was impacted upon due to the police as an institution being "professionally stigmatised" with a historic perception of hostility, anger and mistrust of the police. Therefore, PLT were continually mindful that their "interactions could be misinterpreted and escalated" (2020b: 35). Nevertheless, Kilgallon (2020b: 44) witnessed the development of long-term relationships between PLT and float organisers where "at different points of the weekend each relied upon the other for help or support," which generated the requirement for teamwork between organisers, police and float leaders all working together to maintain order. Kilgallon concluded that the effectivity of the use of PLT was dependent on the fact that PLT were legitimised both internally by police commanders and externally with key float leaders with whom they had built a relationship and jointly negotiated for a successful Carnival.

Conclusion

Within the body of literature examined over the last two chapters, it has become apparent that interaction between the police and protesters is essential in facilitating negotiation. This interaction has been termed differently across the literature: as liaison (for example, Waddington, 2013; Stott, Scothern and Gorringe, 2013); negotiation (for example, Waddington, 1994; McCarthy and McPhail, 1998); dialogue (for example, Wahlström and Oskarsson, 2006; Gilmore, Jackson and Monk, 2016); communication, (for example, della Porta and Reiter, 2006; Gorringe, Stott and Rosie, 2012); and engagement (for example, Tyler and Blader, 2003; Stott, West and Radburn, 2018). Many researchers use the words interchangeably and significance is placed not on the term used, rather the extent to which the parties engage in dialogue and the depth of relationships fostered (for example, College of Policing, 2018; Gilmore, Jackson and Monk, 2016).

The College of Policing (2018) defined the role of PLT as providing the link between the police and groups to "establish and maintain dialogue." This research seeks to examine the use of PLT in considering the contribution that a dialogical approach has made to the policing of protests. Therefore, based on the literature examined in this chapter, for this research, "dialogical" will include all the terms identified above and used interchangeably, and focus will be made not on the term used, but the extent to which dialogue has been entered into, and the impact on all engaged.

In contrast to the abundance of research into protest policing, scant literature examined the implementation and value of a dialogical approach and the use of PLT. This book augments this small cannon of research and provides empirical research into the use of PLT at protest events and marches post their inclusion as a national tactical option (College of Policing, 2013). Exiting research has utilised either ESIM (Gorringe, Stott and Rosie, 2012; Stott, Scothern and Gorringe, 2013) or the Flashpoints Model (Waddington, 2013) as a theoretical framework, with neither considering a blending of both models in analysing data. This research argues that many themes identified, such as relationship building and liaison at an interactional level, transverse both models and both models provide insight into the value of a dialogical approach. Further, this chapter has evidenced that concepts integral in the policing of protest, such as legitimacy and social identity (Reicher, 1996; Waddington, Jones and Critcher, 1989; Gorringe, Stott and Rosie, 2012) and trust (della Porta and Reiter, 1998; Wahlström and Oskarsson, 2006) are also prominent themes in procedural justice theory (Tyler, 2006; Bradford, 2014; Bottoms and Tankebe, 2012). This chapter has explored three theories that have provided an academic grounding for the use of a dialogical approach to the policing of protest and has further explored how different approaches to protest policing are set within this framework. This research argues that all three theories identified are mutually compatible and may be blended to provide a sound theoretical framework in which to further explore a dialogical approach to the policing of protest. Furthermore, this research argues that this framework underpins the different approaches to the policing of protest, providing police decision-makers with a tool kit of strategic options to be applied in different protest situations.

This chapter has established that existing PLT literature is limited to examining dialogue between police and protesters (Gorringe, Stott and Rosie, 2012; Waddington, 2013; Jackson, Gilmore and Monk, 2018), football supporters (Hoggett and West, 2018) or event organisers (Kilgallon, 2020b). The chapter has identified a gap in the literature examining dialogue between the police and other key groups and individuals, such as businesses and partner agencies. Further, the police must operate within the Articles of the Human Rights Act 1998 as both "arbiter" (HMIC, 2009a) and "guarantor of those rights" (Neyroud and Beckley, 2001) balancing the rights of protesters, those wishing to continue their lawful business and the public at large (Mansley, 2014). Published literature examining the balancing act that the police perform through dialogue is lacking.

The research described in later chapters will therefore address this lacuna by considering the application of such a dialogical approach to the policing of protest events, analysing not only the relationship between protesters and police, but the relationships between the police and all engaged in the event. An alternative relational system to Redekop and Paré (2010) will examine the relationships built and maintained between the police and protest groups, counterprotest groups, businesses, local authorities and other interested parties. The research will examine the role of the police as arbiter in balancing the human rights of all interested parties and how utilising a dialogical approach assisted police commanders to balance competing qualified human rights and promote a procedurally fair approach to the policing of protest events. Accordingly, the research will fill the void in the published literature established in the last two chapters by examining the following research questions:

1. What contribution has a dialogical approach made to the policing of protest events in the UK?
2. How might a dialogical approach be extended to include all interested parties affected by a protest event?
3. What does this approach offer in the balancing of the competing human rights of all those engaged in the event?

References

Atak, K. and della Porta, D. (2016) Popular uprisings in Turkey: Police culpability and constraints on dialogue-oriented policing in Gezi Park and beyond. *European Journal of Criminology*, 13(5), 610–625.

Baker, D. (2014) Police and protester dialog: Safeguarding the peace or ritualistic sham? *International Journal of Comparative and Applied Criminal Justice*, 38(1), 83–104.

Bottoms, A. and Tankebe, J. (2012) Beyond procedural justice: A dialogic approach to legitimacy in criminal justice. *Journal of Criminal Law and Criminology*, 102(1), 119–170.

Bowen, C. (2015) *PLO and PLT in NPIA* [email] 14 June 2015. Message to author from christopher.bowen@westyorkshire.pnn.police.uk

Bradford, B. (2014) Policing and social identity: procedural justice, inclusion and cooperation between police and public. *Policing and Society*, 24(1), 22–43.

Bradford, B., Jackson, J. and Milani, J. (2021) Police legitimacy, in Barnes, J. and Forde, D. eds., *The encyclopedia of research methods in criminology and criminal justice*. Volume II. Hoboken: Wiley-Blackwell.

Bradford, B., Murphy, K. and Jackson, J. (2014) Officers as mirrors: Policing, procedural justice and the (re)production of social identity. *British Journal of Criminology*, 54, 527–550.

Bradford, B., Quinton, P., Myhill, A., and Porter, G. (2014) Why do 'the law' comply? Procedural justice, group identification and officer motivation in police organizations. *European Journal of Criminology*, 11(1), 110–131.

College of Policing (2013) *National Police Public Order Training Curriculum: Police Liaison Team trainers guide*. Wyboston: College of Policing.

College of Policing (2016) *Authorised Professional Practice* [online] Available at: https://www.app.college.police.uk/

College of Policing (2017) *Guideline 4: Promoting the right culture* [online] Available at: https://www.college.police.uk/What-we-do/Support/Guidelines

College of Policing (2018) *Police liaison teams* [online] Available at: https://www.app.college.police.uk/app-content/public-order/planning-and-deployment/

della Porta, D. and Reiter, H. (1998) *Policing protest: The control of mass demonstrations in Western democracies*. Minneapolis: University of Minnesota Press.

della Porta D., and Reiter, H. (2006) The policing of global protest: The G8 at Genoa and its aftermath, in della Porta, D., Peterson, A. and Reiter, H. eds., *The policing of transnational protest*, 13–41. Aldershot: Ashgate.

Deutsch, M. (2006) Justice and conflict, in Deutsch, M, Coleman, P. and Marcus, E. eds., *The handbook of conflict resolution: Theory and practice*, 2nd ed. San Francisco: Jossey-Bass.

Drury, J. and Reicher, S. (1999) The intergroup dynamics of collective empowerment: Substantiating the social identity model of crowd behaviour. *Group Processes and Intergroup Relations*, 2(4), 381–402.

Drury, J. and Reicher, S. (2000) Collective action and psychological change: The emergence of new social identities. *British Journal of Social Psychology*, 39, 579–604.

Drury, J. and Reicher, S. (2009) Collective psychological empowerment as a model of social change: Researching crowds and power. *Journal of Social Issues*, 65(4), 707–725.

Drury, J., Reicher, S. and Stott, C. (2003a). Transforming the boundaries of collective identity: From the 'local' anti-road campaign to 'global' resistance? *Social Movements Studies*, 2, 191–212.

Drury, J., Stott, C. and Farsides, T. (2003b) The role of police perceptions and practices in the development of "public disorder". *Journal of Applied Social Psychology*, 33(7), 1480–1500.

Extinction Rebellion (2021) *Statement on police liaison for the impossible rebellion starting*, 23rd August [online] Available at: https://extinctionrebellion.uk/2021/08/11/statement-on-police-liaison-for-the-impossible-rebellion-starting-23rd-august/

Gillham, P. and Noakes, J. (2007) "More than a march in a circle": Transgressive protests and the limits of negotiated management. *Mobilization*, 12(4), 341–357.

Gilmore, J., Jackson, W. and Monk, H. (2016) *Keep moving! Report on the policing of the Barton Moss community protection camp: November 2013 –April 2014*. Centre for the Study of Crime, Criminalisation and Social Exclusion, Liverpool John Moores University: Centre for Urban Research, University of York.

Gorringe, H and Rosie, M (2008) It's a long way to Auchterarder! 'Negotiated management' and mismanagement in the policing of G8 protests. *British Journal of Sociology*, 59(2), 187–205.

Gorringe, H., Rosie, M., Waddington, D. and Kominou, M. (2012) Facilitating ineffective protest? The policing of the 2009 Edinburgh NATO protests. *Policing and Society*, 22(2), 115–132.

Gorringe, H., Stott, C and Rosie, M. (2012) Dialogue police, decision-making, and the management of public order during protest crowd events. *Journal of Investigative Psychology and Offender Profiling*, 9, 111–125.

Her Majesty's Inspectorate of Constabulary. (2009a) *Adapting to protest*. London: HMIC.

Her Majesty's Inspectorate of Constabulary (2009b) *Adapting to protest: Nurturing the British model of policing*. London: HMIC.

Hinds, L. and Murphy, K. (2007) Public satisfaction with police: Using procedural justice to improve police legitimacy. *The Australian and New Zealand Journal of Criminology*, 40(1), 27–42.

Hogg, M. (2006) Social identity theory, in Burke P, ed., *Contemporary social identity theories*. Stanford: Stanford University Press.

Hoggett, J. and Stott, C. (2010a) Crowd psychology, public order police training and the policing of football crowds. *Policing: An International Journal of Police Strategies and Management*, 33(2), 218–235.

Hoggett, J. and Stott, C. (2010b) The role of crowd theory in determining the use of force in public order policing. *Policing and Society*, 20(2), 223–236.

Hoggett, J. and West, O. (2018) Police liaison officers at football: Challenging orthodoxy through communication and engagement. *Policing*, 14(4), 945–961.

Hough, M., Jackson, J., Bradford, B, Myhill, A. and Quinton, P. (2010) Procedural justice, trust and institutional legitimacy. *Policing*, 4(3), 203–210.

Jackson, W., Gilmore, J. and Monk, H. (2019) Policing unacceptable protest in England and Wales: A case study of the policing of anti-fracking protests. *Critical Social Policy*, 39(1), 23–43.

Kilgallon, A. (2020a) Policing in dispute: Academia versus activism. *Policing*, 14(4), 843–845.

Kilgallon, A. (2020b) Police interaction and Notting Hill Carnival. *Policing and Society*, 30(1), 28–46.

King, M. and Waddington, D. (2005) Flashpoints revisited: A critical application to the policing of anti-globalization. *Protest, Policing and Society*, 15(3), 255–282.

Le Bon, G. (1895) *The crowd: A study of the popular mind*. London: Unwin.

Lind, E. and Tyler, T. (1988) *The social psychology of procedural justice*. New York: Plenum Press.

Lydon, D. (2020). The construction and shaping of protesters' perceptions of police legitimacy: A thematic approach to police information and intelligence gathering. *Police Practice and Research*, 22, 1–14.

Maiese, M. (2004) Procedural justice in Burgess, G. and Burgess, H. eds., *Beyond intractability*. Boulder: University of Colorado, Conflict Information Consortium.

Mansley, D (2014) *Collective Violence, Democracy and Protest Policing*. London and New York: Routledge.

Martin, and Bradford, B. (2019) The anatomy of police legitimacy: Dialogue, power and procedural justice. *Theoretical Criminology*, 25(4), 559–577.

McCarthy, J. and McPhail, C. (1998) The Institutionalization of Protest in the United States in Meyer, D. and Tarrow, S. eds., *The Social Movement Society: Contentious Politics for a New Century*, 83–110. New York: Rowman and Littlefield.

Myhill, A. and Quinton, P. (2011) *It's a fair cop? Police legitimacy, public cooperation, and crime reduction: An interpretative evidence commentary*. Bramshill: National Policing Improvement Agency.

Moran, M. and Waddington, D. (2015). Recent riots in the UK and France: Causes and commonalities. *Contention: The Multidisciplinary Journal of Social Protest*, 2 (2), 57–73.

National Policing Improvement Agency (2010) *Trainer's Guide: Public Order Bronze / Silver Interim Course*. Wyboston, Bedfordshire: National Policing Improvement Agency.

Newburn, T. (2016) Reflections on why riots don't happen. *Theoretical Criminology*, 20(2), 125–144.

Noakes, J. and Gillham, P. (2006) Aspects of the 'New Penology' in the police response to major political protests in the United States, 1999–2000, in della Porta, D., Peterson, A. and Reiter, H. eds., *The policing of transnational protest*, 97–115. Aldershot: Ashgate.

Neyroud, P. and Beckley, A. (2001) *Policing, ethics and human rights*. Cullompton: Willan Publishing.

Paternoster, R., Brame, R., Bachman, R. and Sherman, L. (1997) Do fair procedures matter? The effect of procedural justice on spouse assault. *Law and Society Review*, 31(1), 163–204.

Quinton, P., Myhill, A., Bradford, B., Fildes, A. and Porter, G. (2015) *Fair cop 2. Organisational justice, behaviour and ethical policing: An interpretative evidence commentary*. Ryton, Coventry: College of Policing.

Redekop, V. and Paré, S. (2010) *Beyond control: A mutual respect approach to protest crowd-police relations*. London: Bloomsbury.

Reicher, S. (1996) The Battle of Westminster: Developing the social identity model of crowd behaviour in order to explain the initiation and development of collective conflict. *European Journal of Social Psychology*, 26, 115–34.

Reicher, S. (1984) The St. Pauls' riot: An explanation of the limits of crowd action in terms of a social identity model. *European Journal of Social Psychology*, 14, 1–21.

Roadnight, J. (2015) *From PLO to PLT: The development of police liaison teams in the college of policing* [email] 6 July 2015. Message to author from julian.roadnight@college.pnn.police.uk

Rosie, M. and Gorringe, H. (2009) What a difference a death makes: Protest, policing and the press at the G20. *Sociological Research Online*, 14(5:4), 1–12.

Stott, C. (2009) Crowd psychology and public order policing: An overview of scientific theory and evidence, in *Submission to the HMIC Policing of Public Protest Review Team*. University of Liverpool.

Stott, C., Adang, O., Livingstone, A. and Schreiber, M. (2008) Tackling football hooliganism: A quantitative study of public order, policing and crowd psychology. *Psychology Public Policy and Law*, 14, 115–141.

Stott, C. and Drury, J. (2016) Contemporary understanding of riots: Classical crowd psychology, ideology and the social identity approach. *Public Understanding of Science*, 1–13.

Stott, C., Hoggett, J. and Pearson, G. (2012) Keeping the peace: Social identity, procedural justice and the policing of football crowds. *British Journal of Criminology*, 52, 381–399.

Stott, C., Hutchinson, P. and Drury, J. (2001) 'Hooligans' abroad? Inter-group dynamics, social identity and participation in collective 'disorder' at the 1998 World Cup Finals. *British Journal of Social Psychology*, 40, 359–384.

Stott, C., Scothern, M., and Gorringe, H. (2013) Advances in Liaison Based Public Order Policing in England: Human Rights and Negotiating the Management of Protest? *Policing*, 7(2), 212–226.

Stott, C., West, O., Cawkwell, R., Lunn, D., Hughes, D. and Kemp, B. (2015) *Public Order and Public Safety (POPS) policing* [online] Available at: http://www.law.leeds.ac.uk/research/projects

Stott, C., West, O. and Radburn, M. (2018) Policing football 'risk'? A participant action research case study of a liaison-based approach to 'public order'. *Policing and Society*, 28(1), 1–16.

Sunshine, J. and Tyler, T (2003) The role of procedural justice and legitimacy in shaping public support for policing. *Law and Society Review*, 37(3), 513–547.

Tajfel, H. (1978). *Differentiation between social groups: Studies in the social psychology of intergroup relations*. London: Academic Press.

Tyler, T. (2006) *Why people obey the law*. Princeton and Oxford: Princeton University Press

Tyler, T. and Blader, S. (2003) The group engagement model: Procedural justice, social identity, and cooperative behavior. *Personality and Social Psychology Review*, 7(4). 349–361.

Tyler, T. and Lind, E. (1992) A relational model of authority in groups. *Advances in Experimental Social Psychology*, 25, 115–191.

Van Damme, A. and Pauwels, L. (2016) Why are young adults willing to cooperate with the police and comply with traffic laws? Examining the role of attitudes toward the police and law, perceived deterrence and personal morality. *International Journal of Law, Crime and Justice*, 46, 103–116.

van Knippenberg, D. (2000) Work motivation and performance: A social identity perspective. *Applied Psychology*, 49(3), 357–371.

Waddington, D. (2013) A 'kinder blue': Analysing the police management of the Sheffield anti-'Lib Dem' protest of March 2011. *Policing and Society*, 23(1), 46–64.

Waddington, D. (2016) From 'iron fists' to 'bunches of fives': A critical reflection on dialogue (or liaison) approaches to policing political protest. *European Police Science and Research Bulletin*, 1, 30–43.

Waddington, D. (2011) *Policing contemporary political protest: From strategic incapacitation to strategic facilitation?* [online] Available at: http://www.shu.ac.uk/research/cresr/sites/shu.ac.uk/files/

Waddington, D. (2007) *Policing public disorder: Theory and practice*. Cullompton: Willan Publishing.

Waddington D., Jones, K. and Critcher, C. (1989) *Flashpoints: Studies in public disorder*. New York: Routledge.

Waddington, P. (1994) *Liberty and order: Public order policing in a capital city*. London: U.C.L. Press.

Waddington, P. (1998) Controlling protest in contemporary historical and comparative perspective, in della Porta, D. and Reiter, R. eds., *Policing protest: The control of mass demonstrations in western democracies*, 117–142. Minneapolis: University of Minnesota Press.

Wahlström, M. and Oskarsson, M. (2006) Negotiating political protest in Gothenburg and Copenhagen in della Porta, D., Peterson, A. and Reiter, H. eds., *The policing of transnational protest*, 117–144. Aldershot: Ashgate.

Wainwright, M. (2011) Police spend £2m to protect Liberal Democrats at Sheffield conference. *The Guardian* [online], 10 March 2011. Available at: http://www.theguardian.com/politics/2011/mar/10.

Watson, A. and Angell, B. (2007) Applying procedural justice theory to law enforcement's response to persons with mental illness. *Psychiatric Service*, 58(6), 787–792.

Wells, H. (2008) The techno-fix versus the fair cop: Procedural (in)justice and automated speed limit enforcement. *British Journal of Criminology*, 48, 798–817.

Chapter 4

Conducting research
Insider or outsider?

Introduction

The first three chapters of this book have explored existing literature concerning protest policing, human rights and a dialogical approach. Analysis of the available text has identified an absence of research examining the dialogue between the police and all engaged in protest events, as well as its contribution to the balancing of human rights. The final four chapters of this book will describe and analyse the research I have undertaken in exploring this lacuna. In the middle of the two sections is this chapter which describes my journey as a serving police officer and researcher and, as such, by its self-ethnographical nature, I have chosen to write this chapter in the first person.

This chapter initially considers an evidence-based approach to policing and the receptivity of police practitioners to empirical research when balanced with their experiences. I then describe my experience as a serving police officer and researcher and, having examined the existing literature, explore my epistemological and ontological position as insider and outsider researcher. The research focused on conducting interviews with participants who had experienced different aspects of two contrasting events: protests against the badger cull in South West England; and an English Defence League (EDL) march and counterdemonstration in Liverpool. I describe my choice of semi-structured interviews as the main data source and how insider–outsider considerations impacted on decision-making regarding interview locations, dress code, selecting participants and gatekeepers. I examine the ethical considerations that were pertinent as both insider and outsider and describe some of the ethical challenges that accompanied the process. I consider the power imbalances in conducting interviews and describe my experiences in interviewing participants in the two case studies as insider and outsider. Finally, I draw conclusions from my experiences in how I was at times an insider, an outsider and on occasions both simultaneously during the research.

However, initial research considerations focused on how I might select the most appropriate methods for those who may access the study. Creswell (2014: 25) observed that "researchers write for audiences that will accept their research." This provided a starting point for my journey and, following the signposts for evidence-based policing (EBP), I began an exploration through the landscape of methods seeking the most appropriate destination to provide data to further probe a dialogical approach to the policing of protest events.

An evidence-based approach

The concept of an evidence-based practice was initiated in the field of medicine in the 1980s (Eddy, 2005), and was soon adopted in other fields, such as nursing (Melnyk, 2011), probation (Raynor, 2003) and education (Petty, 2006). Such an approach to policing was introduced by Sherman (1998), who observed that using research to guide police policy and procedures ensured that best practice was informed by the best evidence. Sherman concluded (1998: 2) that "police practices should be based on scientific evidence about what works best." In recent years, the burgeoning foothold that an evidence-based approach to policing has gained in UK policing has become palpable through its emergence in both academic institutions and police services (Lumsden and Goode, 2016). What has emerged is an approach which "implicates the use of research, evaluation, analysis, and scientific processes" in police decision-making (Lum and Koper, 2015: 260). Sherman argued (2013: 379) that police practice had changed from a reactionary response-led approach to what he described as "the 'triple-T' of targeting, testing, and tracking" because of implementing an evidence-based approach. However, Lum and Koper (2015) cautioned that an EBP approach appeared to differ from other fields in that the police were the subject of less scrutiny than medicine where interventions negatively impacted on their response.

The advantages of an EBP approach have been well documented, including an increase in police legitimacy, transparency, accountability and improved relationships and trust between the police and the public (Sherman, 2013; Lum and Koper, 2015). Hoggett and Stott (2012: 178) opined that EBP was "not just desirable but essential" and that such an approach professionalised the police and advocated collaboration between police and academic researchers to improve the knowledge and understanding of both. However, Lum et al. (2012) recognised the potential for conflict between the police and academia where the researcher and the practitioner sought to exchange knowledge, skills and products yet still held different expectations and views.

An EBP approach must be accepted both internally and externally for it to impact on UK policing. Lum and Koper (2015: 271) observed that the police "must be receptive to such an approach; the research must be useful, and there needs to be a demand for such knowledge in policing." Sherman (2013) provided evidence where inspections of policing discovered knowledge gaps but then ignored them rather than investing in research to investigate the issue.

Sherman concluded (2013: 395) that research can inform policing by anticipating "chronically recurring issues" and providing evidence in time for the next critical event rather than merely identifying knowledge gaps post incident.

For acceptance internally in policing, researchers must overcome a perception that evidence-based research conflicts with experience. Research in both the US and the UK suggested that police officers have a strong reliance on professional experience and instinct, and where there was a choice between experience and expert opinion, experience was greatly valued over the latter (Palmer, 2011; Lum et al., 2012). Palmer, Kirby and Phythian (2019: 91) found that although police officers recognised the term EBP, the use of an EBP approach was less apparent, and although senior ranks embraced the doctrines, lower-ranking officers were "more likely to value experience over academic evidence and collaboration." Similarly, Jonathan-Zamir et al. (2019) found that while overall police officers supported EBP, they were psychologically inclined to rely not on the evidence of research but on their professional experience. Jonathan-Zamir et al. (2019: 1471) concluded that attempts to implement an EBP approach needed full awareness of this inclination of police officers and rather than suppress it, "EBP initiatives should build on it and 'import' scientifically sound practices into the experience."

Fleming and Rhodes (2017: 3) observed that police officers viewed their experiences as "valuable, practical and conducive to problem solving." However, Fleming and Rhodes also acknowledged the limitation of using experience as evidence, identifying that experience was based on limited history, it simplified stories, was biased, was bended to make it more convenient to the narrative and was political in terms of being partisan. Fleming and Rhodes (2017: 30) concluded that police officers drew on any source of knowledge that helped them do their job and utilised "political knowledge and craft knowledge as well as research-based knowledge in their everyday lives." Sherman (2013: 419) caveated that EBP did not replace the decisions made in policing based on experience, rather "can only inform such judgment, and usually improve it." Dawson and Stanko (2016) further noted the complex challenges of embedding EBP into police organisations, a challenge academic scholars described as resistance to change. However, Dawson and Stanko concluded that such scholars sat overwhelmingly outside of the police organisation and argued (2016: 65) that there was a "wealth of data that is routinely captured within police forces that should be the mainstay information for any new research."

I therefore considered the juxtaposition of research and experience and the methods I would utilise to capture experience in the data acquired. I pondered how, if experience was greatly valued in policing, such experience may be captured and analysed, so that it may contribute to the wealth of data as another source of knowledge to inform police decision-making. I concluded that the contribution that my research may make to the evidence base may not be one of proving an approach is either right or wrong, but rather examining the experiences of all those involved in the events and providing them with a voice (Becker, 1967). This conclusion led me to consider a qualitative approach to data collection to "explore the behaviour, perspectives, feelings and experiences of people and what lies at the core of their lives" (Holloway and Wheeler, 2002: 3). Considering my epistemological position in examining the policing of protests, a field within which I both worked and conducted research, I evaluated that my subjectivity was integral to the research process (Flick, 2009) and as a qualitative researcher I was part of the study, engaged in and integral to all parts of it (Dwyer and Buckle, 2009). As Flick, von Kardorff and Steinke (2004: 3) argued, I aimed to describe "life-worlds 'from the inside out,' from the point of view of the people who participate."

Therefore, I selected a qualitative method to examine and analyse relationships from the perspectives of all those engaged in protest events. It has been established in previous chapters that existing research into a dialogical approach to policing protest focused on the relationship between protest groups and the police and was lacking in examining the wider social relations existing between all those engaged in protest events. This method allowed examination of different viewpoints to analyse protest policing, acknowledging "different subjective perspectives and social backgrounds" related to all engaged in events (Flick, 2009: 16). Easton, McComish and Greenberg (2000) observed that utilising a qualitative approach yielded rich data. Mack et al. (2005: 6) argued that "the great contribution of qualitative research is the culturally specific and contextually rich data it produces." I concluded that it was the richness of data that was most pertinent to the research I was conducting. Despite the recognised limitations, utilising qualitative methods was the most appropriate approach for my research, a pragmatic choice of the most appropriate method for the area explored (Silverman, 1997).

Having selected a research qualitative method pathway, I next considered my position as both a serving police officer and a researcher in the field. Might I be classed as a spy within the police, as Horn (1997) suggested, when attempting to gain access to police forces? How might I gain access to those outside of the police who may also treat my presence with suspicion? My position as insider and outsider and the implications for my research, therefore, needed further consideration.

Insider, outsider or both?

Before embarking on research, it was important for me to assess my position as a researcher in the field of protest policing, an area of policing that I am well versed, and ponder how this may impact on conducting field research through interviews. I reflected on my experience in the policing of public order and public safety events and examined whether as a researcher I might be an insider, outsider or both, when undertaking field work.

I have been serving as a police officer for approaching 30 years and during this time have specialised in the field of public order policing. I have been deployed on numerous public order and public safety events throughout my service, including marches, protests, sporting and music events and serious disorder. I remain an operational Public Order and Public Safety Adviser and have been deployed at over 100 different events across the UK, providing advice at Gold (strategic), Silver (tactical) and Bronze (operational) levels. Such events include high-profile sporting events such as Champions League football matches and the Open Golf tournament, protests and marches such as G8 protest in Northern Ireland and NATO conference marches in South Wales, and serious disorder such as experienced in Liverpool in 2011.

However, as well as being a practitioner, I have studied public order and protest policing, both formally and informally, and have undertaken postings in policing where an understanding of the theoretical framework behind protest policing and decision-making has been essential to the role. I was seconded to the National Policing Improvement Agency and latterly the College of Policing for four years within the Public Order and Public Safety team, where my work impacted upon national policy. I have delivered public order and personal safety training to police officers and staff for over 25 years at operational, tactical and strategic levels, including delivering public order command courses to senior offices from throughout the UK. I have delivered numerous international public order command course, including to officers of the Ethiopian Federal Police, Tanzania Police Force, Royal Anguilla Police Force, Sierra Leone Police and the Republic of Sierra Leone Armed Forces.

I provide this detail not in any way to asseverate any expert status in the field of public order policing, but rather to contextualise the challenges I faced as an experienced police officer conducting academic research, one whom Posner (2009: 16) may describe as a "so-called pracademic" having occupied significant positions as both academic and practitioner. My position as police officer not only provided me ready access to those who had policed protest events but further placed me firmly as an insider within "police (canteen) sub-culture" (Waddington, 1999) in the close-knit public order policing community. As a researcher exploring a cultural setting to which I had a "natural access," I was undertaking what Alvesson (2003: 174) described as a self-ethnographic study in which I was "an active participant, more or less on equal terms with other participants."

Therefore, I was mindful from the outset of my position as insider, as an experienced practitioner in protest policing and acknowledged that my experience was also subject to bias and based on my own partisan history (Fleming and Rhodes, 2017). Alvesson (2003: 189) cautioned that engaging in such research as an insider necessitated some risk, and the challenge for such a researcher was not of going native as the ethnographer, rather making "strong efforts to avoid 'staying native.'" However, Brannick and Coghlan (2007) defended insider research. Despite acknowledging a perception that insiders were unable to maintain objectivity and distance Brannick and Coghlan (2007: 72) challenged the standpoint and contended that insider research was not only of value, but also provided "important knowledge about what organizations are really like, which traditional approaches may not be able to uncover." The approach allowed the insider to use their knowledge and experience to reassess the areas in which they study. Brannick and Coghlan however cautioned that insider researchers needed to pay due regard to the strengths and limitations of their comprehension of the community within which they conducted research.

Burgess (1984) argued that the experiences of the insider researcher who studied a familiar setting would appear to outweigh those of the outsider. However, Burgess guarded that insider researchers must not take situations as read due to their familiarity with the research area and recommended (1984: 28) that researchers "continually pose questions about the settings within which they are located." Al-Makhamreh and Lewando-Hundt, (2008; 19) noted that conducting research "at home" presented the researcher with "dilemmas, but also opportunities and enriches the data." Dwyer and Buckle (2009) acknowledged the dangers of an inside researcher making assumptions, failing to fully explain their experience and potentially shaping interviews based on their and not the participants' experiences. However, Dwyer and Buckle identified advantages that were afforded to an insider in gaining access and concluded that the most significant consideration was not whether the researcher was an insider or outsider, but how they faithfully and accurately represented the experiences of the participants, which required the researcher to be "open, authentic, honest" and "deeply interested in the experience of one's research participants" (2009: 59). Furthermore, Dwyer and Buckle surmised that due to the role they undertake, and their extensive knowledge of the literature surrounding their study, researchers can never fully be either insiders or outsiders, but only ever occupy "the space between" (2009: 61).

Woodward (2008) agreed that the argument for and against insider or outsider research based on the former being subjective and the latter objective was too coarse an antithesis. Woodward argued (2008: 547) that the research process could never be totally inside or fully outside, "but involves an interrogation of situatedness and how 'being inside' relates to lived bodies and their practices and experiences." Such research therefore may produce data that lacks objectivity due to an inside viewpoint but may also provide a richer and more authentic appreciation of the setting. Breen (2007: 163) saw her role as neither insider nor outsider but in the middle. Breen (2007: 163) conjectured that "the role of the researcher is better conceptualised on a continuum, rather than as an either/or dichotomy."

Bartunek and Louis (1996) offered an alternative approach and argued that insider researchers tended to view the research setting subjective to their own positions in the field, whereas outsiders were likely to have greater influence over public interpretation of the research setting. Bartunek and Louis favoured an approach where insiders and outsider researchers worked together, conducting team research. It is worth noting, however, that such an approach does not take in to account the fact that researchers may undertake both roles in conducting field work. Mullings (1999) observed that discourse regarding the position of a researcher as either insider or outsider assumed that being one or other was a "fixed attribute." Mullings argued that such a stance discounted the alternative viewpoints that a researcher may undertake in time and through space and concluded (1999: 337) that "no individual can consistently remain an insider and few ever remain complete outsiders." Similarly, Wegener (2014: 164) suggested that "insider and outsider positions are created, altered and reproduced." Wegener argued that a continuous transition between research viewed from the inside and the outside provided a rewarding perspective from which to observe, and that such positions were not unfluctuating standpoints, but were transient.

It could be argued therefore that my research placed me as an insider, examining an area of policing in which I am very much still an active participant (Alvesson, 2003). Alternatively, as a police officer turned researcher, I might have been viewed by colleagues as "others:" insiders who have become outsiders, which Horn (1997: 299) described as "a particularly dangerous breed since they have special knowledge of the police and aim to make public the secrets of police work." Similarly, conducting field work within the protest community, I was aware that I may be viewed as an outsider, and therefore needed to consider how to negotiate outsider issues (Poulton, 2012) in order to collect and evaluate data. Participants within protest groups may be considered as members of a "service occupation" (Becker, 1963: 82), within which there will be some who have a full-time vocation centred on their principles, and others who have a more casual connection to the cause. Equally, as a serving police officer and outsider, I may have been viewed as a servant of the "client," able to apply sanctions, but perceived by the members as unable to "judge the proper worth" of such protest groups.

I concluded that my field work entailed a transient position as researcher, passing in, out and along the continuum of insider and outsider research (Wegener, 2014: Breen, 2007). The challenge was to avoid the barriers of being on either end of the spectrum and, being mindful of my epistemological position, to provide a voice to all those engaged in protest events without providing a distorted view from one side or the other. In doing so, I sought to understand each participant from their view of reality which "they create by their interpretation of their experience and in terms of which they act" (Becker, 1963: 174).

Therefore, I elected to engage in conversations to elicit information (Reyes-Garcia and Sunderlin, 2011) and capture the experiences of all interested parties involved in protest events. The following section examines my considerations in utilising interviews as the primary data source and the decisions I made in identifying case studies, selecting participants and recruiting gatekeepers, as both insider and outsider researcher.

Utilising interviews: Insider and outsider

Burgess (1984) observed that interviews may be used to gain an insight into situations which either the researcher did not witness or areas where the participants may not wish the researcher to be present. My area of research centred on dialogue and relationships that have been built over time and centred on trust (for example, Wells, 2008; Smith, 2015). Observing such encounters might not therefore be conducive to the circumstances, and the presence of a researcher might hinder the dialogue between parties. Interviews therefore provided me with a window through which to observe the relationships and dialogue without compromising the ongoing interaction, and in so doing provide access to experiences (Silverman, 2010).

Seidman (2006) observed that at the centre of conducting research interviews was an interest in the lived experiences of individuals because they were of worth and having this at the heart of the process assisted in ensuring the researcher centred interviews on the participant and not their own ego. Seidman concluded (2006: 14) that conducting interviews was "deeply satisfying to researchers who are interested in others' stories." This was very much at the centre of my approach in addressing any concerns of participants regarding my insider or outsider status. I chose a less structured interview approach to capture the experiences of participants and to provide insight into "a world beyond the story that the interviewee tells" (Melia, 1997: 34).

Having selected semi-structured interviews as my primary data source and identified an interview strategy, I turned my attention to identifying suitable case studies in which to explore a dialogical approach to protest policing, the selection of participants to interview and recruiting gatekeepers.

Identifying case studies

Stake (2005: 143) observed that research based on case studies was "defined by interest on an individual case, not by the methods of inquiry used." Flyvbjerg (2006: 224) further noted the importance of the study to be close to real-life situations and provide a wealth of details, to provide the "development of a nuanced view of reality." Mack et al. (2005) advocated utilising case studies for the contextually rich data that were produced. I decided to use case studies to provide a framework by which to delve deeper into the practical application of academic theories in protest events and capture the real-life experiences of those involved. Therefore, I endeavoured to select "fertile cases" (Ragin and Becker, 1992: 122), information rich and worthy of in-depth study due to their significance (Patton, 2002).

As Stake (2005: 150) noted, casework often began with studies already identified by the researcher, because they were of "prominent interest." In selecting case studies, I initially considered selecting a variety of case studies to provide data from a wide range of geographical areas in the UK, as I had identified that there was no research into Police Liaison Team (PLT) since their adoption as a national tactic. Through my national role in the College of Policing, I had identified several case studies that might be suitable and had access to gatekeepers. A key factor was selecting case studies where a dialogical approach had been implemented, including the deployment of PLT, noting that not all police forces had such experience in the policing of protest. Being conscious of potential issues in making generally valid statements when basing research on a single study (Flick, 2009), I considered utilising more than one study.

The first case study I selected was the policing of the badger cull and its opposition in South West England in 2016. I chose this study for several reasons: I had spent time in the region during my time in the College of Policing and had anecdotal evidence of the challenges that the policing of the cull had brought; the cull had high-profile media coverage and divided opinion; the policing of the cull provided an opportunity to interview participants from several police force areas in one case study (Devon and Cornwall, Avon and Somerset, Dorset and Gloucestershire); and I had access to gatekeepers within the areas. Analysis of the policing of the badger cull provided an opportunity to examine the value of a dialogical approach to environmental protests in a rural setting where the opposition spanned several weeks. The study provided a rich vein of data which allowed me to select participants from all sides and viewpoints of the cull and opposition to it.

To provide diversity in terms of location, duration and nature of protest, I sought a second case study located in an inner-city setting and naturally gravitated to my home police force area. As well as providing contrast, examining a case study based in Merseyside brought other advantages; the city of Liverpool had witnessed numerous protests and marches over many years; Merseyside Police had embraced a dialogical approach so there was an opportunity to examine its contribution; there was ready access to potential participants and gatekeepers; and there was no existing research examining protest policing in the city. The announcement by the EDL of their intention to march in June 2017 provided a perfect opportunity to study a current case. Support from my home force and particularly one senior officer allowed me to remain external to the event as a researcher rather than taking an active part in planning and policing the event.

Several other case studies were considered and explored as additional studies before I settled on two case studies: less to allow a comparison of one with the other but more to provide a variety of events in terms of types of protests, size, location, geographical and economic considerations. There was an element of pragmatism and logistics in limiting the research to two studies, although the badger cull case study did entail several trips to the South West region. However, the decision was more than a practical one; concentrating on only two studies meant that I was able to interview numerous participants from different viewpoints of each event. This approach allowed me to delve deeper into the case study (Easton, McComish and Greenberg, 2000) and provided rich and thick data (Dibley, 2011) whilst still affording contrasting case studies.

Therefore, my knowledge and experience as an insider enabled a more directed case study selection process. I was very aware that the case studies chosen were ones where a dialogical approach was utilised and therefore specifically sought to evaluate the contribution of such an approach. Had I selected case studies as an outsider, it may have been more difficult to identify events where a dialogical approach had been implemented. This would not have made the research results less valuable but may not have allowed as rich an analysis of where a dialogical approach had been utilised.

I was further aware of being an insider researcher as I considered a sampling process and selected an appropriate nonprobability strategy, basing my sampling strategy on the strength of my experience and knowledge in the field in which I was conducting research. Shively (2011: 62) noted that researchers might employ a process where they actively seek "a sub-group of the population for research focus, subsequently drawing a random sample from the purposively selected group." Thus, my experience in the field engendered my selection of a purposive or judgmental sampling strategy for the selection of participants to interview. Patton (2002) noted that where random sampling addressed the issues of bias in identifying participants by randomising the selection, bias in purposeful sampling was an intentional focus and therefore a strength, yielding information-rich cases. Barbour (2001: 1115) observed that purposive sampling offered a level of control for the researcher "rather than being at the mercy of any selection bias inherent in pre-existing groups." Therefore, the case studies I selected allowed me to carefully choose a sample based on considering the parameters of the groups I was researching.

I further considered an appropriate sample size that would provide suitable representation for all the different groups identified in each study. Guest, Bunce and Johnson (2006) argued that a sample size of as few as six interviews might be adequate to facilitate the development of meaningful themes and interpretations, with a saturation of themes present within 12 interviews. Similarly, Francis et al. (2010) argued that almost all the beliefs of the interviewees were captured if setting a minimum sample size of 13 participants. Ritchie, Lewis and Elam (2003) offered that a small sample size was often applicable in conducting qualitative research as the studies were rich in data, and when suitably analysed a point was soon reached where there was little new data of evidential value obtained from additional interviews. I opted to set my sample size at 20–25 interviews for each case study to ensure that there was representation and voice of participants from members of all the key groups engaged in or affected by the protests in each case study.

Selecting participants

Having selected two case studies, my attention turned to identifying and selecting the most appropriate participants with whom to conduct interviews. Stake (2005: 161) observed that the objective in conducting case study research was "not to represent the world, but to represent the case." Using this as my mantra, I sought to select participants from all key groups able to inform important facets and different perspectives (Sargeant, 2012) relating to a dialogical approach to the policing of protest. I was particularly mindful of identifying participants representing all angles of the discourse to examine the balancing of competing human rights. I therefore identified the following groups from which to recruit participants:

- Police Public Order Commanders.
- PLT officers.
- Members of protest and counterdemonstrating groups.
- Employees of businesses and organisations affected by the protest.

The selection of participants was determined by their involvement in the event, which was the subject of the study. Hence, the police officers specifically approached were those that had occupied key roles during the policing of the protest identified. Likewise, members of protest and counterdemonstrating groups, employees of businesses and other key organisations were also selected by their relevance to the research and the fact that they had been engaged in the protest events identified for the case studies. As I had selected to employ a purposive approach to select the sample, and whilst considering who was best qualified to participate, I also mused over selecting reliable and competent participants. Tongco (2007:155) opined that reliable interviewees may not necessarily be competent, that reliability referred to the honesty and truthfulness of the participant, whereas competency denoted how qualified the interviewee was "to answer questions about the cultural domain the researcher is studying."

I concluded that it was crucial not just to recruit gatekeepers that would provide access to the organisations identified, but to also select sub-gatekeepers within those organisations who might assist me in identifying those individuals to approach as prospective participants.

Recruiting gatekeepers

Gaining access to research participants entails negotiation and renegotiation (Burgess, 1984) and, for access into organisations, necessitates institutions building trust in the researcher, allowing a working alliance to forge where research is possible (Flick, 2009). Nind (2008) recommended approaching the senior figure in an organisation first, as a gatekeeper through whom others with first-hand experience can be recruited as participants. Burgess (1984) posited that researchers should select plural gatekeepers able to provide the researcher with permission and access to different elements of the organisation. Further, Burgess highlighted that where there were no readily available gatekeepers, researchers should consider how to befriend individuals that might promote the research within their social settings.

Brannick and Coghlan (2007) observed that the main challenge for outsiders was in gaining primary access. Once this had been achieved, the recruitment of suitable gatekeepers through negotiation was usually obtained with ease. However, for insiders, the reverse was true in that although primary access was a given, they may not have secondary access to individual departments of the organisation required for their research. Merkens (2004: 166) cautioned that "gatekeepers often link an element of self-interest with their willingness to open one or more doors." Comparably, Wanat (2008) suggested that the gatekeepers' involvement was influenced by whether they saw the research as being beneficial to their cause or a threat.

My status as an insider afforded me primary access to gatekeepers within police organisations. I initially sought senior officers as initial gatekeepers for each case study: a Deputy Chief Constable and an Assistant Chief Constable. Both provided authorisation and validity to the research, often referred to as providing "top cover" in police vernacular and allowed me to recruit further gatekeepers who provided access to the different facets of the organisations. My knowledge and experience allowed identification of the most suitable secondary gatekeepers, and they in turn provided access to further gatekeepers who identified key individuals involved in the case studies researched. Contrary to Merkens (2004) and Wanat (2008), I did not encounter resistance from any gatekeepers in relation to self-interest. In fact, I experienced few questions from any of the gatekeepers I engaged regarding the research that I was undertaking prior to them committing to participation. Instead, I encountered an overwhelming enthusiasm from each gatekeeper and sub-gatekeeper, and a strong desire for them to share their story and experiences. Furthermore, there was a real fervour from gatekeepers and sub-gatekeepers to provide me with access to those with whom they had entered into dialogue during their respective protest events, so that they too could be afforded a voice and share the narrative of their engagement. Such zeal was not limited to providing access to those whom the gatekeepers identified as being supportive of the police. Several sub-gatekeepers furnished contact details for individuals they perceived as being key in the event researched, and even though they supplied a caveat that the person in question might not want to speak to me, suggested that their significance in the case study made it worth me at least seeking their participation.

My evaluation of why I was afforded unabridged support initially drew me to the conclusion that this was partially due to the fact that I was an accepted insider within police circles. As a researcher within my own organisation examining the policing of the EDL march in Liverpool, my experience in public order and protest policing afforded me creditability. This, coupled with the backing of senior officers as primary and secondary gatekeepers, validated my research and status as researcher. Although I was an outsider police officer researching the policing of a badger cull, I was an insider as part of the wider police family, vouched for by senior officers. Further, my years of secondment to the College of Policing Public Order and Public Safety team provided credence, and this position was used by gatekeepers in their introduction of me to further sub-gatekeepers.

However, I concluded that the willingness to participate without protecting self-interest was more than simply because of my position as an insider researcher. There was a genuine enthusiasm from gatekeepers and participants to have the story told from all sides of the issue. This conclusion was affirmed by the eager response of participants from groups who would consider me as an outsider: members of protest groups, businesses and other organisations. Sub-gatekeepers were asked to approach members of the identified groups and seek their permission to pass contact details on to me. Despite the initial concerns of gatekeepers, they reported that all those contacted were very keen to participate and furnish their details. This allowed me to contact prospective participants and outline my ethical position as researcher and police officer. I found that in these groups, where there were no readily available gatekeepers, I did not need to utilise a strategy to befriend individuals (Burgess, 1984) as they were enthused participants. Therefore, although my status provided an introduction, my overwhelming experience was that participants engaged because they wished to provide their narrative and have their voice heard.

Preparing for interviews: Insider and outsider

As I began to identify participants, I also prepared for the interviews to be conducted with selected participants. I had chosen a semi-structured "or 'conversational' interviewing style" (Silverman, 2010) as this appeared ideally suited to my research, which was heavily weighted on dialogue, and would encourage discussion. I prepared question sheets to assist me in formulating questions and keeping me on track, which aided a consistent questioning approach across the interviews and case studies. The questions flowed in a similar fashion for all interviewees: police; protest group members; and other interested parties. The questions asked participants to describe the protest event, their involvement and identify other groups or stakeholders involved in the event. Questions asked participants to explain how they had engaged in dialogue, before, during and after events, about human rights considerations and to what extent they believed a dialogical approach contributed to the balancing of human rights.

I further pondered practical implications in conducting interviews and how my position as insider, outsider or both may impact upon participants and potentially hinder the open conversation I pursued. I considered how open I might be with participants about my own experiences, both as a police officer well versed in protest events and as a researcher. Burgess (1984) observed that the established protocol of researchers avoiding discussing personal experiences became a barrier to relationship building when conducting interviews and ignoring this standard practice encouraged discussions and providing an opportunity for social evaluation. However, Hermanns (2004: 209) guarded interviewers from "appearing to be as wise and omniscient as he or she believes him or herself to be." Despite not needing to befriend participants to recruit them, I still recognised that relationship building was a key element in preparing for interviews. DiCicco-Bloom and Crabtree (2006) established that the act of interviewing was invasive. They identified the importance of building rapport and gaining the respect and trust of the interviewee, creating a safe environment, which was most conducive to allowing interviewees to share their experiences. I recognised that for some participants this invasion might be exacerbated by my position interviewing as a serving police officer.

Atkinson and Coffey (2001) advised interviewers to contemplate their and their interviewee's social roles and acknowledge power differentials. Further, Ribbens (1989: 580) noted that "research interviews may inescapably involve power imbalances." I recognised that addressing such power differentials was key to creating a rapport and breaking down barriers. Being an insider in policing may be an advantage in existing rapport, but also presented challenges in addressing power imbalances, particularly where my selection of participants included police officers senior in rank to me. Conversely, my outsider status may adversely affect the willingness of some participants to share their experiences, particularly members of protest groups who might have had negative encounters with the police. Therefore, in preparing for interviews, I needed a considered approach to best encourage open discourse and so further deliberated the selection of interview locations and even an appropriate dress code for each interview.

Interview locations

Due to my insider status, it would have been simple and convenient to conduct all interviews in the most accessible police premises for each participant. For police officers, this opened up the option of numerous offices and rooms inside the security area of a police premises. For non-police participants, access potentially required meeting security measures, such as providing personal details, unless an external room outside of the security area, like an interview room, was utilised. Both scenarios had the capacity to impact on the openness of interviewees, depending on how they viewed me as insider or outsider, potentially as part of the sub-culture or as a police investigator. I considered alternative options, such as a coffee shop or other neutral public venue, or a room in an interviewee's own organisation or business. My intention was to identify somewhere free from distractions, selected to accommodate the participant, based on their availability and willingness to attend the agreed location (Gill et al., 2008; Rowley, 2012) and one which created "a productive atmosphere for the conversation" (Hermanns, 2004: 209).

However, Herzog (2005) argued that the choosing of an interview venue, and by whom that venue was chosen, was far more than simply selecting somewhere that was comfortable and convenient. Herzog argued (2005: 25) that the location "should be examined within the social context of the study being conducted and analysed as an integral part of the interpretation of the findings" and consequentially the choice of location and how it was determined should itself be an integral part of the research and considered in the analysis of data gleaned. Elwood and Martin (2000) concurred and suggested that deeper consideration should be given to location selection than simply accepting it as a pragmatic solution to suit all involved. Analysis of a chosen location provided a richer and more in-depth picture than considering the interview contents alone and this information allowed the researcher to better understand the experiences of the interviewee. Analysing the location when selected by the interviewee might also shed light on the power differentials. Elwood and Martin (2000: 655) provided an example where organisational directors choosing to be interviewed in their own offices accentuated their directorship, "seemingly to assert their expertise about the neighbourhood and authority in the interview experience."

I therefore chose to hand over the control of selecting interview locations to participants. My rationale was, firstly, to empower interviewees in the decision-making process, allowing them to address potential power differentials and create an atmosphere most conducive to facilitating open conversation (Atkinson and Coffey, 2001; Hermanns, 2004). This would empower participants in their analysis of my insider-outsider status and assist in building a respectful relationship between the participants and me, based on a mutual trust, and assist in creating a "message of dignity and acknowledgment of one's equal right to contribute knowledge and an experience that matches the message" (Karnieli-Miller, Strier and Pessach, 2009: 286). Secondly, the selection might provide further data and allow analysis of the participant's choice of venue, providing "a social-political statement beyond the logistical decision based on the participant's convenience" (Herzog, 2005: 44) which might be revealed directly or indirectly during the interview.

I was mindful that should the participant be given free rein in selecting a location, there might be constraints, particularly in considering risk management, which may result in a compromise being sought (Burgess, 1984). To assist with the selection, I ensured that participants were aware of the nature of the interview prior to selecting the location. This allowed interviewees to make an informed choice of a suitable venue where they could freely share their experiences (Elwood and Martin, 2000). As an option, I was prepared to provide a choice of suggestions should participants ask me to select a venue, which would still address any imbalances of equality that conducting interviews might present. An analysis of the different choices made by interviewees and how providing free choice assisted in breaking down barriers and assisted easier transition through the insider-outsider continuum is provided later in this chapter.

Dress code

Conscious that first impressions were most powerfully communicated non-verbally (Mehrabian, 1972), I further considered how I might present myself as a researcher and interviewer in terms of dress. Coffey (1999) recognised the challenge that researchers encountered in presenting themselves and observed that at times a dress code had been adopted to mirror that of those being interviewed. Poulton (2012) recounted anxieties in selecting what to wear when meeting participants as a researcher. Although not facing the same gendered challenges as Poulton, I still sought to present myself in a way that aided entering and developing rapport. As both researcher and police officer, I particularly wished to appear professional without being officious, especially in situations when I was an outsider, and sought to address potential power imbalances.

Further, when interviewing police colleagues within my own organisation, I considered whether wearing police uniform was applicable, should an internal police premise be selected as the interview location. This I thought might be potentially significant when interviewing commanders of a higher rank than myself. Although the police vernacular in public order command is one of "role rather than rank specific" (College of Policing, 2013), I have discovered from personal experience in delivering command courses the advantages of adopting a non-uniformed dress code to remove barriers of rank. However, allowing the interviewee to select the venue removed the opportunity to implement such protocols, should a uniformed officer select their office as the interview location, and this therefore left me to ponder self-image presentation. I concluded that what was most significant in selecting interview location and dress code was not particularly the choices I made, rather recognising the impact that such dynamics might have on the interview and interviewer. This became part of the study and the impact of the choices made are described for each case study later in this chapter.

Ethical considerations

In preparation for conducting research, I gained ethical approval which provided thought and considerations on how I would conduct interviews. However, I recognised that ethical considerations do not end once approval has been granted and I continued to make ethical decisions throughout the process. I was acutely aware from the outset that conducting interviews and encouraging discussions relating to protest activities might pose the risk that criminal or other disclosures requiring action might occur. My concern was not only that this might compromise me as both a researcher and a serving police officer, but that this would also detract from the research being conducted. The ethical dilemma I faced was not as risk-laden as Yates (2004) encountered in conducting criminal ethnographical research. However, I still concurred that it was important to establish a "defensible ethical stance" and consider the "issues that could potentially arise" (Yates, 2004: 21). Although I assessed the risk in my research as low, I minimised this by ensuring that my ethical position as serving police officer and researcher was clarified in all correspondence prior to interviews being arranged. Further, I outlined the parameters of the interview to each participant in a participant information sheet in advance of every interview and reinforced them verbally prior to each interview. This preparation ensured that neither I nor the participant were compromised during the interview process.

Selecting appropriate interview locations to provide a safe and appropriate place for both interviewer and interviewees required further ethical consideration, particularly relevant once I had decided to ask participants to select interview locations and more so when some chose home addresses and public houses. Due to the nature of the case studies examined and the identity of some participants, this necessitated me, as a serving police officer, notifying my own organisation regarding two interview meetings, complying with the "notifiable association policy" (Merseyside Police, 2021). Despite the policy requiring "strict confidentiality," after both notifications, I was contacted by a member of the intelligence department enquiring about planned interviews. On the first occasion, I was requested to approach the interviewee to ascertain their openness to becoming a covert human intelligence source (Home Office, 2018). On the second occasion, I was tasked to find out more information and pass it back to the individual. Both times I ignored the request and on the second occasion returned to the individual to educate them about my ethical position as a researcher irrespective of my position as a serving police officer. In both situations, I felt very much as an outsider in my own organisation and felt very uncomfortable in receiving the requests and responding. To be clear, neither request was dishonest, rather I believe the approaches were made in good faith as a part of the individual's "drive to get the job done" (UK Government, 2022). However, I perceived that my police colleagues displayed a misunderstanding, both of the role of researcher and of a dialogical approach to protest policing. The requests were a desire to get a result in the here and now. Had I obliged, this may have had a detrimental impact not only on the trust I was seeking to build with participants but also longer term on the relationships that it became evident existed and had developed between police colleagues and those engaged in protest events. On reflection, I surmised that such requests were unlikely to be made of an outsider researcher in this situation. Making a stand against the approaches also made me question my own insider–outsider status and, although uncomfortable to record, was an important experience to document to assist other researchers in considering their own status in conducting field research.

A final ethical consideration concerned the anonymity of interview participants, of which they had been assured, in presenting the research. I was aware that the key individuals in each case study were from a small pool of possible participants and was mindful that if I identified which organisation or group each interviewee participant came from, there was a probability that this anonymity would be compromised. Therefore, I firstly grouped organisations together, providing a collective term and then a distinguishing letter for each participant (the collective terms for each case study are further described in this chapter). Secondly, I decided against preparing a list of participants identifying demographic and organisation. The decisions I made were not without debate and in particular this decision polarised my two academic advisers: one favoured a table to help the reader to know more about the demographics of participants; and the other suggested an approach of withholding the locations of the case studies to provide further anonymity to participants. My decision fell somewhere in the middle, but it was an approach that I believed allowed me to be able to present the case studies in the settings that they occurred, providing analysis at political, ideological, cultural and contextual levels (Waddington, Jones and Critcher, 1989) whilst still maintaining the anonymity as assured to participants prior to their research interviews.

Conducting interviews: Insider and outsider

Now that I had an interview plan and approach prepared, I then commenced conducting 48 interviews across the two case studies. The following describes some of my experiences in implementing the plan and provides considerations for navigating the continuum of insider and outsider researcher in conducting interviews.

Case study 1: The badger cull

Between February and May 2017, I conducted 26 interviews with participants who had been integral to the policing of badger cull protests in South West England. The sample of police officers ranged from the rank of Constable to Deputy Chief Constable and were all serving officers from Devon and Cornwall Police, Avon and Somerset Police or Gloucestershire Constabulary. The group was composed of: police commanders undertaking the role of Gold, Silver or Bronze Public Order Commanders; and Liaison Officers, divided into Police Liaison Officers (PLO) who engaged with protest groups and Cull Liaison Officers (CLO) who engaged with the pro-cull community. Members of protest groups interviewed included those who referred to themselves as "*protectors*," and others who favoured the term "*hunt saboteurs.*" The term *protester* was itself a contentious label that is further examined during later chapters and it was thus avoided within the research findings. Farmers and cull contractors responsible for carrying out the cull were interviewed as those who were affected by the cull and who liaised with the police. To protect anonymity, participants were grouped, and the following collective terms were used:

- **Commander** – Police Public Order Commanders
- **PLT** – police officers liaising as PLO or CLO

- **Protector** – encompassing all those opposing the badger cull
- **Business** – include farmers, landowners and cull contractors

The recruitment of police officers was facilitated through gatekeepers and all commanders that had significant roles in the policing of the badger cull readily agreed to be interviewed. All were asked to choose their preferred locations for interview. The vast majority of police officers chose to be interviewed on police premises. On reflection, here was further evidence where I traversed the insider–outsider researcher status and on occasions felt on both sides simultaneously. Being a serving police officer and having worked nationally I was very comfortable with entering police premises outside my own force. However, although I was an insider in policing terms, I was also an outsider in that I needed to gain access, and so in most cases attended the reception where I was issued with a visitor's pass and needed to wait to be met by the interviewee. From here, I was then taken to the participants' chosen location and the selections appeared to vary between police ranks: more junior ranks chose interview rooms or quiet corners of canteens; more senior officers who had their own officers selected these as interview locations. The one police officer who selected to be interviewed at a neutral venue rather than on police premises chose the location for their convenience. In selecting a dress code that was professional without being officious, I chose to wear trousers and a shirt, rather than a suit or jeans. Although I was there specifically as a researcher, I had been introduced to participants as a serving police officer and was mindful of representing my home police force well.

The recruitment of Protectors was also facilitated through gatekeepers and despite my initial reservations I found that participants were very keen to be interviewed and provide their narratives. Protectors chose to be interviewed at two different locations; despite me being potentially viewed as an outsider, the majority invited me into the homes; the remainder chose a pub or café. Business participants also selected to be interviewed at home. Recruiting business participants was more difficult than any other group. Individuals expressed a fear that their involvement in the cull might be discovered and I had prospective interviews that failed to materialise despite several telephone and email exchanges.

Case study 2: The EDL march

Between July and October 2017, I conducted 22 interviews with participants who had been integral in the policing of the EDL march in Liverpool. The sample of police officers ranged from the rank of Constable to Deputy Chief Constable and were all serving officers from Merseyside Police or British Transport Police. The group was comprised: police commanders undertaking the role of Gold, Silver or Bronze Public Order Commanders; and Liaison Officers, which included PLT who had engaged with EDL or "*left-wing*" group members and police operational planners who had engaged with business and partner agencies. The EDL members who engaged with the police were so identified. Those opposing the

EDL march refuted the suggestion that they were protesters and preferred the collective noun of "*activists*" as most appropriate to describe their involvements. There were several participants interviewed from other organisations and businesses, representing: Liverpool City Council; St George's Hall; Merseytravel; and the Empire Theatre. These participants were also grouped to protect identities. The following collective terms were used:

- **Commander** – Police Public Order Commanders
- **PLT** – including operational planners
- **EDL** – marching members
- **Activist** – encompassing all those opposing the EDL march
- **Business** – interested parties including the local authority

Recruiting police officers for this case study in my home force presented no issues, particularly having a senior officer as gatekeeper sponsoring the research. All chose to be interviewed on police premises and there were varied locations selected, although many senior officers chose more neutral rooms instead of their own offices in which to be interviewed. The EDL members were willing participants from the first requests and selected a pub as the interview location. All business participants except one chose to be interviewed at their places of work which afforded them familiar surroundings and a safe environment (DiCicco-Bloom and Crabtree, 2006). The one exception chose to attend police premises to be interviewed, explaining that they regularly attended the police location in their duties so were familiar with the location.

The most difficult group to recruit were those opposed to the EDL march. Gatekeepers failed to identify suitable participants who had engaged with the police pre-event, describing them as a difficult group to reach, and this became a key area analysed during the study. However, I was keen to hear the voice of all those present including those opposed and therefore sought out potential participants to hear their reasons for not engaging with the police. An internet search produced a list of the groups and trade unions who had been actively involved in the counterprotest (Unite Against Fascism, 2017). Using the list, I searched for email addresses and contacted seven groups identified. I introduced myself as serving police officer and researcher and asked whether a member who was involved in the counterdemonstrations would be prepared for me to contact them. Five failed to respond to email correspondence despite several attempts. However, two organisations did respond, and participants were recruited. One selected to be interviewed at their own business location, the other chose to attend police premises.

Exploring interview locations

I had selected interviews as my main source from which to gather data to examine a dialogical approach to protest policing. In doing so, I had sought to gather their experiences and hear the voice of everyone affected by or engaged in the policing of the events described in both case studies. My approach had been to create an environment most conducive to allowing participants to freely share their experiences and to seek to remove barriers that my insider-outsider status may bring.

The overwhelming response of participants in both case studies was a desire to tell their stories. Each interview was planned to last approximately 30 minutes and every interview lasted at least this length of time However, whether it was due to the choice of the venue allowing participants to freely share, many continued past the planned time with participants eager to talk, and some passed the hour before I was able to conclude the interview. It was also evident, as I transcribed each interview and examined transcriptions, how little I spoke during each one. Many interviews commenced with me asking an open question and then several minutes of the participants describing their experiences. Only two interviews, both of Protectors, were initially more stilted, which was reflected in the one sentence replies to initial questions. However, in both cases, the interviewees seemingly relaxed and later on in the interviews engaged in long narratives describing their experiences.

The interview location choices certainly addressed any concerns regarding power imbalances (Ribbens, 1989). This was particularly evident inside the security of senior officers' inner sanctums, where the power very much lay with the interviewee. For the badger cull case study, these offices were not places I had visited previously. For the EDL case study, I had been inside the rooms several times previously as a Public Order and Public Safety Adviser. In both cases the dynamic was very much of being a visitor in the domain of the senior police officer, and although an insider in terms of being a fellow police officer, very much one of a junior rank. This power balance was noticeable even in the subtlety of the police officer staple of getting a "brew" before the interview started. In the canteens, it was easy for me to offer to buy a drink for interviewees before we started to assist in creating an informal atmosphere. However, in the offices of senior police officers, it was they who offered the drinks, another nuance highlighting where the power lay. This was further evident in examining transcripts of the interviews with the most senior officers. Whereas with other police officers there was more of a balanced question and answer structure, it was noticeable that with senior officers there was an opening question followed by several pages of narrative from the interviewee. This lessened the opportunity of utilising probing questioning as the interviewees effectively took control and provided their accounts. However, the response was consistent and corresponded with the approach I had set in gaining data through hearing the voice of participants and I was still able to steer questions to cover the aspects of research I was examining. Allowing those officers to choose to be interviewed in their own offices allowed participants to assert their expertise (Elwood and Martin, 2000) and provided rich data.

With more junior ranking police officers, I felt more as an insider in both case studies and that I was there to give them voice. There was a sense, particularly with PLT, that they were not always listened to; several commented that "*the bosses just don't get PLT*" and that this was an opportunity for them to be heard not just externally but within their own organisations. The fact that I was one of them, that I understood the language and had experience (Lum et al., 2012) allowed interviewees to freely express in a way that might not have been as open to someone outside of the organisation. However, I was also mindful of my objective role as researcher and to portray this visually I wore casual clothing, even when this meant, in my own force, having to change out of uniform to conduct interviews in my own place of work.

The transfer of power in allowing interviewees to choose locations was also evident when interviewing those outside of policing, since some of them might have found my outsider status potentially intimidating. Those who selected their own homes as the location wholeheartedly received me into them, offering drinks and making me feel welcomed. Several participants chose their places of work as interview locations which also meant that I was an invited guest, beholding to their procedures in entering premises and being shown to interview rooms. Some chose public spaces such as cafes in which to be interviewed. On arrival, I was very keen to allow the interviewee to choose seating arrangements. An EDL member chose a pub as a meeting place, which may have easily encouraged me to make stereotypical assumptions about "lager lout" tendencies (Mann, 2012). However, on my arrival, the interviewee made it clear that they were drinking soft drinks and that the location was one of convenience rather than any significant venue.

The power to dictate the interview location empowered interviewees and allowed them to control the initial elements of the interview, setting the tone and creating an environment most conducive to enabling open discourse. Participants freely opened up about their experiences, both those within hierarchical police settings and those external to policing. Police commanders were able to assert their territorial authority and lower ranks were given a voice to challenge not only external but internal misunderstandings of their role. Those outside of policing were provided with an open setting where they were able to describe their encounters in engaging in dialogue, including real exasperations about how the police had dealt with some situations, which interviewees passionately regaled. One interviewee vented about their frustrations before suddenly apologising, which allowed me to value their responses and assure them of the importance of hearing their experiences. Several thanked me for listening to their "*side*" and one commented that they wished that all police officers had been like me. The willingness for all participants to engage was not because of any particular interviewing skills I may or may not possess, rather, I perceived, due to the interviewing plan implemented which acknowledged my insider and outsider status and sought to build bridges to allow an understanding and valuing of the views of all.

Presenting findings

I transcribed each recorded interview, employing a more naturalistic approach (Oliver, Serovich and Mason, 2005) placing less significance on the mechanics of the interview and more on the meanings and perceptions conveyed. Interviewees had been afforded free rein in response, so little emphasis rested on analysis of pauses and fillers, which I removed so as not to detract from the overall narrative. Coding followed a thematic approach (for example, Robson and McCartan, 2016) using a combination of predetermined codes based on the questions asked and those that emerged during the interviews. These themes were consistent across both case studies and are set out in the following three chapters of this book; one on each of the case studies presenting the key findings; and a further discussion chapter examining the research questions posed across both case studies.

A narrative passage approach was utilised to convey research findings (Creswell, 2014) with interview excerpts blended to form the narrative for each theme heading. To provide the voice of participants, I inserted excerpts in full, mindful of employing "intellectual judgement" (Mason, 1994: 95) in developing the analysis to contextualise the excerpts within the narrative. Each excerpt was attributed to an individual from one of the collective groups identified earlier in this chapter, identified by a unique letter for each participant.

Conclusion

This chapter has provided thought for researchers, particularly when conducting quantitative research, in considering their research status as insiders and outsiders. Throughout my research journey, I have been conscious of my position as both researcher and serving police officer. I have continually assessed my insider-outsider status and concluded that I passed in, along and through the continuum of insider and outsider researcher at different times during the process, and on occasions was both insider and outsider simultaneously. The decisions I made regarding interview location and dress code assisted in building bridges, trust and relationships with those whom I interviewed, which reduced power imbalances and facilitated open conversation. This is evidenced by the lengthy, flowing interviews that were conducted and the access I was provided both physically in being invited into participants' homes and places of work and emotionally through their orating of rich stories. These decisions supported the epistemological stance I had selected as researcher in capturing the experiences of all those engaged in protest events and yielded rich data from which to analyse a dialogical approach to protest policing.

References

Al-Makhamreh, S. and Lewando-Hundt, G. (2008) Researching 'at home' as an insider / outsider. *Qualitative Social Work*, 7(1), 9–23.

Alvesson, M. (2003) Methodology for close up studies: Struggling with closeness and closure. *Higher Education*, 46, 167–193.

Atkinson, P. and Coffey, A. (2001) Revisiting the relationship between participant observation and interviewing in Gubrium, J. and Holstein, J., eds., *Handbook of interview research: Context and method*, 801–814. Thousand Oaks: Sage Publications.

Barbour, R. (2001) Checklists for improving rigour in qualitative research: A case of the tail wagging the dog. *British Medical Journal*, 322, 1115–1117.

Bartunek J. and Louis, M. (1996) *Insider / outsider team research*. London: Sage Publications.

Becker, H. (1963) *Outsiders: Studies in the sociology of deviance*. New York: The Free Press

Becker, H. (1967) Whose side are we on? *Social Problems*, 14, 239–247.

Brannick, T and Coghlan, D. (2007) In defense of being "native": The case for insider academic research. *Organizational Research Methods*, 10(1), 59–74.

Breen, L. (2007) The researcher 'in the middle': Negotiating the insider/outsider dichotomy. *The Australian Community Psychologist*, 19(1), 163–174.

Burgess, R. (1984) *In the field: An introduction to field research*. London and New York: Routledge.

Coffey, A. (1999) *The ethnographic self: Fieldwork and the representation of identity*. London: Sage Publications.

College of Policing (2013) *National police public order training curriculum: Police liaison team trainers guide*. Wyboston: College of Policing.

Creswell, J. (2014) *Research design: Qualitative, quantitative, and mixed methods approaches*. Thousand Oaks: Sage Publications.

Dawson, P. and Stanko, E. (2016) The best-kept secret(s) of evidence based policing. *Legal Information Management*, 16, 64–71.

Dibley, L. (2011) Analyzing narrative data using McCormack's lenses. *Nurse Researcher*, 18(3), 13–19.

DiCicco-Bloom, B. and Crabtree, B. (2006) Making sense of qualitative research: The qualitative research interview. *Medical Education*, 40, 314–321.

Dwyer, S. and Buckle, J. (2009) The space between: On being an insider-outsider in qualitative research. *International Journal of Qualitative Methods*, 8(1), 54–63.

Easton, K., McComish, J. and Greenberg, R. (2000) Avoiding common pitfalls in qualitative data collection and transcription. *Qualitative Health Research*, 10(5), 703–707.

Eddy, D. (2005) Evidence-based medicine: A unified approach. *Health Affairs*, 24(1), 9–17.

Elwood, S. and Martin, D. (2000) "Placing" interviews: Location and scales of power in qualitative research. *The Professional Geographer*, 52(4), 649–657.

Flick, U. (2009) *An introduction to qualitative research*. 4th ed. London: Sage Publications.

Flick, U., von Kardorff, E. and Steinke, I. (2004) *A companion to qualitative research*. London: Sage Publications.

Fleming, J. and Rhodes, R. (2017). Can experience be evidence? Craft knowledge and evidence-based policing. *Policy and Politics*, 46, 1–41.

Flyvbjerg, B. (2006) Five misunderstandings about case-study research. *Qualitative Inquiry*, 12(2), 219–245.

Francis, J., Johnston, M., Robertson, C., Glidewell, L. Entwistle, V., Eccles, M. and Grimshaw, J. (2010) What is an adequate sample size? Operationalising data saturation for theory-based interview studies. *Psychology and Health*, 25(10), 1229–1255.

Gill, P., Stewart, K., Treasure, E. and Chadwick, B. (2008) Methods of data collection in qualitative research: Interviews and focus groups. *British Dental Journal*, 204, 291–295.

Guest, G., Bunce, A. and Johnson, L. (2006) How many interviews are enough? An experiment with data saturation and variability. *Field Methods*, 18(1), 59–82.

Hermanns, H. (2004) Interviewing as an activity, in Flick, U., von Kardorff, E. and Steinke, I. eds., *A companion to qualitative research*, 209–214. London: Sage Publications.

Herzog, H. (2005) On home turf: Interview location and its social meaning. *Qualitative Sociology*, 28(1), 25–47.

Hoggett, J. and Stott, C. (2012) Post G20: The challenge of change, implementing evidence-based public order policing. *Journal of Investigative Psychology and Offender Profiling*, 9, 174–183.

Holloway, I. and Wheeler, S. (2002) *Qualitative research in nursing*. 2nd ed. Oxford. Blackwell Publishing.

Home Office (2018) *Covert human intelligence sources: Revised code of practice*. Available at: https://assets.publishing.service.gov.uk/government/uploads/system/uploads/attachment_data/file/742042/20180802_CHIS_code_.pdf

Horn, R. (1997) Not 'one of the boys': Women researching the police. *Journal of Gender Studies*, 6(3), 297–308.

Jonathan-Zamir, T., Weisburd, D., Dayan, M. and Zisso, M. (2019) The proclivity to rely on professional experience and evidence-based policing. *Criminal Justice and Behavior*, 46(10), 1456–1474.

Karnieli-Miller, O., Strier, R. and Pessach, L. (2009) Power relations in qualitative research. *Qualitative Health Research*, 19(2), 279–289.

Lum, C. and Koper, C. (2015) Evidence-based policing, in Dunham, R. and Alpert, G. eds., *Critical issues in policing*. 7th ed. Long Grove. Waveland Press.

Lum, C., Telep, C., Koper, C. and Grieco, J. (2012) Receptivity to research in policing. *Justice Research and Policy*, 14(1), 61–95.

Lumsden, K. and Goode, J. (2016) Policing research and the rise of the 'evidence-base': Police officer and staff understandings of research, its implementation and 'what works'. *Sociology*, 52(4), 813–829.

Mack, N., Woodsong, C., MacQueen, K., Guest, G. and Namey, E. (2005) *Qualitative research methods: A data collector's field guide*. North Carolina: Family Health International.

Mann R. (2012) Uneasy being English: The significance of class for English national sentiments. *Ethnicities*, 12(4), 484–499.

Mason, J. (1994) Linking qualitative and quantitative data analysis in Bryman, A. and Burgess, R. eds., *Analyzing qualitative data*. London and New York: Routledge.

Mehrabian, A. (1972) *Nonverbal communication*. New Brunswick and London. Transaction Publishers.

Melia, K. (1997) Producing 'plausible stories': Interviewing student nurses in Miller, G. and Dingwall, R. eds., *Context and method in qualitative research*, 26–36. London. Sage Publications.

Melnyk, B. (2011). *Evidence-based practice in nursing and healthcare: A guide to best practice*. Philadelphia, PA. Lippincott Williams and Wilkins.

Merkens, H. (2004) Selection procedures, sampling, case construction in Flick, U., von Kardorff, E. and Steinke, I. eds., *A companion to qualitative research*, 165–171. London. Sage Publications.

Merseyside Police (2021) *Notifiable association policy*. Available at: https://www.merseyside.police.uk/SysSiteAssets/foi-media/merseyside/policies/notifiable-association-policy.pdf

Mullings, B. (1999) Insider or outsider, both or neither: Some dilemmas of interviewing in a cross-cultural setting. *Geoforum*, 30, 337–350.

Nind, M. (2008) Conducting qualitative research with people with learning, communication and other disabilities: *Methodological challenges*. ESRC National Centre for Research Methods Review Paper. Economic and Social Research Council.

Oliver, D., Serovich, J. and Mason, T. (2005) Constraints and opportunities with interview transcription: Towards reflection in qualitative research. *Social Forces*, 84(2), 1273–1289.

Palmer, I. (2011) *Is the United Kingdom Police Service receptive to evidence-based policing? Testing attitudes towards experimentation*. Mst. thesis. Cambridge University, UK. Available at library.college.police.uk/docs/theses/Palmer-evidence-based-policing-2011.pdf

Palmer, I., Kirby, S. and Phythian, R. (2019) Assessing the appetite for evidence based policing: A UK based study. *International Journal of Police Science and Management*, 21(2), 91–100.

Patton, M. (2002) *Qualitative research and evaluation methods*. 3rd ed. Thousand Oaks: Sage Publications.

Petty, G. (2006) *Evidence based teaching*. Cheltenham: Nelson Thornes.

Poulton, E. (2012) 'If you had balls, you'd be one of us!' Doing gendered research: Methodological reflections on being a female academic researcher in the hyper-masculine subculture of 'football hooliganism'. *Sociological Research Online*, 17(4).

Posner, P. (2009) The pracademic: An agenda for re-engaging practitioners and academics. *Public Budgeting and Finance*, 29(1), 12–26.

Ragin, C. and Becker, H. (1992) *What is a case? Exploring the foundations of social inquiry*. Cambridge: Cambridge University Press.

Raynor, P. (2003) Evidence-based probation and its critics. *Probation Journal*, 50(4), 334–345.

Reyes-Garcia, V. and Sunderlin, W. (2011) Why Do Field Research? in Angelsen, A., Larsen, H., Lund, J., Smith-Hall, C. and Wunder, S. eds., *Measuring livelihoods and environmental dependence: Methods for research and fieldwork*, 17–32. Bogor, Indonesia: CIFOR.

Ribbens, J. (1989). Interviewing: An "unnatural situation"? *Women's Studies International Forum*, 12(6), 579–592.

Ritchie, J., Lewis, J. and Elam, G. (2003) Designing and selecting samples in Ritchie, J. and Lewis, J. eds., *Qualitative research practice: A guide for social science students and researchers*, 77–108. London. Sage Publications.

Robson, C. and McCartan, K (2016) *Real world research: A resource for users of social research methods in applied settings*. 4th ed. Chichester, West Sussex: Wiley.

Rowley, J. (2012) Conducting research interviews. *Management Research Review*, 35(3:4), 260–271.

Sargeant, J. (2012) Qualitative research part II: Participants, analysis, and quality assurance. *Journal of Graduate Medical Education*, 4(1), 13.

Seidman, I. (2006) *Interviewing as qualitative research: A guide for researchers in education and the social sciences*. 3rd ed. New York and London. Teachers College Press.

Sherman, L. (1998). *Evidence based policing: Ideas in American Policing*. Washington, DC: Police Foundation.

Sherman, L. (2013). The rise of evidence-based policing: Targeting, testing, and tracking. *Crime and Justice*, 42(1), 377–451.

Shively, G. (2011) Sampling: Who, how and how many? in Angelsen, A., Larsen, H., Lund, J., Smith-Hall, C. and Wunder, S. eds., *Measuring livelihoods and environmental dependence: Methods for research and fieldwork*, 51–70. Bogor, Indonesia: CIFOR.

Silverman, D (2010) *Doing Qualitative Research: A Practical Handbook*. 3rd ed. London: Sage Publications.

Silverman, D. (1997) The logics of qualitative research, in Miller, G. and Dingwall, R. eds., *Context and method in qualitative research*, 12–25. London: Sage Publications.

Smith, M. (2015) *The use of Police Liaison Teams in the policing of events: A review of practice*. Ryton: College of Policing. Available at: http://library.college.police.uk

Stake, R. (2005) Qualitative case studies in Denzin, N. and Lincoln, Y. eds., *The Sage handbook of qualitative research*. 3rd ed., 134–164. Thousand Oaks. Sage Publications

Tongco, M. (2007) Purposive sampling as a tool for informant selection. *Ethnobotany Research and Applications*, 5, 147–158.

UK Government (2022) *Have you got what it takes to be a police officer?* Available at: https://jobhelp.campaign.gov.uk/have-you-got-what-it-takes-to-be-a-police-officer/

Unite Against Fascism (2017) *Merseyside defeats fascist EDL – victory on the Mersey! [online]* 5 June 2017. Available at: http://uaf.org.uk/2017

Waddington D., Jones, K. and Critcher, C. (1989) *Flashpoints: Studies in public disorder*. New York: Routledge.

Waddington, P. (1999) Police (canteen) sub-culture: An appreciation. *British Journal of Criminology*, 34(2), 287–309.

Wanat, C. (2008) Getting past the gatekeepers: Differences between access and cooperation in public school research. *Field Methods*, 20(2), 191–208.

Wegener, C. (2014) 'Would you like a cup of coffee?' Using the researcher's insider and outsider positions as a sensitising concept. *Ethnography and Education*, 9(2), 153–166.

Wells, H. (2008) The techno-fix versus the fair cop: Procedural (in)justice and automated speed limit enforcement. *British Journal of Criminology*, 48, 798–817.

Woodward, K. (2008) Hanging out and hanging about: Insider / outsider research in the sport of boxing. *Ethnography*, 9(4), 536–561.

Yates, J. (2004) Criminological ethnography: Risks, dilemmas and their negotiation. *British Journal of Community Justice*, 3(1), 19–31.

Chapter 5

Case study 1
The badger cull

Introduction

The following three chapters provide an insight into the dialogical process between the police and all those engaged in protest events through the examination of two case studies. The first two examine each case study individually to provide perspective and examine the dialogical process, and Chapter 7 examines both case studies together, providing an analysis of the value and contribution of utilising such an approach.

This chapter therefore introduces the first case study: the policing of the badger cull and its opposition in South West England in 2016. The study examines the experiences of those engaged in or affected by the cull and opposition to it, focused particularly in the locations of Devon and North Cornwall, although many participants shared experiences in other cull areas. The study considers the dialogical engagement that took place between the police and all those affected by the badger cull in the build-up period, during the cull itself, and the period after the cull had ended and examines the balancing of the human rights of all affected parties. The chapter examines the relationship between the police and those wishing to protest or oppose the badger cull, and how such dialogue impacted upon the decision-making of the police commanders and the actions of those in opposition to the cull. The chapter, therefore, opens with an overview of the badger cull and its opposition in South West England, particularly concentrating on events and protests in the area in 2016, to provide a contextualised background to the case study.

However, unlike most existing literature, this study does not concentrate solely on police–protester engagement, rather it examines relationships further afield. The starting point, therefore, in analysing data gleaned in this case study will be to identify the whole range of interested parties who were significantly impacted by the badger cull and who had a vested interest in the cull and in doing so explore their identity and map the dialogue process between the police and each party, pictorially represented in a Dialogical Wheel. The chapter will explore the significance of trust, and in some cases the lack of it, and political pressures that had potential to influence decision-making. The chapter will then contemplate the role of police liaison and the selection of appropriate

DOI: 10.4324/9781003160533-5

officers and examine the police liaison process that was implemented prior to, during and post the cull period, particularly considering human rights implications and the balancing of such rights. Finally, the chapter will examine points of contact and the communication and dialogued enacted and consider reasons why some did not wish to engage in dialogue with the police.

Background to the cull

Badgers are perhaps one of the most popular native wild animals in the UK and a potent cultural symbol of the countryside (Enticott, 2001). However, in recent years, despite its protected status, the badger has been the subject of a cull in designated areas of England, particularly within the South West region (Parliament, 2011) following concerns linking the badger to the spread of bovine tuberculosis (DEFRA, 2016). The cull dichotomised views and opinions in the region and saw an increase in licences for cull operators (Natural England, 2014) coupled with opposition in the form of protests, marches and positive action (Irons, 2016; Cleave, 2016; Carrington, 2013). This section provides an overview of the badger cull and opposition to it to provide contextualisation to the case study and assist with understanding the competing opinions and the challenges that the police needed to address in their decision-making in the policing of protest events, marches and demonstrations as well as in ensuring a lawful, government-driven culling process was not prevented from operation and allowing the community to continue to feel safe and protected.

The badger was voted second only to the hedgehog in a national poll to select the most popular UK wildlife icon (Discover Wildlife, 2013), features on the logo of the Royal Society of Wildlife Trusts (more commonly referred to as The Wildlife Trusts) and is a cherished wildlife species within British history and culture. However, even in British culture, the badger is portrayed as both friend and foe and this can be observed in popular children's literature: 'Mr Badger' in Kenneth Grahame's 1908 novel *The Wind in the Willows* is portrayed as a wise, kind and compassionate fellow, willing to help others; whereas in Beatrix Potter's *The Tale of Mr. Tod*, the badger 'Tommy Brock' is depicted as a grim and deeply unpleasant character (Cassidy, 2012).

The badger has in more recent times found itself at the centre of contentious debate concerning its contribution to the spread of bovine tuberculosis (bTB) and therefore polarised views concerning the merits of culling badgers. The Department for Environment, Food and Rural Affairs (DEFRA) described bTB as "the most pressing animal health problem in the UK" (DEFRA, 2014: 6) and there has been a significant increase in the number of cattle culled due to the disease in recent years (Driver, 2016). Since the 1970s, badgers have been linked to this problem (Enticott, 2001), however, the extent to which badgers spread the disease and the effectivity of an enforced badger cull has been highly contested. The issues are further complicated by the protected status of badgers. Apart from badger baiting, made illegal in 1835, badgers were first given legal protection by the Badgers Act 1973, which was amended by the Wildlife and Countryside Act 1981, and replaced by the Protection of Badgers Act 1992 (Harris et al., 1994). This legislation means that the methods of culling badgers, namely cage-trapping and shooting badgers; controlled shooting; and cage-trapping and vaccination are clearly defined by DEFRA within open and closed seasons (DEFRA, 2016).

In 1997, under the direction of Professor Lord Krebs, an independent scientific review was compiled into the spread of bTB in cattle and badgers, and recommendations were made to the government to implement randomised controlled trails (Krebs et al., 1997), subsequently instigated and lasting for ten years. However, the effectivity of the cull was widely contested, and a report commissioned by DEFRA concluded that "badger culling is unlikely to contribute usefully to the control of cattle TB" (Bourne, 2007: 21). Lord Krebs himself was quoted as saying that the cull was "ineffective" in controlling the disease (Harvey, 2011).

On 14 December 2011, then Secretary of State for Environment, Food and Rural Affairs, Mrs Caroline Spelman, announced "the next stage in the eradication" of bTB, involving a pilot scheme of badger control, which included licences granted by Natural England for the culling of badgers by shooting (Parliament, 2011). On 19 January 2012, DEFRA confirmed that the areas of West Gloucestershire and West Somerset had been selected and invited licence application submissions to Natural England to undertake culling operations (DEFRA, 2012). Natural England, a non-departmental UK public body and "the government's adviser for the natural environment in England" (Natural England, 2017) issued licences later that year, and culling commenced in August 2013, continuing until November 2013 (DEFRA, 2015). After the initial pilot year, DEFRA announced that culling would continue for a minimum of four years, and West Gloucestershire and West Somerset were granted licences for a second year, undertaking culling operations from September to December 2014 (DEFRA, 2015). The third year of culling took place in autumn 2015 in the existing two areas, and an additional licenced area in Dorset (Hirst, 2017). On 17 December 2015, then Secretary of State for Environment, Food and Rural Affairs, Mrs Elizabeth Truss, announced that the cull would be extended for 2016. With changes to the requirements, seven areas were identified with additional areas selected in Cornwall, Devon, Dorset, Gloucestershire and Herefordshire (Hirst, 2017).

Natural England have since 2006 been authorised by DEFRA to discharge their functions in the culling of badgers and provide annual guidance (DEFRA, 2016). DEFRA clearly define the methods of culling badgers within open and closed seasons, namely: cage-trapping and shooting badgers; controlled shooting; and cage-trapping and vaccination, to "deliver an effective cull" (DEFRA, 2016: 4). Natural England are then empowered to issue licences and set minimum and maximum cull numbers for each area, based on advice from an Independent Expert Panel (Natural England, 2014). Natural England also have responsibility for developing a monitoring regime alongside DEFRA and the Animal Health and Veterinary Laboratories Agency (AHVLA), including monitoring accuracy of shooting (Natural England, 2014).

The debate on the effectivity of a badger cull continued. The cull was supported by the National Farmers' Union (NFU) who described it as a vital component in the plan to "control and eradicate bovine TB where the disease is endemic" (Batters, 2015). However, The Wildlife Trusts (2017) voiced concern that available scientific evidence did not support a cull, because a cull would not decrease occurrences of bTB to cattle from badgers, rather "disperse badger populations to the detriment of the countryside."

Opposition led to numerous protests, demonstration and marches throughout South West England, starting in 2013 in Gloucestershire, with marches organised by Gloucester Against Badger Shooting and supported by national wildlife charities such as Badger Trust, Born Free and Animal Aid (Green, 2014). Other groups such as the Stop the Cull group and hunt saboteurs groups, some of which included members "who acknowledge past convictions for aggravated trespass and criminal damage but condemn intimidation or violence" (Carrington, 2013) used more direct actions in protesting, such as publishing the details of farmers or landowners signed up to the cull, and deploying "an arsenal of proven, non-violent, direct tactics" (Hunt Saboteurs Association, 2013). As the culling operation increased and contractors in other areas of the South West region gained licences, so those opposed to the cull made their voices heard through a variety of mediums, including protests, marches, demonstrations, badger patrolling and direct action.

2016 heralded the first licences for the culling of badgers in Devon and Cornwall. The cull period lasted for over six weeks, between 29 August and 18 October 2016 (DEFRA, 2016). However before it had even started, those in opposition took to the streets. March 2016 saw the first significant demonstration, organised by the Badger Trust, and involved an assembly of over 200 anti-badger cull protesters at Plymouth Hoe before they marched through the city (Irons, 2016). In August, it was reported that members of Devon and Cornwall Against the Badger Cull (DCABC) joined with other groups to hold "a peaceful protest against badger culling" at the Holsworthy and Stratton Agricultural Show (Cleave, 2016). The culling operation commenced in September and coincided with protests in Bideford (Keeble, 2016), as well as near to the office of the NFU Exeter (Sleightholme, 2016) and inside the Totnes Civic Hall, where a meeting was called by the Devon Badger Group and Cornwall Against the Badger Cull (Acourt, 2016). The protests gained media coverage, and the cause was supported by celebrities, including Queen guitarist Brian May (Winter, 2016). Alongside protests and demonstrations, others took a more active role by undertaking badger patrols on a regular basis (Derrick, 2016) and support was provided after Camp Badger was established

(Birchall, 2016) to accommodate anti-cull supporters. As the cull moved into October, protests continued to occur in places such as Ashprington, where it was reported that a group of around 25 protesters marched through the village carrying flags, wearing masks and "clashing with a parish councillor" (Dennis, 2016). Further protests were reported in the streets of Launceston and on the beaches of Bude.

By the end of the cull period in December 2016, DEFRA reported that all cull areas had achieved their minimum number and did not exceed their maximum number of culls, with a total of 10,866 badgers killed; just under half (5,219 badgers) were caged and shot while the remaining 5,672 were shot (DEFRA, 2016). The NFU praised the safe, humane and effective way the cull operatives had carried out the cull (DEFRA, 2016). DCABC however criticised the "unscientific and unethical badger cull" and claimed that the target number of culls were "mysteriously halved" in the week before the end of the culling period, seriously questioning the "supposed science behind the cull" (DCABC, 2017).

The culling of badgers continues to be a present government strategy central to the eradication of bTB, with the overall aim of achieving Officially Bovine Tuberculosis Free status for England by 2038 (DEFRA, 2021). Opposition to the government also continues, including permission granted by the Court of Appeal at the Royal Courts of Justice to challenge the bTB eradication policy (Langton, 2021) and Dr Jo Smith, CEO of Derbyshire Wildlife Trust expressing sympathy to the "great hardship" caused to the farming community through bTB but stating that the government has "failed to listen to the public" who want to see the cull ended immediately and that culling badgers is an ineffective way of halting the spread of bTB (Derbyshire Wildlife Trust, 2021). Protests also continue against the cull, both in existing cull areas, with groups vowing to go out every night to stop the shooting of badgers in Devon and Cornwall (Greaves, 2020) and ongoing protests and peaceful demonstrations in newer cull areas such as Cheshire (Farrington, 2021).

This case study, therefore, provides insight into the policing of such a contentious government policy and allows consideration into how the police implemented a dialogical approach in the South West region of England in 2016 as their key strategy to allow them to balance the competing rights of all those who were affected by the badger cull.

The preponderant portion of this chapter will now focus on the experiences of those who were significant social actors in the South West region prior to, during and post the badger cull period of 2016 based on their views expressed during semi-structured interviews conducted with each participant. The responses were analysed and key themes emerged from the data, forming the headings for the following section and allowing opinions to be collated and grouped. Many of the responses of participants have been transcribed verbatim, to provide a voice in their own words to those who had been integral in the policing responses to the badger cull in 2016.

Interested parties

There has been a tendency to locate the police as in opposition to protesters in national and international media, describing the tensions and "clashes" between police and protesters (for example, Dresch, 2021; Zahir, 2021). The focus of existing research into protest events similarly centres on the relationship between police and protesters and the small body of literature examining communication in such events concentrates solely on dialogue between police and protesters (for example, Gorringe, Stott and Rosie, 2012; Waddington, 2013) or event organisers (Kilgallon, 2020).

However, there are various social actors engaged in such protest events and it is facile to simply examine the protester–police or police–organiser relationship. There are numerous other interested parties who are affected by such events and who engage in dialogue with the police in lieu of and during events. This research examines relationships built and dialogue enacted between the police and a whole host of interested parties alongside event organisers and protesters, and in so doing provides an insight into the process and an evaluation of the value of such an approach.

To analyse the contribution that a dialogical approach may have made to the policing of protest, it is important firstly to establish with whom such dialogue was undertaken. Therefore, the starting point in analysing the research data from this case study and examining the dialogical process was to identify all the interested parties who engaged in dialogue with the police in this case study. This following section therefore initially explores the complex picture that emerged when identifying interested parties and examines the significance that understanding identity and nomenclature had on this process. Further, numerous communication channels were established between the police and interested parties during the cull period, and this dialogical process is mapped, pictorially depicted in the Dialogical Wheel. Other factors recognised in identifying interested parties, such as illegitimacy, trust and political pressures, are also discussed.

Identifying interested parties

Button and John (2002) observed that there existed a complex range of interested parties involved in the policing of environmental protest. Such a complexity was immediately evident in this case study as participants described the large number of diverse interested parties involved in the badger cull. It was apparent that there were groups within groups in the anti-cull community, and a crossover of membership was described, consistent with the Elaborated Social Identity Model (ESIM) (for example, Reicher, 1996; Drury and Reicher, 2000). However, there were also numerous groups and organisations identified in the research who might not have been readily considered to be interested parties to the onlooker that not only became ensconced in the cull but were engaged in dialogue with the police during that period. Identifying interested parties allowed a consideration of institutional, organisational, cultural and contextual levels of analysis as presented when applying the Flashpoints Model (King and Waddington, 2005; Waddington, 2013).

There were various interested parties identified in this case study who engaged in dialogue with the police during the badger cull period. One Police Liaison Team (PLT) officer observed that although many outsiders often simply divided parties into two groups, either for or against the cull, it was much more nuanced. To consider the contribution of a dialogical approach, it was therefore paramount to first identify interested parties and their identity and map the dialogical process.

Every participant who engaged in this case study research identified that there were different groups of people who opposed the cull, and the actions and responses of each group varied. One of the significant groups identified as opposing the badger cull were often referred to by Commanders and PLT as the "*Middle England*" group, although one PLT caveated, "*We've got to be careful about the terminology.*" The term was used by many police and Business participants to describe those opposing the cull who attended cull areas to walk the pathways and support wounded badgers. The group were described as "*moderate,*" "*engaging,*" "*law abiding,*" "*haven't got a confrontational bone in their body,*" who had "*never had any contact with the police*" and who "*wouldn't dream of having contact with the police.*" One Commander summarised:

> You had the Middle England brigade, who were passionate about badgers, and still are. And what they didn't want to do is see badgers being culled. They thought this was an illogical approach, why not vaccinate? They were the Badger Trust people. They were Middle England. They were completely lawful. They would never dream of coming across police officers, you know, they would never dream of disagreeing with the police officers. They didn't particularly even like trespassing; they would if they had to. But they would carry out sett surveys to identify where there were badgers.
>
> (Commander C)

Many members of the group referred to as "*Middle England*" were members of badger groups, such as the Cornwall Badger Group, the Devon Badger Group and the Somerset Badger Group. Many PLT and some Commanders referred to these groups specifically, identifying them as people from all walks of life: "*they could come from anywhere,*" "*one was a postal worker, someone who just felt very strongly about it,*" "*they would be at work all day, come out in the evenings, were knackered, were very engaging with what we were trying to achieve as the police.*"

One Protector explained that the badger groups comprised people who wanted to protect badgers and help injured badgers. Some of the badger group members also belonged to groups specifically opposing the cull, for example, Devon and Cornwall Against the Badger Cull. This provided a point of contact for people that opposed the cull and wanted to get involved in activities such as the patrols. The Protector explained how they had become involved in the badger group:

> *I suppose I have liked badgers since a very early age. I think they are cute, mysterious. So, when the cull first came about in Devon and Cornwall, I started looking at it, thinking, 'Why are they doing this?' Looking at what had happened previously. And I had started signing petitions and making my own posters, and I thought that I need to do more. So, my first event was a march in Exeter, which was a real eye-opener, to go along with so many other like-minded people. And, from there, I joined the Devon Badger Group, and gradually, progressively, became more involved with the group.*
>
> (Protector C)

Another Protector also explained how they as an animal lover had also become involved in opposition to the cull:

> *I saw a thing on the TV. They were going to cull badgers in Somerset. And, well I thought, 'I don't think that sounds right,' even though I didn't know the pros and cons of it. So, I just knew I had to do something about it. So, I Googled Somerset Badger Group and I rang, and I spoke to [Protector] and I went up there on a walk. And that was it, really, I got involved then. And went up about two or three nights a week for the whole of the six weeks of the cull ... Of course, the first year, none of us knew what we were doing. We were just sent down the lane, 'Oh, go and walk up and down there, until you can't do it anymore, and then go home, and come back the next night.' So, we did that. We did feel that we were doing something useful.*
>
> (Protector A)

Such groups would turn up to patrol every evening in the various cull areas, meet in local car parks, don high-visibility jackets, carry torches and undertake injured badger patrols along public footpaths. However, participants also described another group of those opposing the cull, who were described by Commanders as "*more active,*" with a "*much more hardened edge*" and as "*people who are willing to take more direct action.*" One Business participant shared their perception regarding the differing approaches:

> *There was the middle-class, the ones that came out 8 o'clock in the evenings. They done peaceful protest, they kept to the footpath, they made a few noises, flashed a few lights, caused disturbance, all within the law, and they probably went home at 11 o'clock. Totally lawful. And then there was probably a harder protest group, where they came and they were not lawful. They did trash some of our equipment. They damaged fences, left gates open, and they would not be within what we perceived was lawful.*
>
> (Business A)

Many participants located the hunt saboteurs (sabs) in this group of "*political activists*" and "*domestic extremists,*" and noted that, whereas the badger groups were predominantly from the South West area, various hunt sab groups attended from elsewhere in the country. A Business participant explained that this group had two objectives: to locate and destroy cage traps; and to disturb those contractors culling the badgers at night, thereby disrupting the cull. One Protector assisted in outlining sabs' objectives:

> *You know, the whole idea is to blend in and just get on with what we do, without causing any problems for anyone. But I do know in other areas of the cull, there's all different groups involved, and in some areas, there has been intimidation of farmers, and vice versa, intimidation of activists. But my main aim is to not cause anyone any problems.*
>
> (Protector B)

Although groups were united in opposing the cull, differences and disagreements were apparent in their respective approaches and tactics. One PLT explained that the structure was quite complex, and there were groups that did not talk to each other or disagreed with others' tactics. A Protector described "*in-house fighting*" and "*things getting nasty*" within an anti-cull community consisting of "*people from all walks of life, with all different lifestyles,*" and "*egos that try to make things bigger than the issue.*" Another observed that some had "*gone further,*" destroying cages and entering farms in the middle of the night, actions they believed to be "*intimidation*" and "*wrong.*" Conversely, another Protector observed some were not prepared to engage in activities that others might do, but they still were "*a useful group of people to have on board.*" This Protector favoured a more direct approach to the badger patrols, but added:

> *Basically, it is a good working relationship with them [badger patrols]. If there was areas we wanted to visit, they acted as a good decoy to get us into areas that we found it difficult to get into. They'd maybe go and patrol an area and draw the attention to themselves, whilst we could go about our work.*
>
> (Protector B)

A further group were identified as anti-cull, which were described as the "*top end category; animal rights extremists.*" A Business participant however observed that the presence of this group was limited as the cull was "*probably too low-key for them.*"

Camp Badger was referred to by many as a key location for those opposing the cull, providing accommodation and food. The camp was open to the "*Middle England*" groups and hunt sabs alike and became a meeting place and focal point as well as a target during the cull period. Although there was opposition to the camp in the local community, there was also lots of support "*on the *quiet*" demonstrated by constant donations of food. One participant explained how the camp originated:

> We became involved firstly, because we did a sett surveying course down in our woods, at the beginning of last year. Because, we wanted to understand more about how to spot what the badgers were doing and understand about our sett. And, from that, we met a few people, and we went to a meeting in [location], to find out what was happening with the cull. And, after that, we had an email from one of the ladies, who'd been at the sett surveying weekend here. And, she asked us if we knew anybody who had some land and who would be prepared to host a cull [opposition]. And, we had already thought about it previously, and so, we said yes, we would host the cull [opposition], and so that … Camp Badger, so, that's how it started, basically.
>
> (Protector D)

Several Protectors explained that as well as the activities at cull locations, they wanted to raise public awareness of cull sites as a part of their opposition and so organised demonstrations aimed at certain organisations. One explained:

> We have had demonstrations outside the NFU and DEFRA and Natural England, to try and draw attention … Well, we have had some media attention as well, just to raise the profile as it got a little bit nearer to the cull. But we've also tried to get meetings. Twice, probably three times I have asked personally the NFU to come and sit around the table with us, because, you see, they haven't really got any scientific argument.
>
> (Protector A)

However, as established earlier, analysis did not concentrate solely on the relationship between the police and the protest groups and this case study unearthed a whole host of other interested parties who were ensconced in the cull process with whom the police engaged in dialogue. If charting the identity of those opposing the cull was complex, establishing the identity of those the subject of this opposition similarly produced an intricate picture. Participants identified several key interested parties which included governmental departments, particularly DEFRA and the Home Office. There was great interest from Chief Constables from other police areas as well as from Police and Crime Commissioners who wanted to voice their "*different views on how things should be done.*" Natural England were identified as key in the culling process and perceived by many as a lead pro-cull agency, although one Commander advised that because of their affiliations and protection of animal health, they had encountered several people within Natural England who were "*less than pro-cull.*" Another stakeholder identified was the Animal Plant Health Agency (APHA), a subsidiary of DEFRA who, one participant explained, oversaw the humaneness of the cull by monitoring the contractors. Another described APHA as "*more animal loving*" rather than pro-cull. The contractors and culling companies themselves were significant players, with several companies involved, all "*separate entities*," as were the landowners who were required to sign and apply for a licence before the cull could take place.

The most complex and diverse group as identified by every participant in the research was the farming community and some Commanders suggested that this was a group often missed. The farming community ranged from smallholders with a couple of fields and few livestock up to 1,000-acre farms. Some farmers, as landowners, were licenced for cage-trapping or shooting, and farmers would actively take part in the cull. However, every participant made it clear that there were different communities within farming, and it was wrong to label them all as pro-cull. One PLT explained that within farming there are some who are pro-cull, pro-hunting and "*pro lots of different farming activities*," but then there are also people in the farming community who aren't pro-cull, who may be pro-hunt, but see the cull as government-driven and do not support it. Another PLT explained that some farmers would not sign their land over because they did not agree with the scientific evidence and favoured a vaccination approach. Several Protectors concurred and provided examples of farmers who disagreed with the cull, favouring evidence that the main transmission of bTB was from cattle to cattle rather than through badgers. One Protector explained that the badger groups were not "*anti-farmers*," but that this was the rhetoric that was being promulgated to alienate Protectors from the farming community.

A Commander suggested that many anti-cull farmers came from the non-beef or non-dairy farming population. A Business participant suggested that support for the cull was often location related, with farmers in more rural areas tending to either support or at least have no issues regarding the validity of the cull. However, others noted that one of the locations where the anti-cull group met was on a rural farm, where the farm owners were against the cull. What was agreed by several responders was that those farmers that were anti-cull would tend to be less overt about their opinions. One Protector recounted the pressure that they had witnessed applied on individual farmers by the local community for opposing the cull, and several Protectors pointed to the NFU as having "*intimidated*" and "*put huge pressure*" on farmers if they did not sign up.

The NFU were therefore also key stakeholders within the cull, described as "*a very powerful body*" by one Protector, "*the ones that are driving this policy*" by another, and became the subject of protests at their offices. However, even with the NFU support was not clear-cut. One Protector and farm owner explained that they were members of the NFU, as it was an insurance requirement due to owning thatched-roofed buildings, even though they were vehemently anti-cull. Another Protector recounted that they had spoken to lots of members of the NFU who do not agree with the cull, which they found *"quite surprising."* Contrastingly, a Business participant involved in the cull stated that they were not affiliated to the NFU because they were *"not from that background"* and that in their area it was very much independent farmers who were behind the cull.

As well as the farming industry, there were numerous ancillary industries linked to farming with whom the police liaised, including a large creamery, feed merchants, poultry merchants, egg suppliers, farm shops and supermarket chains. Other interested parties who engaged in dialogue were those involved in pheasant shoots, hunting, fisheries and gun sports. Some of the ancillary industries themselves became the subject of protests and demonstrations. A PLT described how they had liaised with one feed company who were *"being targeted quite regularly"* and receiving nuisance phone calls.

The extended community also emerged as significant stakeholders. One Business participant recounted how anti-cull posters had brought fear of live firing in the area. Local authorities and town councils were identified interested parties, and PLT explained the variance in different areas: some communities were predominately pro-cull but there were towns where councillors were *"openly anti-cull"* and one Commander described a town where a protest of 3,000 participants would occur *"at the drop of a hat."* Neighbourhood Watch teams and coordinators wanted information from the police regarding what was lawful and legal. Other members of the public expressed concerns to the police regarding the number of resources dedicated to policing the cull and protests. One PLT explained that they had dialogue with local schools who wanted to know what stance they should take with pupils regarding the cull. Several Commanders observed that Devon and Cornwall Police were also internally divided: some for the cull, some against, and some indifferent. Finally, the cull and opposition played out in local and national media, and this was augmented by support from *"other interested parties, such as Brian May, Queen's guitarist,"* who attended protest events and marches.

It was clear therefore that not only were there numerous interested parties, but that the police had made a concerted effort to identify each and every group and sub-group, and through the use of PLT made attempts to enter into dialogue with each group to understand their viewpoints, their raison d'être, and thus both educate other police officers to assist with decision-making and facilitate lines of communication between groups who would not ordinarily interact with each other.

Identity and nomenclature

The sense of group identity and the power of a name emerged as a key theme for all those interviewed in the badger cull case study. Participants were unanimously keen to assert that the dialogue and engagement process was more than simply identifying stakeholders; there was a need to understand the identity of key groups to build relationships. This section seeks to establish the identity of interested parties and examines the importance that groups placed on terminology used to describe their perspective, and how understanding the distinctions of nomenclature was key for the police in fostering a dialogical approach.

Button, John and Brearley (2002) described an emergence of "full-time protesters" in their research into environmentalist protests. However, it was apparent from all participants in this research that the term "*protester*" was itself problematic, and all Protectors vehemently distanced themselves from the label, which they felt was forced upon them and had negative connotations. The suggestion that they might be "*professional protesters*" was seen as particularly offensive. Participants who opposed the cull were asked how they would describe themselves. Their responses provide an insight in their perspective and identity:

Passionate. Angered. And feeling that I can make a difference by standing up and saying, "No!"

(Protector C)

Just normal! We are just people ... We are just a family who live here, who want to save our badgers.

(Protector D)

It's not about the cull. We are a badger group, and so we deal with garden problems, planning and development, road casualties, all that sort of thing. But obviously, the cull is always in the back of everybody's minds.

(Protector A)

We are not protesters. It's not a protest. We are people who don't agree with the unjust law.

(Protector F)

I'm not a protester, I'm a hunt saboteur. I go out and stop fox hunting actively in the field. I don't go protesting, I actually go out with the hunt and stop them killing animals. Same with the badger cull, I go out and stop them killing badgers.

(Protector B)

The government have forced the cull here, it is going to happen on your doorstep. We don't agree with it. So, they've labelled us as protesters. No, we're not! We just, we want to live our life, and be normal. But, hang on a minute! You've decided you're going to kill all the badgers in your area, to protect the cows. Wrong, anyway. But you can't just let it go on. We didn't move here to deliberately stop anything like that happening, we were already here! They brought that in to create us as protesters, so they've labelled us with that. We are not! We just want them not to do what they are doing. Protester is the wrong word.

(Protector E)

There was a clear feeling amongst all those opposed to the cull that there was a human element to their opposition which was being overlooked. The negative connotations that they felt were attached to the label of protester meant that they were not being seen as individuals within a larger group, but rather stigmatised and limited by the term. These participants wanted to describe the diverse nature of the individuals who had coalesced to oppose an unjust cull. One Protector explained, "*Good people are against the cull. Educated people. Doctors, scientists, lawyers. Not idiots with guns!*" Another observed that those opposing included social workers, lecturers and a senior person in Citizens Advice Bureau. A further Protector described people from all walks of life: "*a mum and her two children came along to the protest, because the little boy loves animals, badgers being one of his favourites.*" One Protector described how a couple had joined the opposition to the cull after being alerted about ongoing protests when stopped by the police. The couple had a Wildlife Trusts sticker depicting a badger displayed in the car and the police stopped them because they thought the couple were Protectors! Another described their personal sacrifices in opposing the cull:

It's a huge involvement. It's been a massive part of my life. I've spent a considerable amount of my own money and a considerable amount of time and effort on it, you know, and having to use five weeks' holiday as block holidays from work to be able to go and do this. I take every single bit of leave in one go.

(Protector B)

The human element of opposing the cull was very much also recognised by those police officers who had engaged as PLT, who recognised the barriers that using the collective noun of "*protester*" caused in building relationships and understanding the person or group behind the cause. All PLT participants recounted occasions when they had been corrected for using the word "*protester*" and through their liaison had recognised the negative connotations associated with the term and accepted the explanation that this label might wrongly lead the wider community to view those opposing the cull as aggressive and violent. A Commander described the dangers of labelling and recognised that there was affiliation and crossover within groups and individuals should not be "*pigeon-holed.*" A PLT reaffirmed the negative subtext and explained that the terminology used in police briefings had painted the "*protesters*" as the "*bad guys*" and the farming community as "*victims.*" The PLT explained how they had challenged both commanders and officers in nomenclature and this approach had subsequently been addressed. "*Protector*," PLT explained, became an accepted term to describe the activities of the badger groups, although some anti-cull identified as "*hunt saboteurs*." PLT explained how there was an education for police staff in terminology, with "Protector" being provided to press departments and Commanders as the preferred collective noun. A Commander simply summarised, "*We'll call them whatever they ask us to call them.*" A PLT explained that they tended not to refer to them as a group at all, rather individually, to make it personal.

It was not only those opposing the cull that expressed concerns that the human aspect of the badger cull has been significantly overlooked. Farmers and contractors commissioned to carry out the cull also personalised their supported of the cull and observed that this had been disregarded by many in the debate. Business participants described the threats on their livelihoods caused by bTB and explained that they were attempting to protect their livestock, seeking to reduce bTB "*by the best means possible*," as directed by the government. One Business participant told of the losses that he and others had suffered to bTB. Another outlined the colossal impact on farmers and landowners and spoke of six farmers who had committed suicide in a six-month period post the foot-and-mouth outbreak. They recounted that pressures were continuing to mount on farmers thorough bTB, which massively affecting their well-being and mental health.

Image 5.1 Members of the Somerset Badger Group on badger patrol at night. Used with permission of *Somerset Against the Badger Cull*

116 Case study 1

Image 5.2 Protectors outside the library in Bideford, Devon protesting against the badger cull. Used with permission of *Graham Hobbs*

Image 5.3 Members of the Badger Group as they prepare to undertake their patrols and walk the public footpaths. Used with permission of *Somerset Against the Badger Cull*

Case study 1   117

Image 5.4 A public vigil held by those opposing the badger cull. Used with permission of *Somerset Against the Badger Cull*

Image 5.5 Protectors display a placard in memorial of badgers killed during a public vigil. Used with permission of *Somerset Against the Badger Cull*

Image 5.6 A police liaison officer at a protest event, wearing their light blue tabard. Used with permission of *John Gomez/Shutterstock.com*

Illegitimacy and lack of trust

Throughout the research, it became apparent that many interested parties saw their own actions as legitimate and proportionate, whether that be in carrying out the cull, opposing it or maintaining business as usual. However, there was a common perception expressed by participants from all interested parties that the actions of outgroups, individuals and groups outside their circle with dissimilar ideologies, were not lawful or legitimate. This sense of illegitimacy extended to police responses and resulted in some expressing a lack of trust in and with outgroups.

Business participants were explicit in how they believed some of those opposing the cull had acted illegitimately. They explained how some anti-cull had *"trashed equipment," "damaged fences," "intimidated," "destroyed cage traps," "left gates open"* and acted outside *"what we perceived was lawful."* Participants explained that there had been times when the police had been called to respond but did not take any action because they said there was insufficient evidence.

Protectors described incidents that evidenced how those carrying out the cull had in their opinion acted unlawfully. They explained that on occasions, cull operatives had reverted to free shooting and described incidents where live shooters were operating near Protectors, *"totally contrary to all the guideline that are issued by Natural England and DEFRA."* One described how they had witnessed *"dogs being set on wounded badgers."* Another commented:

> *If they were to carry out the cull as it's properly supposed to be carried out, I might have a slight bit of respect for them. But, not when we're finding illegal snares on badger runs.*
>
> (Protector B)

Some Protectors described how they had also been intimidated by other individuals and groups who were either pro-cull or anti those opposing the cull. Protectors described alarming actions from outgroups which included *"throwing firecrackers"* and *"shining laser lights"* into where the Protectors were located. Most appalling was the description by one Protector of a *"dead deer outside the gates, skinned, with its feet cut off and put on top of it."*

The perception of legitimacy has been identified as a key component of both ESIM and procedural justice theory (for example, Drury and Reicher 2000; Tyler and Lind, 1992). Legitimacy also emerged as a significant theme in this research, and all parties described incidents where they perceived the actions of outgroups as illegitimate. This belief led to the perception that those outside of their group were acting in an unlawful or unacceptable manor and consequently exacerbate a lack of trust and created a barrier to engagement. Often such incidents were marked by participants feeling that out-groups did not understand them or their motives or reasons for their behaviours.

Protectors described some incidents where their interactions with the police were strained and where they believed that the police acted in an illegitimate manner. Notably, all such incidents referred to interactions with the *"ordinary police"* who were described as *"not so friendly,"* rather than with PLT. One Protector described how they had initial been told by a police patrol that they were being arrested under the Protection of Badgers Act and searched until then being informed it was mistaken identity. A Protector described how they had been *"accosted, pretty much, by a police officer"* whilst walking a footpath. Another observed that when Protectors were stopped by the police for doing *"something that is perfectly legal,"* it dissuaded others to join their patrols. Several felt that the police as an organisation sided with the farmers, supporting the cull and those undertaking it, and classing Protectors as *"criminals."* One shared:

> *The police are being influenced by the farmers. Because, the farmers are seen as the legitimate part of the community. Protesters are labelled with being a certain type of smelly, dirty, horrible person that doesn't do anything, has no brains. When it's actually the complete opposite way around.*
>
> (Protector D)

PLT also recognised that there were police internal issues and misperceptions regarding the legitimacy of protests. One PLT observed:

> *There is still often a generic mistrust of the term protester within the organisation, and if there are a protester, they must be a trouble causer. That's not generic, obviously. But there are still some people that hold that real archaic opinion.*
>
> (PLT A)

However, it was not only Protectors who had experienced mistrust with the police; this was also identified internally, where PLT felt marginalised and treated as an outgroup within their own organisation. PLT described how their own colleagues received them *"with mistrust,"* *"with joviality,"* and how *"sometimes people questioned the role,"* consistent with challenges recognised by Stott, Scothern and Gorringe (2013). PLT described how their own colleagues needed educating and several described how PLT had influenced police briefings and challenged terminology when the anti-cull community were depicted as *"the bad people"* and the farming community as victims. One PLT noted:

> *If an anti-cull was to be a victim of crime, that wouldn't be reflected in that terminology in the briefing, which of course put somebody in the mind-set that the bad guys already are the protesters. And they're not.*
>
> (PLT D)

Another PLT who had engaged with the farming community described how colleagues misunderstand their role:

> *Because, the other thing is, they [police colleagues] all think I'm having a laugh out and about with farmers, and eating cake, drinking tea at the farmers table. It's not that at all. I'm in some shitty cow shed talking to 50 farmers to say, "Look, we're here for you. Anytime you want to phone me, I'm available." I get phone calls at 10 o'clock at night, but I never book my time off. I don't put any overtime in when I do 12, 14 hours a day, when I get phone calls at nine o'clock in the evening from a farmer. I don't want a gold medal. I'm not interested in being bigged up. I just want to make sure that these communities are getting the service that we are giving to the protesters.*
>
> (PLT E)

Police responders also described difficulties experienced with police intelligence departments requesting information gathering by PLT and how PLT had refused this to protect their relationships with those with whom they were engaging. Several described the challenge PLT faced in not being perceived as intelligence gatherers, and how this was a barrier to their relationships with those with whom they were engaging. One PLT explained how they had dealt with internal requests from intelligence departments:

> *We just go straight back and say, "No! Sorry, that's not our role." And so, if the people in our own establishment don't know what we do, that there is no hope for people in the protesting community. So, that's a massive difficulty that we come up to quite a lot, and it's one that we can just repeat over and over again to any protesters, that we are not there to get as much information, we just want to facilitate people's protest.*
>
> (PLT F)

The perceived illegitimacy of outsider groups led many participants to describe a sense of injustice on occasions in how certain incidents were addresses. One Protector voiced their frustration:

> *They [cull operatives] gone there, half the time, covering up their number plates. And I've got [PLT] on the phone, saying to me, "Oh, well, we've made the decision. We are not going to let them get away with covering up their number plates anymore." If my lot would have covered up their number plates, they would have been arrested straightaway! They stopped cars continually, all the time. That lot locked people in! Had guns on the floor in their car, not sheathed. Have cans of beer in the car! We've got videos of everything everywhere. And driving around with their number plates disguised, and the police do nothing, and openly say, "Oh, we're not going to let them do it anymore." And you say, it's fair, and we haven't been put in this position, and we aren't there having to defend ourselves*

against all these hooligans. They are the hooligans! They are the ones who go out at night and think it's fun to go out legally shooting everything, scaring everything at night.

(Protector D)

It became evident during the research that there was in fact a level of trust built between the police and all the interested parties during the badger cull. However, it was also clear that the trust was intrinsically linked to perceptions of legitimacy driven through dialogue, themes which will be further explored.

Mapping the dialogue process

This case study provided clear evidence that a dialogical approach was implemented by police decision-makers throughout the badger cull period. PLT were used in both problem-solving and mediation between Protectors and Commanders, as advocated by Waddington (2013) and Stott, Scothern and Gorringe (2013) and this research reinforces the positive impact of deploying PLT to engage with protesters. However, this case study also provides further evidence supporting the use of PLT not just with protesters but extending further to liaise with all interested parties. This dialogical process was not therefore a simple linear process of mediation by PLT between Protectors and Commanders rather the process embraced all interested parties and provided voice and interaction with police decision-makers. The process necessitated utilising numerous communication channels and the following section examines and maps this dialogical process.

The use of dialogue was identified by police participants in this research as a key strategic intention in policing the badger cull and its opposition. From the outset Commanders sought to engage in dialogue with all the interested parties and implement a process that provided every individual and group a pathway to communicate with the Silver Commander. PLT and Commanders recognised that the process became more convoluted in time with further groups identified and new relationships continually being forged. Commanders needed to balance between recognising the diversity of groups and memberships with a pragmatic approach to dialogue. A Commander explained:

It's wrong to say two sides of this, because that suggests a kind of differentiation already, in relation to parties. But the reality is, there are people that are pro-cull, and there are people that are anti-cull.

(Commander B)

Despite the complexity, Commanders explained that the solution was "*extremely simple*": implementing a single command structure with command protocols. All PLT were aligned via team leaders (Police Sergeants) to PLT sub-Bronze Commanders in each police force area, and they in turn fed in to one overall PLT Bronze for the region, responsible for all engagement relating to the various stakeholders involved. Therefore, there was a network of dialogue mapped out, with some PLT liaising with those opposing the cull, and other PLT liaison with those engaged in the cull and providing the links with the farming communities. (These officers were designated as "*Cull Liaison Officers (CLO)*" in the South West area for this role, although are encompassed in the generic term of "*PLT*" for this research.) A Commander explained that this ensured an independent chain of command for the dialogical process rather than PLT working to geographical Bronze Commanders in their force areas.

This research therefore saw a complex map emerge depicting the interaction and dialogue between the police and interested parties. To assist in understanding this complexity, a diagram has been prepared to outline the interactions identified in this research and provide a pictorial overview of the dialogue undertaken prior to, during and post the cull period (see Figure 5.1).

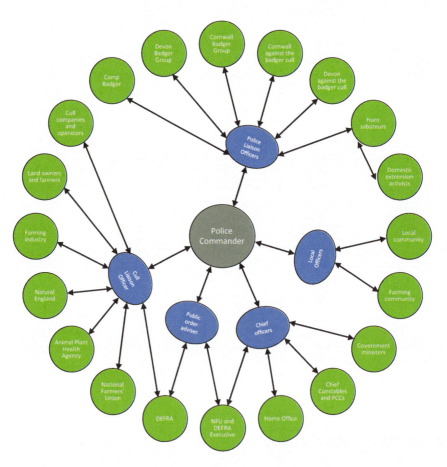

Figure 5.1 The policing of the badger cull dialogical wheel.

This Dialogical Wheel visually portrays the numerous interested parties that were identified as being engaged in dialogue with the police during the research, and the officers who acted as liaisons between the police commander and the groups.

PLT were aligned either with anti-cull groups or with pro-cull and the farming community, and one explained that "*never the twain shall meet.*" This allowed Commanders to dissemination information and keep a sterile corridor between the groups. A Commander explained, "We wouldn't necessarily pass all of that information, all of the stakeholder feelings, across to the other groups." PLT explained that PLT and CLOs worked from different police stations and in many cases did not know the identity of their counterparts. A PLT working with Protectors observed:

That was good, to me. I wouldn't have liked to have known any more information. You know, the fact that we didn't know where the cull was specifically taking place. We weren't party of any of that information. That worked.

(PLT G)

A PLT liaising with cull companies also advocated the structure and observed that this negated confidentiality issues presenting potential risks for people initiating cull companies and this further promoted the development of trust, further discussed later. The police were open and clear about the structure to all engaging with the police. One Protector summarised their understanding of the policing response:

We've got our liaison police, and then the farmers have got their liaison police, and they've got liaison between the two. And then, you've got the regular police, who would turn up when you are doing patrols, or who would drive up and down, shining their lights in if someone had seen someone walking up the road.

(Protector D)

PLT aligned with those opposing the cull therefore sought to engage in dialogue with groups such as the badger groups, individual Protectors and hunt sabs. A Protector explained how they had been approached by a PLT at the camp gates of where they were staying and "had various conversations throughout the cull" with them. Another explained how PLT had asked them to become a point of contact for the Protectors in liaising with the police, and how this had become "very difficult" for them when asked by Protectors to deal with numerous incidents reported to them day and night and balancing this with working full-time.

PLT aligned as CLOs engaged with cull companies, contractors, parish leaders and the farming community. PLT held meetings with Natural England, the NFU, APHA and DEFRA and liaised with other stakeholders, such as feedstuff companies, the dairy industry, deer hunter packs and fisheries. One Business participant explained how the liaison worked:

> We then had a police liaison officer assigned to the cull area, who attended all of meetings, we had meetings prior to the cull and during the cull, who kept us in the picture really, of what was happening, along as we did with him if we saw any activities or any sort of strange cars, we would speak to him.
>
> (Business A)

PLT were of the lowest police ranks: Constable and Sergeants. However, rank did not present a barrier to those engaging, and participants commented that their PLT provided them access to the decision-makers. One Business participant outlined how the PLT would hold meetings and feed information in to their "*hierarchy.*" Another observed that the process worked "*really very well,*" and although they had previously met with officers of a higher rank, having a designated PLT provided understanding and accessibility. One Commander recounted that, initially, Natural England and DEFRA wanted to go directly to the Commander but were encouraged instead to engage through PLT and "*after the first couple of months finally got the message and went through the cull liaison leads.*" Another Commander described how there was a command structure escalation system in place where people from both sides were able to access the senior police Commanders (Gold or Silver). They observed:

> *The protest liaison side were very good. They only pulled the card to communicate with Gold once, and Silver twice, which during an operation that started planning in December 2015, and didn't finish until the start of November 2016, I think was really good. I would say that the governmental departments were a bit more free with that card, shall we say.*
>
> (Commander A)

The police approach of mapping the dialogical process concerning the badger cull and its opposition was consistent with ESIM, Flashpoints and procedural justice theories, which allowed police commanders to identify numerous groups and sub-groups (Drury and Reicher, 2000), understand their goals and values (Waddington, Jones and Critcher, 1989) and engage in a manner which allowed a fair and transparent approach (Lind and Tyler, 1988). Seeking to engage with all groups, Commanders evidenced an approach largely of strategic facilitation (Waddington, 2011) in facilitating protest which, contrary to Gilmore, Jackson and Monk (2016), was not limited to protest sanctioned by the police. However, other approaches to the policing of protest were deployed. For example, there was an element of a strategic incapacitation approach (Gillham, 2011) evident where police commanders sought to engage with those not wishing to enter dialogue, such as the "*more direct action*" groups. Furthermore, police liaison with government departments was very much one of negotiated management (McCarthy and McPhail, 1998). Therefore, the police approach was tailored to the circumstances rather than set in stone and Commanders demonstrated a flexibility in how they addressed different situations.

Political pressure

The role of the police in balancing competing rights has been established in earlier chapters. This role entailed balancing the objectives of each of the interested parties, which included the government, who were clearly major stakeholders in the badger cull. All Commanders spoke of the political pressures they faced in their decision-making. Waddington (1998), della Porta and Reiter (1998) and King and Waddington (2005) described political influences that implanted on police responses and similarly Commanders in this research described "*Ministerial pressure*" for the cull to pass "*with as little incident as possible*" and to ensure that the "*cull operatives were able to work unfettered.*" However, there was a clear defiance expressed that the police would not move away from a negotiation approach. One Commander posed the question:

> *At what point do you allow central government to dictate police policy around policing protest? That's almost a dangerous step, isn't it?*
>
> (Commander F)

Several Commanders observed that the situation was augmented by internal pressure from Chief Constables and Police and Crime Commissioners who became involved outside of the command structure because of political questions asked of them. One Commander expanded:

> *There are obviously times when political pressure, there's an immediate imperative to get an answer for something. The Home Office weren't so forthcoming. They would go directly to Chief Constables, or the Gold Commander, when they wanted an answer, which resulted in a difficult phone call or conversation. And sometimes a quite honest answer, "I don't know that information, and when I do know, I'll phone you back and let you know if I'm able to tell you that information." The whole concept of the operation being that if you didn't need to know something, you didn't need to know something. And that involved a lot of managing upwards.*
>
> (Commander A)

Another Commander provided a frank insight into how they had managed some of the political pressures, including at the Prime Ministerial level. The Commander described how they would have a ministerial phone call with DEFRA on average once a week after an incident had been "*phoned in*" directly from a landowner to the Prime Minister or the Secretary of State, following which "*they would then raise it, and they would then discuss it with me.*" The Commander explained how they had managed the political intrusions, acting as the police liaison between governments and their tactical police commander, allowing them to concentrate on operational decision. The Commander explained:

> *I'm now on my fifth Secretary of State. One Secretary of State was so demanding. Because they lived there, they were getting phone calls from farmers who are demanding action of them. And I was having to deal with the political pressure. And of course, the Prime Minister was getting these phone calls as well. So, you're dealing with the highest-level scenarios where the Prime Minister is demanding that the police arrest people, and we are saying, "No." That was again PLT to a certain degree. That's effectively what I was doing on a Ministerial level.*
>
> (Commander C)

Other Commanders also experienced political pressures whilst seeking to balance competing human rights. One Commander described how they had received a telephone call mid operation after "*a call had been made from a landowner to the Prime Minister directly, to the Secretary of State and the Home Secretary and then to the civil servant*" who contacted them on their mobile phone. The Commander explained:

> *There was an incident where some anti cull had some weapons with them, and there was a bit of disorder. And I had a phone call from someone who works in the Home Office to find out what I was doing. Now, they only had my number because we'd given this presentation, so they wouldn't have phoned any officer. But, I'm there, and like at 10 o'clock at night in the middle of nowhere, thinking, I've got this pressure ... Live in the field, while it's still going on! And I'm thinking, I'm not even sure I know my powers of arrest!*
>
> (Commander D)

However, it was not only the police that recognised the significance of the political landscape: Protectors also identified how politics had a major impact on how they were able to voice their concerns and they also viewed the government as a significant stakeholder. Protectors observed that only scientists with a vested interest, such as the Chief Veterinary Officer and the Chief Scientific Officers for the government, believe or opined that the cull would address the prevalence of bTB. Protectors shared significant scientific evidence that disproved the effectiveness of the cull, "*if only the government would listen.*" One said of the government, "*They're spending £26 million on 6% of the problem. It is utter madness.*" Another stated:

> *Scientifically, it doesn't work, and this is my biggest issue with it. And the fact that the government will not listen to anyone makes me get up and do something. The*

biggest thing for me is actually keeping it in the public eye and making government accountable.

(Protector C)

The dissent by those against the cull naturally led Protector groups to demonstrate outside government establishments. Their presence required police attendance to facilitate peaceful protests, and evoked discussion on where the police sat as servants of the government.

The police as the state?

Whenever there is protest against government policy, there will naturally be questions regarding police impartiality. This was certainly considered by those interviewed in this case study and participants from both pro and anti-cull stances questioned *"on whose side"* the police sat. A Protector questioned the fairness in which the cull was policed and concluded:

It was totally biased on the side of the farmers, with our side, being the outsiders, being looked at as criminals. There's no two ways about it.

(Protector E)

However, Business participants saw the situation from a different viewpoint, that their *"lawful activity"* was being *"interfered with,"* and one expressed the opinion that the police could have been firmer with the Protectors instead of allowing them so much leeway in their opposition.

Police officers recognised the challenge that policing a state-supported badger cull presented. One Commander explained that there would usually be a presumption that the government, like the police, would *"occupy the centre line."* However, in reality, because this was a government-led cull through DEFRA, the government *"were on the pro-cull side of the business."* This presented a conundrum for the Commander, who observed:

If a democratically elected government has said that this is the way that we need to go, in relation to our policy, if that particular operation is not safe, the licence cannot be granted. So, there's also something here around, you know, not allowing small groups of people to destabilise what is democratically elected policy from the government.

(Commander B)

Mansley (2014) argued that the police are the embodiment of the state at political demonstrations. However, all police participants distanced themselves from being servants of the state in their decision-making processes instead strongly asserting that the police had sought a position in the centre of all interested parties to safeguard everyone. A Commander observed that the job of the police was to make sure that law was upheld rather than enact it. One Commander described the police strategic approach as "*the style of British policing, where the police are the public, and the public are the police,*" and another summarised:

> We as the police have kind of made sure that, in terms of the Code of Ethics and our unique position in relation to the British Policing Model, we've positioned ourselves right at the centre of impartiality and proportionality in relation to how we police everything.
>
> (Commander B)

Police participants suggested that the strategic approach allowed them to get amongst the community and understand their needs. A PLT explained that the police could not function "*without the consent of the public, and that was our most valuable commodity, and we've got to do everything we can to preserve that and to protect it.*" Another PLT further outlined how they saw the police strategy:

> Right from the word go, Devon and Cornwall's stance was, "We are right down the middle with this. The cull is lawful, and we will police to allow that cull to take place. However, people have a right to protest and as long as they protest in a lawful way, we will facilitate that protest."
>
> (PLT B)

Several Commanders suggested that it was through the use of PLT that the police had facilitated an understanding of their position in relation to the state with those that opposed the cull and who may have initially perceived the police as actors of the state. One commented:

> In the past, there has been a feeling of anti against the police with some of these groups. So, having the PLT has helped to break these barriers down, and it's made the Protectors trust the police more, and actually see they're friendly people, rather than the police as a part of the state.
>
> (Commander H)

A PLT explained how they also had to manage the expectations of those who were pro-cull, particularly when there were protests at government establishments and where there was a presumption that the police would side with the state:

> I think the difficult thing came up probably with regards to the protests at government establishments and convincing the government establishments that the individuals have got a right to protest. Because some of them in the establishment had the view, "Well, you're the police, you're on our side. They're protesters. You're on our side, and we don't want them here, so stop them!" You know, wave the magic wand. And it was getting this appreciation to one

side, "Well, hang on. They have got rights. Just as you've got rights, they've got rights as well. And you have to appreciate that."

(PLT H)

This chapter has so far established that the police employed a strategy based on dialogue in policing the badger cull and those opposing it. It has described how the police sought to identify every conceivable interested party involved and engage with each to assist in their decision-making on balancing the competing human rights and has mapped the dialogical process. This chapter now turns to examine how the liaison process was undertaken.

Police liaison

A definition of the roles and responsibilities of a PLT as the link through dialogue between the police and groups can be found in Authorised Professional Practice (College of Policing, 2018). However, this case study provided the first research of the application of the role of PLT post its designation as a national police tactic. This section therefore provides an insight into the perception of the role undertaken during the badger cull as viewed by those engaged in the dialogical process. It examines the selection process and qualities that make a good PLT officer, the command and management of PLT and how PLT engaged pre, during and post the badger cull.

The role of a PLT and selecting appropriate officers

The role of a PLT was described by those who performed it as "*literally facilitation,*" "*providing reassurance*" to those with whom they were engaging, "*enabling*" and "*quelling fear.*" A Commander described the role as "*community engagement and negotiation.*" One PLT describe how their role was not to change people's mind-sets, rather to facilitate their needs in expressing their opinions. Several PLT expressed that there was nothing special about the role: "*it is good old-fashioned policing;*" "*it's not complicated;*" "*it's just policing skills, it's just being able to speak to people;*" and "*it's just about having a little bit of knowledge.*" One PLT summarised:

> It's about being able to talk to people. But all's it is, it's a skill of talking to people. And I don't care if it's the Queen or a tramp, I'll talk to anyone.
>
> (PLT E)

It became apparent from all PLT that there was some level of personal commitment and on occasions personal sacrifice that, although was not found in any definition, they felt went with the territory. PLT expressed how they undertook the role for specific reasons: because they believed in the rights of everyone to express their human rights; because they wanted to make a difference to people's lives; and because they wanted to serve their communities. One described the fact that the role was "*liaison 24/7,*" despite the fact that they never claimed or received extra pay or time off for answering calls off duty. Several PLT described regularly receiving phone calls in the middle of the night and when on leave, and there was an overall acceptance that although they were not required to take the calls, by so doing they continued to foster relationships with those with whom they were engaging. One explained:

> *My phone never stops, and I probably take on too much, but I'm pleased. That's my main role as I see it.*
>
> (PLT E)

Protectors also provided an insight into the role of the PLT. Most felt that PLT offered them a level of protection: from pro-cull individuals but also from the "*regular police.*" One recalled:

> *And I know I rang [PLT], and I said, "Well, I can't get hold of your team, I don't know where they are." We felt as though they were there to protect us, we needed protecting. He said, 'That's not the role of the police liaison.' But, it ended up, that's how it felt, they were there to protect us against other people.*
>
> (Protector A)

Commanders and PLT alike articulated it was paramount that the most appropriate police officer was selected to liaise with interested parties. Two common themes were prevalent: officers identified needed to have the "*right skill-set*" and "*personality type;*" but also, there should be a matching of the "*right person to the right group.*"

The importance of selecting an officer who is willing to talk, listen and engage rather than one with public order knowledge, as identified by Gorringe, Stott and Rosie (2012), was a key criterion identified in selecting suitable PLT. One Commander described selecting officers who had the "*gift of the gab.*" "*Patience,*" "*perseverance,*" "*empathy*" and "*flexibility*" were other qualities recognised. Commanders observed that a PLT must not be "*too judgemental,*" but can "*see both sides of the argument,*" and be able to "*bite their lip on occasions.*" One Commander responded that a PLT must be "*Approachable. Honest. Good communicator. Happy to talk. Even happier to listen.*"

Further, many police responders suggested that the liaison officer must be able to communicate appropriately with those with whom they were liaising. Commanders explained selection was not about choosing officers who necessarily agreed with one side or another, rather identifying PLT who would connect with the groups and to whom the groups might "*warm,*" and not selecting PLT "*who will wind them all up.*" Those that had been deployed as PLT with anti-cull groups often described their passion for facilitating the rights of those who wanted to protect the badgers. One explained:

> *My view on people's rights and ability to protest and get their point across lawfully is that I've as strong a view about that as people do about the badger cull, or about animal rights, or about whatever. I feel really passionately about it. So, if you get key people with that kind of ethos into a particular environment that can be useful. In the protest community it has a massive, massive impact.*
>
> (PLT C)

Commanders also described how they selected "*the right PLT to engage with the right farming community,*" officers who had existing links with the rural communities, understood the "*communication channels*" and therefore were best placed to "*build up a good rapport and a good working relationship within limitations.*" One PLT explained they were selected "*because the boss said I speak the local dialect!*" Another explained that in their liaison with the farming community, rather than wearing police uniform and the traditional PLT blue tabard, they dressed in "*farmer's uniform*" to fit in, as the non-verbal communication of dress code was "*massively important, and the farmers didn't want to see a uniform down their lanes.*" Contrastingly, one commander described issues they had encountered when utilising a PLT with the anti-cull groups who "*looked, felt, tasted like a member of the pro-cull community,*" which became a barrier to communication. Another Commander summarised how PLT were chosen because of their understanding of the communities within which they liaised, and provided an example:

> *We've also got a PLT who was born and bred in the country, lives down in darkest, deepest [rural location]. In terms of their accent, demeanour, style, they are very farmer-ish, very at ease sitting around a farmhouse table eating cake and drinking mugs of tea. And, that whole concept, which links back to that strategic style that I mentioned around the style of British policing, where the police are the public, and the public are the police, we have found really, really works in relation to getting amongst the community, understanding the community's needs. And so, by positioning those PLTs within those particular groupings, not only are they identified as part of that group, and people feel more at ease with that particular group and are able to communicate with that group.*
>
> (Commander B)

As well as the farming and protector communities, liaison was also affected with other groups such as DEFRA, Natural England and the NFU, on occasions at chief executive and ministerial level. In such circumstance, Commanders explained that liaison was often undertaken not by formal PLT but by other officers, including public order tactical advisers and senior officers as the liaison conduit. One PLT suggested that for future selection, specialist officers such as Wildlife Crime Officers might be ideal in a PLT role, because of their existing relationships. The consistent message from participants was that, rather than utilise any randomly chosen trained PLT officer, it was vital to select the right person to liaise to encourage open dialogue. Consistent with Waddington (2007), selecting officers who already had relationships fostered with communities aided both the police and the communities they served in facilitating their needs.

"Stockholm syndrome" and the role of PLT Bronze

Although commanders and PLT observed that liaison was most effective when the *"right person for the right job"* was selected, there was a concern that in so doing so, officers and ultimately those with whom they were liaising might become compromised. This was recognised both by Commanders, several of whom identified the presence of elements of *"Stockholm syndrome,"* and by PLT themselves, particularly in a long-running operation as the badger cull.

Many PLT spoke passionately about those with whom they had liaised. On rare occasions this went further, with PLT expressing an affinity for the cause with which the group were concerned, although this was predominantly observed in the responses of PLT working with the farming community. For example, one PLT described their role as *"looking after the interests of the farming community,"* and added *"that's what I'm quite passionate about."* Another talked about how they shared a little of their background with those the farming community and explained to them, *"I'm on your side of the fence."*

However, even in such cases, PLT were very keen to stress their impartiality particularly when it came to matters of law. Generally, PLT expressed a desire not to be seen to be taking sides, but still voiced a *"sympathy"* with the plight of their groups, a *"frustration"* that the groups were not being listened to or there was inaction when they had cause for complaint, and a desire to champion the rights of their groups. PLT who liaised with farmers talked about understanding situations from their viewpoint, such as farm gates being deliberately left open and stock put in danger. PLT liaising with Protectors recounted the conversations that had occurred, where Protectors had shared with PLT the *"facts and figures"* and *"evidence"* against the cull, which had affected them too. One PLT observed that they found the evidence interesting and even compelling, but also felt like the Protectors were justifying their cause and trying to recruit them onto their *"side."* They talked of the challenge of remaining impartial, showing an interest in their arguments without *"passing any view, if you can help it, either way, because you don't want to be seen to be taking sides."*

Often the source of the frustrations for PLT was perceived fairness and parity, echoing procedural justice theory (Tyler and Lind, 1992). A PLT commented that farmers weren't getting the *"same level of service that I think they deserve,"* in comparison to Protectors. Contrastingly, another PLT felt that police officers responded differently to farmers than Protectors when an offence was disclosed. They concluded:

> *Officers were more inclined to believe the farming community were the victims of what was going on but were less likely to believe that the protectors were to be victims of crime themselves; more likely to be the perpetrators.*
>
> (PLT D)

Commanders acknowledge the juxtaposition and potential for "Stockholm Syndrome." There was an acceptance and an "*inevitability*" that PLT would align themselves to the groups to whom they were appointed and feel responsible and protective of those communities. Indeed, as previously identified, this alignment was encouraged when selecting appropriate PLT. However, to ensure impartiality in command decisions, Commanders explained that a "*conduit*" was utilised in the command structure, with liaison officers working to a Bronze PLT, who recognised the allegiance but also sought to realign PLT (see Figure 5.2).

A Commander explained, "*There will be that drift. We've got to bring them back together.*" Another Commander shared how there was the "*opportunity for a little bit of Stockholm syndrome to come into play*" and described how PLT became aligned with the groups that they liaised with and on occasions adopted their stance. The Commander described how they had pre-empted such tensions and observed:

> *We must build in to these long-running operations a point whereby we reset the compass to true north. Because, as the cull goes on, the CLOs, the compass needle will go to the cull side, and the PLT, the compass needle will go towards the protest side. And I think it's very important that there's reset points, where we come together and we recognise how it's going, and we reset ourselves to true north.*
>
> (Commander H)

Dialogue pre-event

Gorringe, Stott and Rosie (2012) observed that utilising PLT pre-event provided an opportunity to maximise perceptions of the legitimacy of police action. Similarly, Watson and Angell (2007) supported pre-emptive dialogue and observed that a procedural justice approach had most impact early in police encounters. All participants in this research concurred that the pre-event period was the most important dialogue phase. It was described by different Commanders and PLT as "*really important,*" "*massive,*" "*key,*" "*crucial,*" "*paramount,*" "*like gold dust*" and greatly assisted in building up rapport and trust from an early stage. One PLT suggested that their role would not have been anywhere near as successful without pre-engagement. Another summarised:

> *I think the pre-event stuff is probably the most important part of it. You get the pre-event stuff right, you will make the event part of it got so much more smoothly.*
>
> (PLT I)

Case study 1

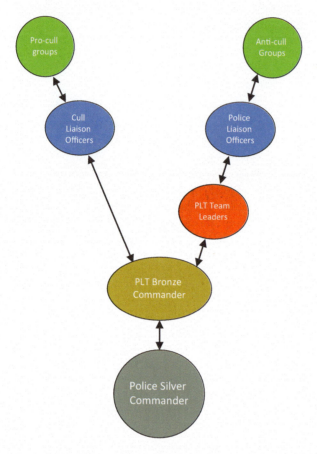

Figure 5.2 Bronze PLT command structure for the policing of the badger cull.

Pre-event engagement took many forms. PLT supporting pro-cull groups attended training days and debriefs, to inform farmers and cull companies about the police perspective and operational processes, as well as providing conflict management and expectation management presentations. With Protectors, PLT attended weekly meetings, maintained one-to-one contacts, which included meeting in person and email correspondence and often daily phone calls. Liaison with DEFRA, Natural England and NFU included inputs from Public Order Tactical Advisers and Public Order Command Trainers in conjunction with PLT and allowed all present to explore legislation and considerations through training and table-top exercises. Relationships were built and maintained between the police and outlying through social media.

Commanders and PLT extolled the benefits of pre-event dialogue. They believed that the engagement provided reassurance for groups, education and guidance in matters of legislation, and insight in to how the "*other side*" might react. It also gave an opportunity for the police to explain their tactics in an open and transparent way, break down fears, manage expectations of what the police could and would do or not do, and thereby provided an understanding of legitimacy.

PLT observed that pre-event dialogue also provided the farmers, contractors and Protectors with a voice. One PLT commented that the process paid "*dividends for everyone.*" Another saw this as crucial, observing that some Protectors had never had any contact with the police at all prior to the cull. Protectors and Business participants concurred. A Protector explained how the PLT had helped them to make contacts at some of the locations where they were going to demonstrate, when previously they had been "*hitting a brick wall*" in trying to make direct contact. A Business participant outlined the value of prior liaison which afforded them an understanding of the police role and consideration of "*various different scenarios, and how to deal with them.*" Another Business participant wanted to "*praise the police for their involvement during the run-up to the cull, because otherwise I think it could have been fisticuffs, and then we would have lost the battle.*" *(Business A)*

There was therefore universal acclamation for the pre-event dialogue that occurred between the police and the different groups involved. One Commander summed up the value they placed on pre-engagement:

> *It reduces the tension, it reduces the conflict, it reduces the fact that both sides will scream "foul" when those things happen. It reassures the community that we understand their issues while at the same time are tolerant of a democratic society. And sometimes the farming community didn't like it because they didn't really understand what the police role were. But, when we explained it, they got it. Conversely, when we use to discuss it with the protesters, they also appreciated that, you know, the farmers have a perfect right to do it. They just don't agree with this tactic.*
>
> (Commander C)

Dialogue during the event

Pre-engagement dialogue provided a platform for ongoing liaison between PLT and groups during the six-week period of the badger cull. PLT explained how "*key players from the Protector world*" would contact them to inform them where they were meeting daily and their plans and intentions for the evening. PLT would then meet with Protectors in locations such as public car parks and at Camp Badger and were then able to update Commanders with the views and intentions of those in attendance, and any tensions or concerns raised. PLT explained that often at the meetings they would engage with other Protectors, and there was a "*natural link*" that would also form with them.

Having PLT deployed regularly in their distinctive blue tabards provided a clear branding, as recognised by Waddington (2013). This insignia encouraged

Protectors who had not previously liaised to approach and engage with PLT officers during events. Further, PLT explained how their daily presence facilitated engagement with "*more challenging extremer activists*" and hunt sabs. One PLT explained:

> Some of them would really engage, no issue at all about engaging, and were very clear to us that we knew that they were up to illegal activity but knew that we couldn't do anything about it until we could prove or have any evidence that they had committed illegal acts, criminal damage, theft or whatever.
>
> (PLT A)

PLT working with the farming communities also spoke about how they maintained daily dialogue with the various groups and individuals, at meeting and on occasions at people's homes. One Business participant explained about how having that dialogue during the cull allowed them to continue to adapt and work around anti-cull activities.

The presence of PLT "*on the ground*" was advocated by many, with several Protectors and police officers explaining how there were situations where PLT had defused flashpoints. However, participants consistently linked the success back to the work that had been undertaken by all engaged parties pre-event, and one Commander summed up the generally held view that "*the fact that they were able to engage on first name terms was brilliant, a real positive*" (Commander F).

Dialogue post-event

The dialogical process was described by participants as cyclical in nature, supporting observations of della Porta and Reiter (1998), with post-event engagement preceding pre-event engagement for the next event or year. Although this was the first cull in Devon and Cornwall, participants who had been involved in previous culls in other police areas recounted how the approaches had been "*tinkered*" with and improved to meet the needs of all parties, based on post-cull dialogue.

PLT explained how they conducted informal debriefs after the cull period with those with whom they were liaising, which maintained relationships. Some Protectors opined that there should have been a formal debrief held by Devon and Cornwall Police, which although had been muted, had not occurred: one felt that they had not had "*closure.*" Several PLT recognised that this was an identified gap, although one explained difficulties that had been encountered in arranging such a debrief. It was however evident that post-event dialogue had not only occurred, but that this had impacted upon Commanders in their decision-making. A Commander shared that feedback they had received indicated that Protectors were pleased to have a conduit through PLT but were not always satisfied with the service that was provided by the police in general.

Maintaining open channels of communication post-event featured highly on the agenda of all those engaged in the dialogue process. Commanders referred to the *"long-term investment"* of having PLT *"running in the background."* It was identified that there were organisational pressures in releasing PLT from their *"day jobs"* to maintain relationships, however all police participants advocated the approach, and expressed that it was foolhardy not to do so. Several suggested that the approach was one of *"investing to save"* in that releasing PLT would ultimately reduce the costs of deploying numerous officers to police events in the future. Some PLT suggested that this process was still lacking, and police forces should do more to maintain an open two-way dialogue process utilising the same officers to develop relationships post-event that had been initiated pre and during the cull.

Participants described how dialogue was ongoing post-cull, and a Protector shared during their interview that they had even called *"their"* PLT earlier that day, some four months after the cull period, to discuss matters. Another Protector offered:

> We kept in touch right the way through, even after the cull. I have had various phone calls off [PLT] since the cull. You know, updating me on that particular case. I wouldn't want to get them into any trouble but even, even as far as, "We'll have to go for a pint next time you're down."

(Protector B)

Commanders however identified post-event engagement with the wider farming community as lacking. One Commander stated this was because the police *"haven't maintained those identified individuals that have built that rapport."* Another concurred, explaining that the cull was temporal, and afterwards most who opposed it left the locations, however, the local community was there permanently, and there needed to be a *"buy in"* with continuing liaison.

Human rights

At the heart of this case study was an examination of the human rights of all of the interested parties and how these competing rights were balanced by police commanders in their decision-making. Earlier chapters of this book have established limited existing literature that examines the relationship between the police and protesters and such research has assessed how the rights of those protesting have been balanced with maintaining public order. However, this case study provided evidence that the balancing act was much more intricate for the police and there were numerous parties whose human right were both engaged and required careful consideration for the police to enable a simultaneous achievement of the competing aims of diverse groups. The following therefore identifies human rights implications through this case study and considers the role and location of the police in balancing the competing rights of all parties.

Human rights implications

As Mansley (2014) observed, it is incumbent for the police to protect the rights of both those engaging in protest and those wishing to continue their lawful business. Police officers had to examine each of the Articles of the Human Rights Act (HRA) 1998 pertinent to the policing of the cull and consider which Articles were engaged during the cull period for each interested party. For Commanders, the right to life (Article 2, HRA 1998) was "*paramount*," in terms of being absolute, particularly with firearms present in cull activities, and there was an acceptance from Business participant and Protectors of the dangers of live firing. However, the perceived human rights implications for participants varied depending on the responder's viewpoint.

Protectors described their human rights in terms freedom of speech and freedom of assembly (Articles 10 and 11, HRA 1998). Protectors described how tradition methods such as writing to MPs and holding protests had been tried without success and therefore, they wanted to exercise their rights through being allowed lawfully to walk public footpaths and make their points, "*without threat of any harm.*" One explained:

> *As an individual, I wanted my voice to be heard, and I also had the right to do what I was doing, because I was within the parameters of the law. And I think we are in a place at the moment where little else works. So, as a person, I want to see that challenged.*
>
> (Protector C)

Some Protectors explained that they felt that their rights included the right to protect the badgers and provide voice for all creatures. One expanded:

> *The only sort of human right I would sort of say, it's my right to defend the voiceless. Animals are voiceless, they get persecuted by humans constantly, and it's my human right to defend the voiceless.*
>
> (Protector B)

Mobbs (2009) claimed that the state, namely the government and the police, sought to stamp out any protest that proposed change and that in the UK this had limited protests to activities that do not promote change, such as letter writing and lobbying MPs. This research refutes the claims of Mobbs and provides evidence which argues that the police facilitated protest even where this caused disruption to local businesses and the community. All police participants articulated that the police had recognised their positive obligation to facilitate peaceful protest in a democracy and had accepted that this had included occasions when there was an intention to disrupt the local community, DEFRA and the NFU, when it included trespass and "*even when it's unlawful.*" One Commander responded that it was "*highly appropriate*" for people to "*use legitimate ends to try and influence that democratically elected policy,"* and the police were very keen to facilitate this, because *"that is our independent role."* Another Commander added:

> *Our job is to keep the peace, our job is to facilitate peaceful protest, our job is to allow, if necessary, illegality, but being very clear on when we will take action, when we won't. And we do so because we are not law-enforcement officers, and we have discretion. We do so because we believe in a fair and legitimate society. And all of these are value driven rather than legality driven. Now, that does mean that we don't arrest everybody just because they commit a criminal offence.*
>
> (Commander C)

Business participants opined that they had the right to go about lawful activities. They expressed their main objective was to *"make a living without living on compensation,"* and to carry out the cull as per government policy without interference. Police responders also recognised the right for people to enjoy their property (Article 1 of Protocol 1, HRA 1998), and go about their lawful business. There was also a recognition of the right to family and private life (Article 8, Human Rights Act 1998) and inferences with this right. Some Commanders commented that they felt the community were *"let down quite severely,"* with an overemphasis by the police on peaceful protest.

Balancing human rights

Existing research into the balance of human rights at protest events primarily examined the balancing of protesters' rights with maintaining order (for example, Reiner, 1998; de Lint, 2005; Werren 2014). The limited research that has recognised that there is a balance to be struck between the rights of those demonstration and the wider society described the process as difficult and challenging for the police (della Porta, Peterson and Reiter, 2006; Donald, Gordon and Leach, 2012). Gravelle and Rogers (2011) described this as an "unenviable task" for the police service. This research provided evidence of the conundrum that existed in balancing the competing qualified human rights of all involved in the cull.

The badger cull case study gave insight into the challenges that befell the police in identifying what each group and sub-group sought to achieve and seeking to allow the aims and objectives of all: those in opposition; those undertaking lawful cull operations; farmers and landowners; and the local communities in which this played out. Police officers described how they had sought to allow everyone to exercise their rights and yet that it was impossible to achieve. A PLT described the challenge as *"the real fine balancing act,"* in protecting the right to express an opinion, yet *"balancing that with insulting someone who does not share that point of view."* Another spoke of balancing facilitating protest with ensuring lawful activity could take place, and observed, *"That's the fence we had to sit on all the way through."* A Commander provided an example of where they had encountered this balancing act:

> We had one farmer cornered by what he termed as "protesters" on his land. They are saying they are lawfully protesting on his ground, not on a footpath. So, immediately that balance comes into play, doesn't it, where he said he was out with a rifle on his ground, because he had to go put a calf down, something like that. And, the protesters weren't having it, and they were expressing their opinion to him, and what they thought he was doing with that firearm on the ground at night. So, you've got human rights of the cull operatives who were acting lawfully on their grounds, their right to do lawful activity on private ground, balanced against those who wish to protest. And whether they need to protest on private land, whether they could assemble on public ground and make their protest from outside. They were the big issues.
>
> (Commander F)

It was evident from the responses that there was subjectivity in where the balance lay. A PLT observed that the balance *"differs depending on the individuals that you discuss that with."* Another concurred:

> I met people with a vast array of opinions in relation to what they considered acceptable in terms of human rights, in terms of what they considered lawful and peaceful protest, and what wasn't.
>
> (PLT C)

Commanders' descriptions of how they balance the competing rights demonstrated this subjectivity. One commented that there was *"no right and wrong answer in relation to the various Articles that we try and balance, because there could well be Articles 9, 10 and 11 on both sides."* Another Commander talked about a *"line"* that Protector groups *"stepped over,"* thereby infringing on the right to family life. Yet another referred to a *"level of harassment that is not acceptable,"* and *"intimidation tactics which went too far."* One shared their *"perspective,"* that there are responsibilities encompassed within any rights, and in making decisions regarding competing rights, the Commander should consider *"which group is irresponsibly conflicting on the other."*

The views of Protector and Business participants were also subjective in relation to what was considered *"lawful activity."* A Business participant observed that the right of peaceful protest became an issue *"when it interfered with what we were doing, a lawful activity."* Another stated that they felt that the Protectors *"exceeded more than their rights,"* whereas their stance was to *"keep the moral high ground and keep law-abiding."* A Business participant gave an example of *"an invasion of about 50 balaclava-clad people"* turning up on a farm, causing *"massive trauma*" to the family inside, which they described as "*a serious issue on breach of human rights, to the rights of someone to live a peaceful life.*" Similarly, a Protector described breeches of human rights they had experienced, where "*shooters*" were "*driving around with guns in an unsafe manner,*" obscuring vehicle number plates and "*not going about their duties in a lawful manner.*"

Commanders observed that ultimately the final decision regarding balancing competing human rights lay with them. There was universal agreement from all police participants that the police positioned themselves in the middle of this balancing act, which composed not of opposing views, but of multi-sided issues, human rights and opinions. In doing so, police participants refereed to their role not as agents of the state, but under the British Model of Policing, sat at the "*centre of impartiality and proportionality.*" A Commander explained the significance to the police of this approach:

> *It means that we can retain our moral high ground. It means we can retain our position in the community, which is one of respect and independence and legitimacy. We are not seen by either side as being heavy-handed. We are seen as being reasonable all the time.*
>
> (Commander C)

Another explained how this positioning assisted their decision-making:

> *Because the moral compass decision that I make as a Commander is not really based upon the world according to me, it's really based upon the views and opinions of all the stakeholders, and all the lessons learned. And by assimilating all of that information, and then comparing and contrasting that information against what, hopefully, is a very well written gold strategy, the decisions for me drop out of that fairly clearly, particularly if you're operating in the middle ground.*
>
> (Commander B)

A PLT succinctly verbalised how they saw the role of the police in balancing competing human rights:

> *Not just the PLT role, but the police role is about facilitation. Just being that, dare I say, piggy in the middle, and not taking sides, but being there to reassure them and explain it to them.*
>
> (PLT A)

The case study, therefore, highlighted the role that police officers are necessitated to undertake in balancing competing rights. The research demonstrated the method that the police undertook in identifying a range of groups and individuals, nurturing and building relationships through dialogue to allow them to ascertain the aims and objectives of each interested party and allow them to balance these rights against the overarching need to protect the public and the communities they served.

A dialogical approach

It has been established that for the period prior to, during and post the badger cull the police implemented an approach centred on a strategy of engaging in dialogue with all interested parties throughout. The final section of this chapter examines how designating a point of contact assisted in this approach and fostered strong relationships through communication and dialogue. Finally, an examination is made of the reason why there existed reluctancy for some to engage with the police and offers thought into contributing factors.

A point of contact

For a dialogical approach to be effective, there was an agreement that having a point of contact was of great benefit. Business participants explained that this provided them with someone who was contactable, able to respond to incidents if required, and someone always available even if their specific PLT was not. Protectors also advocated having a point of contact, providing "*someone who is on your side,*" to whom issues could be raised.

A point of contact provided participants with someone who knew the situation, rather than a cold call to the police. One Protector expanded:

> *Yes, it definitely helped having a single point of contact. Because, having dealt with the police and badger incidents, trying to go through the whole system and get to speak to someone is quite a difficult process. So, having someone you can go to straightaway to say, "This is what is happening," was definitely easier. And it also felt that there was someone out there that, if we had any problems, they'd be able to deal with it.*
>
> (Protector C)

Building a connection with the point of contact was of most significance to responders. Participants talked about having "*a face,*" "*a name,*" "*a regular contact,*" someone they "*will see again,*" and this further elicited discussion regarding relationships that were formed and developed throughout the cull period. One Protector explained that they had found it intimidating to deal with the police and the PLT "*wasn't just another faceless person when dealing with official people.*" Commanders also identified the significance of having a consistent point of contact. Several recognised that although it caused a strain on resources, it was an "*invest to save,*" reducing resourcing in the long term.

Relationships

Hinds and Murphy (2007) recommended that the police seek to build relationships between themselves and their communities in advocating a procedurally fair approach. Relationship building was unanimously described by PLT in this case study as invaluable in implementing a dialogical approach. Relationships were described *as "valuable," "massive"* and *"key."* PLT described how they proactively sought to build relationships during the pre-event phase, and how liaising before the event helped them *"on the day"* to link in with those with whom they had engaged, which aided building *"valuable relationships."*

Several PLT described the investment required for relationship building, which had to be balanced with day-to-day roles. One explained how they tried to maintain their relationships whether on duty or off duty, answering phone calls any time of the day or night. The PLT described the pressures that this had caused in family life but justified this as they *"wanted to keep that personal relationship going."* Similarly, another PLT explained that this was *"more than work,"* however strong relationships *"depict whether the event is successful or not, ultimately."*

Being in a relational system (Redekop and Paré, 2010) allowed PLT to be on occasions *"quite stern"* with those they were liaising, even when they needed to have *"quite frank conversations"* or justify police decisions. A PLT recalled an incident when a NFU representative made *"quite strong representations"* after the police had taken action against another member, causing the PLT to take an uncompromising stance with the NFU representative. The PLT recounted:

> *And, within 15 minutes, he phoned me back, and he said, "Look, I've thought back on what you've said. Yes, I appreciate you're a police officer. I appreciate that you've got to be beholding to the law. I appreciate what I was asking you to do was unreasonable, and please accept my apology." And I wouldn't have got that, I don't think, unless we'd built that relationship up beforehand.*
>
> (PLT H)

Protectors similarly reflected on relationships they had built with PLT over the period. Several provided examples of where this relationship had allowed them to contact PLT at varying times of the day and night, when the *"normal police"* had not been able to address the issues. A Protector observed:

> *It was a relationship built on respect, more than anything. At the end of the day, [PLT] was making sure that their side of it knew that when they were overstepping the mark, that it had to stop as well. You know, he was being quite fair with both sides, to be honest.*
>
> (Protector B)

A Business participant also described the building of relationships with PLT:

> *I think that has been a relationship built up with the liaison officer, because I think there's been an understanding. I mean, you know, it's always been very clear where their line is, and what he can and cannot do. But I think I think we do have a very good understanding of each other.*
>
> (Business B)

Evidence of significant relationships forming was provided by participants' descriptions of those with whom they engaged, consistent with Waddington's (2013) observations of the PLT being perceived as a "kinder" police response. Several Protectors referred to their PLT as "*our police,*" in contrast to "*the normal police,*" "*the cull police*" or "*the regular police.*" Similarly, PLT described themselves and the "*normal police*" as different entities. This sense of ownership supported the overarching evidence that relationships were built on shared experiences. PLT were aware of the significance of relationships, and several described being "*on edge*" in situations whilst liaising with groups on the ground. One spoke of the relationships that they had developed with individuals as providing "*comfort*" in such situations.

Relationships were not without issues, and like many relationships there were "*ups and downs.*" PLT described occasions when relationships were "*dented,*" each time as a result of command decisions. Similarly, a Protector recounted that they had told their PLT that they were "*not dealing with them anymore*" because they had not accepted the Protector's point of view, although the relationship was restored a short time later. The PLT concerned also recalled the incident and described the breakdown due to "*misinterpretations,*" explaining how it required a meeting with the Protector to rebuild the relationship. Another PLT recalled a fellow PLT taking a "*bloody great knock*" when encountering a breakdown in their relationship with Protectors.

Even when PLT faced challenging conversations, explaining legislation and decision rationale, PLT observed that existing relationship made them the most suitable officers to do such. One summarised:

> *And as much as you build up those relationships, they can be broken very, very quickly. Not necessarily by us, but by decisions that are made within the organisation. And we have to obviously go and try and let them know why, and how those decisions came about. You know, it may not be that we agree with those decisions, or they're not going to like what we tell them. But, if you've been working with them for the last two weeks, and you have to let them know like a Section 60, for example, is in place, at least then, they've got a little bit of ... They've got respect, really ... Relationships did deteriorate, and then they built up again. And that's only through consistency of the officers, really, I think.*
>
> (PLT G)

Existing relationships also provided opportunity for Protector and Business participants to question the police and voice (Watson and Angell, 2007) their opinions, even when the PLT provided what one Protector, with laughter, referred to as "*bullshit reasons*" why Commanders had made particular decisions. The responses of Protectors also evidenced an understanding of the human element present within relationships, and a reciprocated empathy. Several

Protectors recognised the "*aggro*" that PLT received and that PLT appeared on occasions "*overwhelmed*" by the process. One Protector shared:

> *I think probably, it could be improved if the actual liaison officers themselves didn't feel that they weren't actually getting the support they wanted from higher up within the police force. I think that they don't feel that they can deliver what we need, because they don't get what they need from the commanders.*
>
> (Protector D)

The proof of the ongoing relationships was most evident in the fact that all PLT, Protectors and Business participants were still in contact with each other at the time that interviews were conducted, several months after the cull period, and the relationships were described in terms of moving forward towards the next cull period rather than looking back. Several participants commented that the relationships were ones of continual learning, and although "*tetchy*" at times with some individuals, generally the relationships were "*fantastic*." One PLT provided an example:

> *It might sound very, very minor, but for me was quite a major thing, getting a text at Christmas, wishing me and my family a Happy Christmas from a couple of the organisers. That shows that there is a relationship there, and a mutual relationship. There is still so much work to be done, and it will never be perfect, we've got to accept that. There is a long, long way to go.*
>
> (PLT A)

As well as being advantageous to the police, all non-police participants advocated to varying degrees building relationships with liaison officers. One Protector summarised:

> *It's better to have a working relationship with the police than to not have any relationship with them at all, in my book. That's what I found from 20 years of experience, and more so now, nowadays. It's much better to explain to the police what you're about rather than them thinking you're just a bunch of who knows what.*
>
> (Protector B)

Most participants explained that the building of relationship was intrinsically linked to a developing trust between individuals, later further discussed. One Protector however did voice that although there were "*benefits that you do have some kind of a relationship,*" trust was not a given, "*in that I don't trust their motives, and they don't trust me.*" Building relationships, therefore, emerged as a key aspect of a dialogical approach and allowed honest dialogue to materialise and open communication to flow.

Communication and dialogue

De Lint (2005) described communications as the best way to improve public order practice. This research evidenced that the relationships developed were very much based on two-way communication and dialogue, and face-to-face contact was integral in this process. Several Commanders shared their thoughts:

> *So, it ain't just a one-way, it's a two-way street. We are explaining to the protest groups or the farmers, "This is what's acceptable, this is what we expect from you," and they are coming back to us. It's just getting that two-way.*
>
> (Commander D)

> *And, actually, it's a two-way flow. I'm happy for the Protectors to gather intel and information via PLT, and back. Because, that's the point, isn't it? It's a two-way flow of information. I want them to understand how we will respond, how we will police them. We are in essence negotiating with them over what is or isn't acceptable. Yes, you know, how far will we let them go, before we unleash the nasty police commander and his PSU officers? It is a negotiation.*
>
> (Commander E)

Commanders also recognised a requirement for continued communication with consistent officers, which was integral in the decision to dedicate specific officers as PLT. This process promoted a communication flow leading to the building of relationships. There was also a sense of empowerment expressed by Commanders, letting PLT "*get on with it.*" PLT concurred with the views of their Commanders:

> *It is two-way. They are very passionate about what they do, and it would tend to be for them, talking, quite rightly, about … to do with the badger cull. They were trying give you lots of information, which would support their cause. I don't know if there are trying to justify what they were doing. They didn't need to.*
>
> (PLT D)

> *We always made sure that we had face-to-face contact, whilst planning any protest marches, which we just think is important, because then they have got used to the … it's not just a voice in a phone.*
>
> (PLT F)

The two-way nature of communication was also evidenced by non-police participants, who described the "*good dialogue*" between the police and those involved in the cull:

> *[PLT] would give feedback, you know, the information he'd gathered that week. There are weekly meetings that were held during the six-week period … He would tell us what action was being taken, if the was any incident, you know, how it was being dealt with. It was a two-way thing.*
>
> (Business A)

> *We were allocated a liaison officer. And I've tried to work very closely with him, being engaged with other contractors, and other cull companies and everything else. So, I've just ... I think that with these things you either, you know, if you work together, sometimes you might have difficult conversations, but at the same time, if you work together, you will achieve what has to be done in a sensible way.*
>
> (Business B)

> *It's much better to have a bit of a working dialogue with the police ... by having a little bit of dialogue and [PLT] saying, "I'm not happy about this," then we can level it off and stop it escalating.*
>
> (Protector B)

Non-engagement

Despite the overwhelming evidence supporting a dialogical approach in this case study, all participants identified that there were some who would not engage in dialogue with the police. All Protectors and Business participants who were interviewed for this research had engaged with the police, however some had expressed an initial reluctance to engage and identified others with whom they associated who had made the decision not to engage with the police. Participants provided insight into some of the barriers to engagement and why they believed that others did not wish to do so.

For Business participants, the main barrier to engagement was the preservation of anonymity. Participants admitted a "*reluctance*" to get involved, not wanting to "*advertise the fact*" that they were involved in the cull. One Business participant explained their views:

> *The law-abiding people in this, especially in terms of things like the cull, they are ... most people are not going to put their neck above the parapet, because they know, or they've seen a perceived intimidation that will lead to a lot more.*
>
> (Business B)

For Protectors, lack of trust appeared as the most common reason suggested for non-engagement, supporting research by Gilmore, Jackson and Monk (2016). One Protector offered that some "*don't trust the police from previous run-ins of previous campaigns that they've been involved in.*" However, one Protector observed that some Protectors wanted to "*just do their own thing,*" which prevented dialogue with the police, implying that some Protectors believed police engagement might hinder their activities.

Some Commanders noted that there had been "*criminality*" committed by some opposing the cull, such as criminal damage, and provided this as a reason for non-engagement. A Commander suggested that one protest tactic employed was to "*cost the police and government more money,*" and engagement hindered this tactic.

Another described an occasion when the police had to warn individuals regarding their actions, and this elicited discussion as to what constituted engagement. Engagement described included communication, dialogue and relationship building on different levels between individuals and the police during the cull.

PLT provided several reasons from their experiences of why some chose not to engage. Anonymity was a reoccurring theme: PLT described *"extremer activists"* wearing *"balaclavas, disguise themselves, and would not speak to us at all."* One PLT suggested that some would not engage because they were *"going out and causing damage."* Another PLT recounted a conversation with activists who informed them that they did not want attention drawn to themselves from the pro-cull community and felt that engaging with PLT would attract attention. One PLT however suggested that it was wrong for the police to presume that those more likely to be involved in criminality would not engage. They observed:

> *I have had some fantastic engagement from some of the absolute activist sabs. There is no doubt, I am confident that they are out committing crime when I'm not talking to them. But they've been really open and engaging and quite honest actually. Whereas some of their colleagues who won't talk to us, won't acknowledge that we are out there, whether it be PLT, whether it be a patrol cop. Not interested at all.*
>
> (PLT A)

The suggestion that the desire to engage related to an individual's disposition or experiences rather than their intended activities was supported by many PLT. One PLT described several groups within which individuals would not engage. Another noted that those individuals *"weren't rude, they weren't offensive, that's their chosen thing."* Several PLT suggested that non-engagement was linked to Protectors having *"deep suspicion,"* that PLT were *"intelligence gatherers."* One PLT offered that there was from some *"a mistrust which still goes on from historic encounters where the police got it wrong."* A PLT explained how they had continued to try and engage and *"not give up on them."* Another explained that they did not want to *"push"* people into engagement, because they did not want to lose the relationships with those that were willing to talk. However, several PLT described situations where they had gained the trust of individuals who had originally not wanted to engage with them, because they had managed to change their perceptions of the role of a PLT.

Non-engagement was not limited to Protectors. PLT liaising with the pro-cull community described many issues in encouraging engagement. This is supported by the difficulty experienced in recruiting participants from the pro-cull community for this research, as described previously, and provides further evidence of the desire for anonymity. One PLT voiced the difficulties they had experienced:

> *Natural England are sometimes hard work, quite a secretive organisation, and I've banged the drum, saying, "Come on! Four years. Start trusting me!"*
>
> (PLT E)

Therefore, although there was a predilection to engage in dialogue predominate in those interviewed in this case study, and an eagerness to advocate the benefits of such an approach, there was a recognition of the barriers that existed which precluded dialogue. Such barriers needed to be identified and addressed to ensure that there was access for all interested parties to have their voices heard and their opinions recognised by the decision-makers.

Conclusion

This chapter has explored a case study examining the policing of the badger cull in South West England in 2016. The data gathered from interviews provided a view of the cull period through the eyes of those integral to the policing of events: police officers commanding the response; police liaison officers engaging with those for and against the cull; those opposing the cull; those carrying out the cull; and those whose business was affected by the cull and the protests against it.

It was evident from the outset, through the experiences of participants, that there were numerous interested parties and groups integral in the cull policing process. Consistent with ESIM, this research mapped groups within those that opposed the cull, for example, Badger Groups, hunt saboteurs and Camp Badger. The case study extended ESIM and identified groups and subgroups across all interested parties. The study evidenced that identity was "*more nuanced*" than simply pro or anti-cull, with for example the farming community falling into both categories. A Dialogical Wheel provided a pictorial illustration identifying the diverse groups and interested parties engaging with the police during the period. An overview of the case study, through open source material, provided a cultural, contextual and situational analysis of the policing of the cull, consistent with the Flashpoints Model, and this allowed a deeper analysis of participants' accounts of their experiences. The study also provided a political/ideological analysis, both of the climate regionally and nationally and within each of the interested parties and evidenced the political pressures on police commanders and their strategic intentions to remain "*at the centre of impartiality*" and "*right down the middle.*"

At the heart of this research, the case study allowed analysis of the dialogical approach of the police at an interactional level (Flashpoints Model) recognising that the protests, as crowd events, were characteristically intergroup encounters (ESIM). Further, analysis of dialogue allowed an examination of the relationships and social experiences consistent with procedural justice theory. This case study identified that the presence of trust and perceived legitimacy, central themes found in all three theoretical frameworks, were integral to the policing of the badger cull. Participants identified a lack of trust between in- and outgroups and described how dialogue between police liaison officers and individuals engendered trust and became the foundation of relationship building. Dialogue pre-event was described in the case study by all participants as being key to building trust. The case study also purported that selecting the most appropriate officers to engage as liaison officers was significant and highlighted the need to temper the potential of "*Stockholm syndrome*" by deploying a PLT Bronze to "*reset the compass to true north.*"

Through the evidence presented in this case study, this research has provided evidence that a dialogical approach allowed the police to hear the voice of all interested parties and build relationships and trust through liaison officers prior to, during and post the badger cull. The case study demonstrates that by implementing such an approach the police sought to remain impartial in their decision-making, undertaking the role of "*piggy in the middle*" in policing the badger cull and attempting to balance the competing human rights of all interested parties engaged in, opposed to or affected by the cull. Chapter 7 will further examine the views of participants engaged in the badger cull case study to consider the value of utilising a dialogical approach and the benefits this may afford to all those involved in such events.

References

Acourt, S. (2016) New badger cull protest clash. *Totnes Times* [online] 6 September 2016. Available at: http://www.totnes-today.co.uk/article

Batters, M. (2015) Badger cull is a key part of tackling bovine TB. National Farmers' Union [online] 8 September 2015. Available at: https://www.nfuonline.com/sectors

Birchall, B. (2016) Controversial badger cull to be extended. *ITV NEWS* [online] 23 August 2016. Available at: http://www.itv.com/news/westcountry

Bourne, J. (2007) *Bovine TB: The Scientific Evidence. A Science Base for a Sustainable Policy to Control TB in Cattle.* Independent Scientific Group on Cattle TB. Available at: http://webarchive.nationalarchives.gov.uk

Button, M. and John, T. (2002) 'Plural policing' in action: A review of the policing of environmental protests in England and Wales. *Policing and Society*, 12(2), 111–121.

Button, M., John, T and Brearley, N. (2002) New challenges in public order policing: The professionalisation of environmental protest and the emergence of the militant environmental activist. *International Journal of the Sociology of Law*, 30(2002), 17–32.

Carrington, D. (2013) Badger cull activists can 'bend the rules' during protests, say police. *The Guardian* [online] 13 June 2013. Available at: https://www.theguardian.com/environment/2013/jun/13

Cassidy, A. (2012). Vermin, victims and disease: UK framings of badgers in and beyond the bovine TB controversy. *Sociologia Ruralis*, 52(2), 192–214.

Cleave, S. (2016) Protesters gather at Holsworthy show entrance to voice their feelings over badger culls. *Bude and Stratton Post* [online] 31 August 2016. Available at: http://www.bude-today.co.uk

College of Policing (2018) *Police Liaison Teams* [online]. Available at: https://www.app.college.police.uk/app-content/public-order/planning-and-deployment/

de Lint, W. (2005) Public order policing: A tough act to follow? *International Journal of the Sociology of Law*, 33, 179–199.

della Porta, D., Peterson, A. and Reiter, H. (2006) *The Policing of Transnational Protest.* Aldershot: Ashgate.

della Porta, D. and Reiter, H. (1998) *Policing Protest: The Control of Mass Demonstrations in Western Democracies*. Minneapolis: University of Minnesota Press.

Dennis, A. (2016) Anti badger cull protestors make their voices heard in Launceston and Bude. *Bude and Stratton Post* [online] 19 October 2016. Available at: http://www.bude-today.co.uk/article.cfm?id=106232

Department for Environment, Food and Rural Affairs (2012) *Written Ministerial Statement 125: Bovine TB*. 19 January 2012. Available at: http://www.parliament.uk/documents/commons-vote-office

Department for Environment, Food and Rural Affairs (2015) *2010 to 2015 government policy: Bovine tuberculosis (bovine TB)*. Available at: https://www.gov.uk/government/publications/2010-to-2015-government-policy-bovine-tuberculosis-bovine-tb

Department for Environment, Food and Rural Affairs (2021) *Bovine Tuberculosis: Consultation on Proposals to Help Eradicate the Disease in England*. Available at: https://assets.publishing.service.gov.uk/government/uploads

Department for Environment, Food and Rural Affairs (2016) *Guidance to Natural England: Licences to Kill or Take Badgers for the Purpose of Preventing the Spread of Bovine TB Under Section 10(2)(a) of the Protection of Badgers Act 1992*. London: Crown Copyright.

Department for Environment, Food and Rural Affairs (2014) *The Strategy for Achieving Officially Bovine Tuberculosis Free Status for England*. Available at: https://www.gov.uk/government/publications

Derbyshire Wildlife Trust (2021) *Government Approves Badger Culling to 2026 and Ignores Public Consultation*. Available at: https://www.derbyshirewildlifetrust.org.uk/news

Derrick, C. (2016) Patrolling the badger culling fields across the South Hams. *Totnes Times* [online]. 28 September 2016. Available at: http://www.totnes-today.co.uk/article.cfm?id=103175

Devon and Cornwall Against the Badger Cull (2017) *About us* [online]. Available at: https://dcabc.wordpress.com

Discover Wildlife (2013) Britain's national species revealed. *Discover Wildlife* [online] 30 July 2013. Available at: http://www.discoverwildlife.com/british-wildlife/britains-national-species-revealed

Donald, A., Gordon, J. and Leach, P. (2012) *The UK and the European Court of Human Rights*. London: Equality and Human Rights Commission.

Dresch, M (2021) Kill the Bill protesters clash with police officers as thousands march across UK. *Mirror* [online] 3 April 2021. Available at: https://www.mirror.co.uk/news/uk-news/breaking-kill-bill-protesters-clash-23848597

Driver, A. (2016) TB toll on the rise as 36,000 cattle slaughtered in 2015. *Farmers Guardian* [online] 16 March 2016. Available at: https://www.fginsight.com/news

Drury, J. and Reicher, S. (2000) Collective action and psychological change: The emergence of new social identities. *British Journal of Social Psychology*, 39, 579–604. The British Psychological Society.

Enticott, G. (2001) Calculating nature: The case of badgers, bovine tuberculosis and cattle. *Journal of Rural Studies*, 17, 149–164.

Farrington, J. (2021) Cheshire groups stage peaceful protest against 'heinous' badger cull *Winsford and Middlewich Guardian* [online] 23 July 2021. Available at: https://www.winsfordguardian.co.uk/news/19464356

Gillham, P. (2011) Securitizing America: Strategic incapacitation and the policing of protest since the 11 September 2001 terrorist attacks. *Sociology Compass*, 5(7), 636–652.

Gilmore, J., Jackson, W. and Monk, H. (2016) *Keep moving! Report on the policing of the Barton Moss community protection camp: November 2013 –April 2014*. Centre for the Study of Crime, Criminalisation and Social Exclusion, Liverpool John Moores University: Centre for Urban Research, University of York.

Gorringe, H., Stott, C and Rosie, M. (2012) Dialogue police, decision-making, and the management of public order during protest crowd events. *Journal of Investigative Psychology and Offender Profiling*, 9, 111–125.

Gravelle, J. and Rogers, C. (2011) Engaging protesters: A smarter way for policing demonstrations. *The Police Journal*, 84, 5–12.

Greaves, P. (2020) Badger campaigners vow to disrupt cull underway in Devon countryside. *Devon Live* [online] 16 September 2020. Available at: https://www.devonlive.com/news/devon-news

Green, E. (2014) Anti-badger culling protest planned this weekend Vet Times [online] Available at: https://www.vettimes.co.uk/news/

Harris, S., Jeffries, D., Cheeseman, C. and Booty, C. (1994) *Problems with Badgers?* 3rd ed. Horsham, West Sussex. Royal Society for the Prevention of Cruelty to Animals.

Harvey, F. (2011) Badger culling is ineffective, says architect of 10-year trial. *The Guardian* [online] 11 July 2011. Available at: https://www.theguardian.com/environment

Hinds, L. and Murphy, K. (2007) Public satisfaction with police: using procedural justice to improve police legitimacy. *The Australian and New Zealand Journal of Criminology*, 40(1), 27–42.

Hirst, D. (2017) *Badgers: Culls in England*. House of Commons Briefing Paper No. 6837. London: House of Commons Library.

Hunt Saboteurs Association (2013) *Huntsabs Pledge Direct Action to Prevent the Killing* [online]. Available at: https://www.huntsabs.org.uk/index.php/92-news/press-releases/

Irons, A. (2016) Hundreds of badger cull protesters make voices heard at Plymouth march. *Plymouth Herald* [online] 19 March 2016. Available at: http://www.plymouthherald.co.uk

Keeble, A. (2016) Government figures show nearly 3,000 badgers killed in Devon cull. *North Devon Gazette* [online]. 16 December 2016. Available at: http://www.northdevongazette.co.uk/news

Kilgallon, A. (2020) Police interaction and Notting Hill Carnival. *Policing and Society*, 30(1), 28–46.

King, M. and Waddington, D. (2005) Flashpoints revisited: A critical application to the policing of anti-globalization. *Protest, Policing and Society*, 15(3), 255–282.

Krebs, J., Anderson, R., Clutton-Brock, T., Morrison, I., Young, D. and Donnelly, C. (1997) *Bovine Tuberculosis in Cattle and Badgers: Report by the Independent Scientific Review Group*. London: The Ministry of Agriculture, Fisheries and Food. Crown copyright.

Langton, T. (2021) *Help Stop Badger Culling Adding to England's Biodiversity Catastrophe*. Available at: https://www.crowdjustice.com/case/stop-badger-culling

Lind, E. and Tyler, T. (1988) *The Social Psychology of Procedural Justice*. New York: Plenum Press.

Mansley, D (2014) *Collective Violence, Democracy and Protest Policing*. London and New York: Routledge.

McCarthy, J. and McPhail, C. (1998) The institutionalization of protest in the United States, in Meyer, D. and Tarrow, S. eds., *The Social Movement Society: Contentious Politics for a New Century*, 83–110. New York: Rowman and Littlefield.

Mobbs, P. (2009) *NETCU, WECTU and NPOIU: Britain's Secretive Police Force: Politicising the Policing of Public Expression in an Era of Economic Change*. The Free Range Electrohippies Project. Available at: http://www.fraw.org.uk/fraw_admin

Natural England (2017) *About us*. Available at: https://www.gov.uk/government/organisations/natural-england/about

Natural England (2014) *Badger Control Measures Authorised in West Gloucestershire and West Somerset*. Available at: https://www.gov.uk/government/news

Parliament (2011) *House of Commons debate: Wednesday*, 14 December 2011. Available at: https://www.publications.parliament.uk/pa/cm201011/cmhansrd

Redekop, V. and Paré, S. (2010) *Beyond Control: A Mutual Respect Approach to Protest Crowd-police Relations*. London: Bloomsbury.

Reicher, S. (1996) The battle of Westminster: Developing the social identity model of crowd behaviour in order to explain the initiation and development of collective conflict. *European Journal of Social Psychology*, 26, 115–134.

Reiner, R. (1998) Policing, protest, and disorder in Britain, in della Porta, D. and Reiter, R. eds., *Policing Protest: The Control of Mass Demonstrations in Western Democracies*, 35–48. Minneapolis: University of Minnesota Press.

Sleightholme, D. (2016) Protestors angry with badger cull roll out. *ITV News* [online] 2 September 2016. Available at: http://www.itv.com/news/westcountry

Stott, C., Scothern, M., and Gorringe, H. (2013) Advances in Liaison based public order policing in England: Human rights and negotiating the management of protest? *Policing*, 7(2), 212–226.

The Wildlife Trusts (2017) Badger: Meles meles. *The Wildlife Trusts* [online]. Available at: http://www.wildlifetrusts.org/species/badger

Tyler, T. and Lind, E. (1992) A relational model of authority in groups. *Advances in Experimental Social Psychology*, 25, 115–191.

Waddington, D. (2007) *Policing public disorder: Theory and practice*. Cullompton: Willan Publishing.

Waddington, D. (2013) A 'kinder blue': Analysing the police management of the Sheffield anti-'Lib Dem' protest of March 2011. *Policing and Society*, 23(1), 46–64.

Waddington, D. (2011) *Policing Contemporary Political Protest: From Strategic Incapacitation to Strategic Facilitation?* Available at: http://www.shu.ac.uk/research/cresr/sites/shu.ac.uk/

Waddington, D., Jones, K. and Critcher, C. (1989) *Flashpoints: Studies in Public Disorder*. New York: Routledge.

Waddington, P. (1998) Controlling protest in contemporary historical and comparative perspective, in della Porta, D. and Reiter, R. eds., *Policing Protest: The Control of Mass Demonstrations in Western Democracies*, 117–142. Minneapolis: University of Minnesota Press.

Watson, A. and Angell, B. (2007) Applying procedural justice theory to law enforcement's response to persons with mental illness. *Psychiatric Service*, 58(6), 787–792.

Werren, C. (2014) Intelligence gathering and the need for control: Managing risk in public order policing. *Criminal Justice Matters*, 96(1), 22–23.

Winter, S. (2016) Queen legend Brian May tells Cameron: Your badger cull cost millions and is not working. *Express* [online] 13 July 2016. Available at: http://www.express.co.uk/news/nature/689008

Zahir, N. (2021) Tensions grow between protesters and scandal-hit police. *Aljazeera* [online] 20 April 2021. Available at: https://www.aljazeera.com/news/2021

Chapter 6

Case study 2
The EDL march

Introduction

This chapter further explores the role of the police in utilising a dialogical approach in facilitating protest and balancing human rights by examining a second case study: the policing of the English Defence League (EDL) march in Liverpool on 3 June 2017. The chapter provides insight into the experiences of those involved in the event: marching, counterdemonstrating and responsible for policing the march, as well as others external to the event but affected by it. It has been identified earlier in this book that established research focuses on the relationship between police and protesters in considering the value of engagement, rather than considering the whole range of social actors with whom the police engage in dialogue, prior to, during and post an event. This chapter, therefore, evidences the wide range of different interested parties with whom the police engaged and maps out the complex dialogical process. After providing a contextualised background, the chapter focuses on identifying this wide range of interested parties, the dialogical process that the police implemented, the challenge of facilitating a balancing of competing human rights and reasons for non-engagement with the police.

Background to the march

The city of Liverpool has witnessed numerous protests, marches and demonstrations over many years for a variety of causes from diverse groups. In August 2017, an art exhibition entitled "Liverpool: A city of protest" celebrated the tradition of standing up for social justice and equality. In launching the event, curator Amanda Atkinson described Liverpool as a city that "is often associated with defiance and non-conformity and spoken about in a way that sets it apart from the usual narrative of modern British political history" (Bido Lito!, 2017).

The EDL march of June 2017 was the third march in Liverpool city centre within a two-year period that attracted a large counterdemonstration and had reports of disorder occurring during the event (Maxwell, 2015; Weston, 2016; Dunn, 2017). Neither of the first two marches included an appearance by the EDL, despite rhetoric that implied that the EDL march in 2017 heralded a return of those involved in previous marches. It did however become apparent in the EDL march case study that the previous marches had an influence on those involved in this march and almost all participants that were interviewed for the EDL case study referred to the previous two events. Therefore, this section provides a short overview of the first two events, and a more detailed examination of the EDL event, to provide context in which to consider the experiences of those participating in this case study.

On 15 August 2015, a "white man march" was organised in Liverpool by "right-wing" group National Action (Atherton, 2017). The marchers were reportedly "given the green light" by Merseyside Police, who quoted the Human Rights Act 1998 "in their defence" and an obligation to facilitate peaceful protest (Joseph, 2015). National Action were greeted at Lime Street railway station by anti-fascist protesters, who turned out to show their opposition (Atherton, 2017). Counterdemonstrations were held by the Anti-Fascist Network and Unite Against Fascism and the march was cancelled after "rival groups fought inside the train station" (Joseph, 2015). National Action reportedly "ended up locked in left luggage at the city's Lime Street train station, surrounded by the Police for their own safekeeping" (Maxwell, 2015). Two further National Action marches were subsequently planned in the following weeks; however, despite the presence of counterdemonstrators in the city awaiting their arrival, National Action failed to materialise either time (Thomas, 2015).

Further incidents of disorder involving National Action occurred around the UK in 2016 (Elgot, 2016). Subsequently, in December 2016, National Action became the first extreme right-wing group to be proscribed as a terrorist organisation, under the Terrorism Act 2000, following "an assessment that it is concerned in terrorism" (Government, 2016). Further far-right groups Scottish Dawn and NS131 were prescribed by Home Secretary Amber Rudd in September 2017, having been identified as alternative names used by National Action. Rudd described the group as "vile, racist, homophobic and anti-Semitic" and stated that she would not allow them to "masquerade under different names" (Travis, 2017).

In February 2016, the Liverpool Echo reported that "far-right group North West Infidels" intended to stage a rally the following day in Liverpool, rather than Manchester as originally planned, to exercise their "democratic rights to freedom of expression, speech, movement and assembly" (Weston, 2016a). The report stated that "according to opponents, the group originally broke away from other racists like the English Defence League because the latter were not racist enough for them" (Weston, 2016a). On 27 February 2016, the Liverpool Echo reported that the city centre had "erupted into violence" as the North West Infidels "clashed with anti-fascist protesters" outside St George's Hall, where the police were "heavily outnumbered" and a number of the Infidels group "broke through the cordon and fought with anti-fascists" (Weston, 2016b).

Events were again focused along Lime Street and near to the train station, the main inter-city rail access to Liverpool, and culminated in disorder outside

St George's Hall on the Plateau, where it was reported that swastikas had been daubed on the walls of the building (Culley, 2016). A number present were identified by the wearing of jackets bearing a "Hooligans Poland" motif on the back (Weston, 2016b). Merseyside Police were reported to have said that the incident involved missiles being thrown and scuffles among protesters, resulting in one police officer being struck by brick and hospitalised, and several arrests (Wheatstone and Weston, 2016).

In May 2017, it was reported that "far-right organisation" the EDL were intending to march in Liverpool. An organiser from the EDL was reported to have told the Liverpool Echo that they wanted to have a peaceful march and make speeches, and further stated, "Originally when we started it was violent – we can't deny that, but we've got rid of the violent element. There has been lots of violent confrontation in Liverpool in the past, that isn't what we want" (Atherton, 2017). The event was confirmed on the EDL website, where it was described as a demonstration "in support of British values and free speech, and in opposition to the Islamisation of our country and left wing ideologies, bullying and violence that enable this Islamisation" (EDL, 2017b). The EDL press release explained that the group had been invited to the city by their supporters and were "delighted to respond positively." Further, the release stated that they would be "focusing on free speech, the roots of political correctness in 'cultural Marxism', left-wing councils and council employees and their virtue-signalling support for 'refugees' over Liverpudlians in need" (EDL, 2017b).

However, the opposition was also announced, with "anti-Fascist activists" planning a "mass mobilisation" to stop the march. A representative from Unite Against Fascism (UAF) was quoted as saying, "Our priority is to keep Liverpool fascist-free, so that these organisations cannot march or speak freely" (Atherton, 2017). Reticence to the EDL was also voiced by Liverpool Mayor Joe Anderson, who was vocal in calling for the government to give him the power to ban outright "far-right groups like this" from coming to the city. Anderson stated that the march was not a matter of allowing freedom of speech for the EDL, rather "about a group that wants to intimidate and bully people" (Thorp, 2017a). An alternative "peaceful, multi-faith event" was also planned at the Hindu Cultural Centre in Edge Lane, with speakers including Merseyside Police Chief Constable Andy Cooke, Police and Crime Commissioner Jane Kennedy and members of the Tim Parry and Jonathan Ball Foundation for Peace (Thorp, 2017c).

On 3 June 2017, it was reported that a march by "right-wing group" EDL "erupted into violence in Liverpool city centre" (Dunn, 2017), after "supporters of the far-right group scuffled with anti-fascists close to Liverpool Lime Street Station" (Burke, 2017). The incident included confrontation between the EDL and anti-fascist protesters, the Merseyside UAF group, on St George's Plateau. It was reported that missiles, which included bottles and what were believed to be firecrackers, were thrown between the opposing groups (Burke, 2017; Dunn, 2017; Mansfield, 2017). The police presence was described as "heavy" (Mansfield, 2017), and Deputy Chief Constable Foulkes from Merseyside Police described the support that the force had received from British Transport Police and colleagues from Lancashire, Cumbria, Cheshire and North Wales (Dunn, 2017), with a reported 12 arrests and the use of public order legislation to disperse demonstrators (Mansfield, 2017).

The response to the EDL march was varied across news reports and social media. The Liverpool Echo recorded that the event was a success for the left-wing demonstrators in blocking the "far right," who were "laughed out of Liverpool for the third year running – as thousands of protesters forced them to cut their march short" (Hughes, 2017). Although this was an EDL march, a different group to previous marches by National Action and North West infidels, the reports suggested that they were in fact one and the same group: "the far-right group attempted to march through the city again, but it didn't really work out for them, again" (Dunn, 2017). The Liverpool Echo also published "Faces of hate: 8 pictures that sum up the EDL" (Hughes, 2017). Further afield, it was reported that the EDL were prevented from marching through Liverpool despite "an unprecedented level of police protection" (Heneghan, 2017). Liverpool Councillor Sean was reported to have posted on Twitter, "Liverpool sends the EDL packing again. Lots of love to @MerseyPolice@ MerPolChiefCon managing situation so well Liverpool heroes" (RT News, 2017). The Socialist Worker reported that thousands had stopped "Nazis from marching through Liverpool," and that this was the "fourth time in the last two years that fascist groups have been met by mobilisations against them in Liverpool" (Jenkins, 2017). UAF listed on their website some of the groups and individuals involved in protesting against the EDL:

> Merseyside UAF's protest was supported by seven Regional Trades Unions: CWU, FBU, GMB, NUT, PCS, UNISON and Trade Union support: Unite, over 25 local Councillors, Show Racism the Red Card and others. The day started at noon with the UAF rally featuring speakers from the local trade union movement and cultural figures from the city, including: Deputy Mayor of Liverpool Ann O'Byrne; Julie Ward MEP; Lynn Collins, Regional Secretary of North West TUC; Martin Cavanagh of the PCS union; Tony Kearns, acting General Secretary of the CWU; Writer Alan Gibbons; Mark Rowe, local Regional Secretary of the Fire Brigades Union, and others.
>
> (UAF, 2017)

The EDL unsurprisingly reported the events of the day differently:

> We were outnumbered 10 to 1 in Liverpool by a largely left-wing crowd. We were bombarded with about 200 rotten eggs, 50 drink bottles (at least one was a glass bottle), 25 full drink cans and bananas and a handful of smoke bombs, darts, large fireworks and coins. We threw nothing – other than a few returns. We were there for the victims (and victims-to-be) of

grooming, abuse, bombings, vehicle attacks and attempted beheadings. And we are not going away.

(EDL, 2017a)

The EDL claimed that those opposing their march had "blood on their hands," a chant that had been heard from the EDL during the event and stated that they were overwhelmed by the support that they had received in marching, despite the opposition from the "regressive left" in Liverpool, who revealed their "seditious intentions" (EDL, 2017a).

The EDL emerged in 2009 as a mass street protest movement able to attract supporters in the thousands to demonstrate against "Islamic extremism" in towns and cities across the UK (Kassimeris and Jackson, 2015: 1) and during the following ten years organised over 450 protest events (Allchorn and Dafnos, 2020). There is much debate regarding the status of the EDL, particularly in the claims of those opposing that the EDL are far-right extremists, fascists and "Nazis" (Jenkins, 2017). At the time they emerged, then Commissioner of the Metropolitan Police, Sir Paul Stephenson, was reported to state that the EDL "per se" were not viewed as "an extreme right wing group in the accepted sense" and that the group had the right to protest (Pitt, 2009). In 2010, Chief Superintendent Adrian Tudway, then National Co-ordinator for Domestic Extremism, wrote that the EDL "are not extreme right wing as a group" and that their published material indicated that they were actively moving away from the right and away from engaging in violence (Dodd and Taylor, 2011). Lord Tebbit in 2013 challenged the founder of an anti-Islamophobia monitoring group to prove the group adhered to far-right principles and said calling the group "right-wing" was "an attempt to smear mainstream conservatives" (Elgot, 2013). That same year, the leader of the EDL at the time, "Tommy Robinson" (real name of Stephen Yaxley-Lennon), when interviewed, declared that he was "not a Nazi, and that he hated Nazis and hated fascism" (Hope, 2013).

The EDL stated in their mission statement that they stand for human rights: that their activities are peaceful: and they are committed to non-violent street protests to further their mission. The statement claims that EDL demonstrations provide the opportunity for a collective voice, and whilst other groups may make their protests through writing articles, debate or violent activities, the EDL are "loud and proud, but then we go back home to our families." The group states that they "stand firm in support of the right of both Muslims and non-Muslims to speak freely" (EDL, 2016).

Research into the EDL also differs in establishing the political and social stance of the group. Morrow and Meadowcroft (2019: 544) consider the EDL as a "far right" organisation however noted that contrary to other "far right" activists "the EDL does not espouse biological racism." Copsey (2010: 25), observed that the EDL is "not an archetypal far-right party or movement." Meleagrou-Hitchens and Brun (2013: 25) observed that the EDL's political stance could be most accurately described as "a new form of cultural nationalism." Pilkington (2016: 123) concluded after three years of research into the EDL that there was "a genuine aspiration to non-racism among grassroots members of the movement." This, Pilkington noted, was evidenced in an organisational commitment to make the group accessible for all, by excluding racism from the EDL and creating clear demarcation lines between the EDL and groups and movements perceived as racist.

However, Kassimeris and Jackson (2015: 12) stated that whether the EDL leadership sincerely believed the group not to be Islamophobic was "a moot point" as the EDL "employed a culturally racist discourse of Islamophobia." Further, Meleagrou-Hitchens and Brun (2013: 12) observed that whether intended or not, the EDL message and tactics used were "bound to attract race nationalists, and there is plenty of evidence that it has." Nevertheless, Meleagrou-Hitchens and Brun warned against using terms such as racist and fascist, acknowledging that although such traits may exist in some within the organisation, this was not representative of the EDL ideology. They concluded that such terms were unhelpful, as they provided a biased and inaccurate analysis of the EDL, which was unhelpful both to those making policy decisions and to the general public in their understanding of the EDL.

Allen (2011: 290) observed that as far as placing the EDL in the far right, the group "undoubtedly resembles other organizations within that milieu," and therefore, despite the EDL protesting to the contrary, concluded that it was very difficult not to place them politically as such. However, Allen cautioned that in doing so, there was a danger of underestimating the strength of support for the EDL, and not recognising that their ideology was different from traditional far-right groups. Further, Allen observed that the appeal of the EDL to, and incorporation of, minority groups often excluded by the far right, bucked the trend from other historical far-right groups. Oaten (2014) concurred and noted the EDL's inclusivity in attracting supporters from different religious faiths and sexual minority groups, evidenced for example in the existence of the EDL Lesbian Gay Bisexual and Transgender Division, who stand alongside the traditional right-wing supporters. Oaten concluded (2014: 333) that the key to understating the EDL was in "understanding the EDL's identity as collective victim." Pilkington (2016: 229) observed that despite the ideology and political activity of the organisation, EDL members often "articulated a rejection of politics per se," perceiving this as meaningless discussion.

This case study explores the experiences of those that marched with the EDL, opposed the march or who were in some way affected by the march and allows an insight into how the police utilised a strategy based on a dialogical approach with everyone affected by the EDL march to assist their decision-making and balancing of competing human rights. Consistent with the previous chapter, the remainder of this study examines the experiences of those who were engaged in or significantly affected before, during and post the EDL march and counterdemonstration in Liverpool on 3 June 2017 based on participant views expressed during semi-structured interviews. The responses were analysed and the same key themes emerged, which for consistency also form the headings for the following section and allow opinions to be collated and grouped. Many of the responses of the participants have been transcribed verbatim, to provide responses in the words of those who had been integral in the policing responses to the EDL march in 2017.

Interested parties

As presented in the previous chapter, existing research into a dialogical approach to the policing process concentrates solely on the dialogue between police and protesters (for example, Gorringe, Stott and Rosie, 2012; Waddington, 2013) or event organisers (Kilgallon, 2020). However, as identified in the badger cull case study, there are numerous individuals and groups that protest events impact on and dialogue prior to and during events is enacted not solely between the police and protesters or event organisers, but rather with a multitude of interested parties, allowing the police to build relationships and allowing voice to those engaged in or affected by the protest event.

The initial approach in analysing data gleaned in researching the EDL march in Liverpool was to identify the wide range of interested parties with whom the police engaged in dialogue, prior to, during and after the march. The following therefore describes and identifies the various interested parties, examining identity and nomenclature, and maps the complex dialogical process, which is illustrated in the *Dialogical Wheel*, recognising impact factors such as illegitimacy, lack of trust and political pressures.

Identifying interested parties

The most obvious interested party in this case study was the event organisers, the EDL. Unsurprisingly, the presence of the EDL brought opposition with counterdemonstrating groups unified politically and culturally (Waddington, Jones and Critcher, 1989) in a city that had witnessed serious disorder during previous marches. However, consistent with the badger cull case study in the previous chapter, this study evidenced numerous other interested parties aside from those marching or counterdemonstrating with whom the police engaged. The starting point here, in analysing the research data from interviews conducted, is therefore to identify and list the interested parties, consider their identity and map the dialogue they undertook with the police.

The EDL provided six weeks' notification to Merseyside Police that they intended to march through Liverpool city centre on 3 June 2017. Although Section 11 of the Public Order Act (1984) states that advance written notice of a public procession is required "not less than 6 clear days" before an intended march, such early notification afforded the EDL and their legal and media teams an extended period to prepare but also to engage with the police through liaison. The EDL selected one of their members as their intermediary, as "*a communication point,*" who "*sat down*" and liaised with Police Liaison Team (PLT) officers and police operational planners during the planning phase. The EDL explained that they always provide notification much earlier than legally required, usually six weeks' notice for national events, and research the location prior to this to ensure there are no other marches or football matches planned for the day. For this event, Liverpool was selected over other "*left-leaning cities such as Brighton*" because of the historical issues that some groups had experienced in the city from counterdemonstrators who in their view had "*stopped marches by massive violence*," preventing "*free speech in our democratic rights in this country.*" They expanded:

> *The main reason we went to Liverpool was because Liverpool is the centre of Antifa, and black bloc, and Social Workers Party. That is where the left are centred and originate from. We went there because we had observed certain behaviours from the left in Liverpool, where they stopped marches by massive violence. Our argument with that was we don't agree with certain directives that the groups were doing, because as far as we are concerned, they are racist, like being Nazis, and stuff like that.*
>
> (EDL A)

This advance notice of a public procession notification provided by the EDL marked the start of the police response, with Commanders identified to plan and prepare for the event. In doing so, Commanders began to question who would attend and march and whether the EDL would "*bring anyone else with them,*" or attract "*other interested parties*" in support. Despite this being the first time in several years that the EDL as a group had a march in the city, Commanders voiced concerns that those attending under the banner of the EDL may have been involved in other more recent events. One Commander spoke from the experience of having been "personally involved in various incidents and court cases" with certain groups who "badged themselves" as one right-wing group, became another group name, and then "*became EDL, became other right-wing factions, depending on what the sort of current politics or influences were at any given time.*"

As soon as it became public knowledge that the EDL intended to march, a counterdemonstration group coalesced, an opposing group which most participants referred to as the "left-wing." This collective response was orchestrated largely by a group known as Unite Against Fascism (UAF). Activists described how the UAF had contacted their unions and asked them to participate in the counterdemonstrations. One explained how the UAF were an organised regional body with a presence and links to other groups nationally and internationally and described their stance:

> *The core aims and objectives are on the internet, but they are very much about the 'fascists off the streets', whether that's locally, whether that's nationally or internationally. And they are not a group that actually resorts to action in terms of actual physical action. They just peacefully counterdemonstrate. But they always are able to galvanise large groups of people together, and put the call out, and likeminded people will then come to have a counter-protest.*
>
> (Activist A)

162 Case study 2

Despite the unity of opposition to the EDL, it was clear from every participant that they had identified numerous groups within the counterdemonstration opposition: UAF members; trade unions such as Unison, Unite the Union and the Communication Workers Union; student groups; the Anti-Fascist Network (Antifa); politicians and local councillors; and the public. Police participants described the component elements that they identified within the opposition group, which included students; "*the public-spirited citizens, the people of Liverpool who have left-wing views;*" those passing by; some "*who are troublemakers*" intent on engaging in disorder; and causing trouble; and "*a hard-core element of left*" who were "*identifiable by clothing, flags*" and who were "*intent on causing issues.*" Some described the complexity of the group makeup:

> *I think the left-wing, you could go on and on and on in terms of breaking them down, and what people's involvement may be.*
>
> (Commander K)

> *Certainly, my reflections after the event, this morphous body called the left-wing. And they ranged from the general community of Liverpool, who are more left-leaning than most other cities in the country, and have a very powerful, political voice, based on history, to the more extreme left-wing, the anarchist bloc that would do anything, can tend to use violence et cetera to achieve their aim.*
>
> (Commander L)

> *All different banners, all different people. There were some with the anarchists' symbol for the left-wing, with face coverings, dressed all in black, and bits of red, carrying flags. Through to people identifying themselves as teachers. There were union members there. I saw a number of Unison banners. Members of the local community. People who they identified themselves as, "We are not part of the counter-protest as such, we are here to just tell these people they can't come to our city." And people who just identified as being Liverpudlians, and people from Merseyside, not wanting the EDL to be there. Definitely not a homogenous group.*
>
> (PLT J)

> *Even young people, even teenagers from some of the tough areas. They thought it was hilarious. Get the bus into town, have a laugh at these, what's going on here.*
>
> (Commander O)

Police participants recognised that although the group were united in opposition to the EDL, each individual group still had their "*own crusades.*" One Commander cautioned against using "*left-wing*" as a collective noun:

> *You've got everything from your anti-fascist, black bloc type groups, who will use violence and will potentially call themselves communists if you spoke to them*

one-on-one, with what could be considered very left-wing views. But you've got groups of black lads from L8 [postcode district of Liverpool including Toxteth] who might not think of themselves as political at all on that continuum. You've got mums with pushchairs. Trade unionists, who maybe would consider themselves just left of centre. You've got literally every man and his dog, doesn't really want these people in the city. So, I don't think we should use left-wing in that respect.

(Commander O)

There was clearly diversity within the group of those opposing the march despite the common aim of opposition to the right of the EDL to have a procession in the city One Activist described the makeup of the counterdemonstration against the EDL march and identified sub-groups including anti-fascists, different trade unions and student groups, augmented by members of the public:

Some of the Antifa, as they are called, they were present. We actually had some community members, as in people who were from different diverse groups, who'd come along, because they'd heard that the EDL were coming to Liverpool, and they wanted to come to demonstrate. And officially, there were community organisers present as well. So, people from the Irish community, people maybe from the black community of Liverpool et cetera that came along to actually say, "Sorry, we don't want the EDL on the streets of Liverpool." We had the Deputy Lord Mayor was present. And there was media ... There was quite a lot of groups that came together in a uniform voice to actually say, "Not on our streets!"

(Activist A)

Local and national media (for example, Hughes, 2017; Mansfield, 2017) sought to polarise opinion on the EDL march in Liverpool, portraying the EDL "faces of hate" who "didn't get very far" in their attempt to march and instead were "escorted" and "laughed out" (Hughes, 2017) of a city united against them. However, there were numerous other groups and interested parties aside from the EDL and the counterdemonstration groups who were neither pro nor anti the march but who were affected by the events of 3rd June. Many of these groups engaged with the police prior to and during the event and this research identified such interested parties who were key in the dialogical process. Participants described the local authority as "*key stakeholders,*" and this included elected members and those involved in "*building work or cleansing works in the city centre in and around such events.*" The retail sector was an interested party, and this included the Liverpool One shopping complex and the "*Business Improvement District that represents 650 retail businesses.*" Pubs were also identified as key stakeholders. One Commander observed:

You had the Wetherspoon's that closed down, and other public houses that had to consider their approach. And, even then, within a small geographical area, you

> had some pubs say, "We are closing down," and then you had another pub who was willing to accept them [EDL]. So, even when you group the pubs together as a party, within that, you've got people who are supportive and willing to host, and you've got others who aren't.
>
> (Commander K)

Other businesses were identified, particularly those located near to the start of the march route. These included Lime Street train station, the Liverpool Museums, the Empire Theatre with "*up to 2,380 attending a matinee performance at the same time,*" and St George's Hall, where there was "*quite a bit of damage and a lot of violence on the steps during the previous event.*" The wider impact affected the transport network and interested parties were identified from Merseytravel, Network Rail, individual train operating companies, train stations and bus companies, who were duty-bound to as far as possible "*create a safe environment for passengers and to make sure the network keeps running.*"

The emergency services were unsurprisingly key stakeholders: Merseyside Fire and Rescue Service; North West Ambulance Service; Merseyside Police; and British Transport Police (BTP). Despite relationships existing between the police services, there was an identified difference in the approach of Merseyside Police and BTP. A Merseyside Police Commander commented of BTP that "*they are a business, and that's challenging.*" Contrastingly, a BTP Commander observed that they had challenges further afield, including the UEFA Champions League final in Cardiff on the same day, which resulted in "*specific key strategic objectives*" peculiar to BTP "*that may not necessarily reflect strategic priorities with Merseyside Police.*" The presence of the EDL had further reaching implications for BTP:

> We also had notification that there was going to be a simultaneous protest outside Birmingham New Street, in the West Midlands. So, again, part of who were the interested parties who were involved right up until the last week, were senior stakeholders in Merseyside Police, and senior stakeholders in West Midlands Police, senior stakeholders in terms of British Transport Police strategic command. I had senior stakeholders in terms of very powerful and influential train operating companies, and that multi-billion pound industry that moves those billion odd passengers around the UK every year.
>
> (Commander P)

Even within policing there was a diversity of approaches, and police participants described the natural internal conflict that will occur during any high-profile event with media and political interest. The perceptions and experiences of Commanders differed from those of other police officers more junior in rank and deployed in different roles during this event. Further, the size and scale of the event required Merseyside Police to bring in mutual aid support from neighbouring police forces and therefore the event was policed by officers from BTP, Cheshire, Cumbria, Lancashire and North Wales police forces under the command of Merseyside Police and this resulted in nuanced responses with many police officers deployed in a city of in which they had little or no experience of policing, deployed in a variety of dress codes depending on their roles. The difference in approaches was recognised not only by Commanders but also those they policed. One Activist described how they interacted with police officers on the ground and the differences in police responses:

> *The police approach before the EDL got in was so light, and it was just banter, chatting to the officers, apart from those Welsh bastards! I didn't have any engagement with them [PLT], but I seen them. I seen also the poor buggers who got to walk around with the video cameras, following everyone. I seen those as well. But mostly, it was just general bobbies on the beat. Obviously, they all had their combat gear, protective gear that they were wearing.*
>
> (Activist B)

Finally, there were the group which many described as "*the population of Merseyside*" who were "*going about their normal daily business.*" One participant explained that the Liverpool city centre population had risen from 3,000 in 2001 to 40,000 at present, further augmented by visitors on a busy Saturday afternoon. Another expanded:

> *There's lots and lots of people. People just going about their general daily business as well. Wanting to take their kids to the museum, wanting to go on the ale, you know what I mean, the old fellas on a Saturday afternoon. You've got all that movement where people just want to carry on as normal. But something like this can just cause gridlock because there's the traffic footfall as well.*
>
> (Business G)

Identity and nomenclature

For participants in this case study, recognising interested parties required understanding their identity. Superficially, the event was labelled as an EDL march opposed by protesters. However, all participants in this case study sought to further delineate the opposing groups and sub-groups and recognise the intentions and identity of different elements.

The identity of those marching, the EDL, was particularly significant in light of previous "right-wing" marches in Liverpool resulting in disorder (Maxwell, 2015; Weston, 2016a), and all participants referenced previous events and their impact on planning for this march. All police participants were very clear that the identity of the EDL was very different from the Polish Hooligans, National Action and North West Infidel groups. Police participants unanimously agreed with Copsey (2010) and Allen (2011) that, despite local and national media references (for example, Burke, 2017; Hughes, 2017) the EDL were not a far-right-wing movement. Consistent with Meleagrou-Hitchens and Brun (2013) and Pilkington (2016), police participants saw a danger in branding the EDL as far right. However, most located the EDL right of centre. One PLT explained how they had conducted research in lieu of dialogue:

> *If you look at the ideology, it's not as far right as you think it is. And there's probably common areas that a lot of the population would agree with.*
>
> (PLT M)

A Commander concurred:

> *I don't see a danger, personally, in relation to the EDL as categorising them as right-wing. We've all had briefings and see the different categories and where people sit on some sort of continuum. And, I like that briefing, and I know that we show the EDL just to the right of centre, not too extreme. And that's fine by me, and that category sits well for me in relation to the EDL.*
>
> (Commander O)

Some police participants expressed a fear in the planning stage that members of *"far-right"* groups might return and be *"rebranded"* as EDL, however this fear was alleviated through the dialogical process implemented. An EDL member explained:

> *I pointed it out to the liaison, and said, "We are nothing to do with the NWI. They are a splinter group." The North West Infidels. Who teamed up with the Polish lot. I said, "We had nothing to do with them." At the end of the day, most of their leaders are in nick, anyway. We was quite aware that their presence affected the police decisions outcome, on the way they treated us. But I think we put it forward enough, and professionally enough to sort of say to the police, "Well, look! We're not that sort of group. We do understand people's rights, other people's rights. We know it needs to be proportional."*
>
> (EDL A)

However, Activists described the EDL in the same vein as previous marching groups, referring to the EDL as *"neo-Nazis"* and *"fascists,"* and suggesting that despite the ideology, those marching displayed *"extreme right-wing"* tendencies. One Activist observed:

> *We see them as fascists. Well, it's what they stand for. Their terminology that they use, they try to twist it.*
>
> (Activist B)

Despite the labelling of the EDL as *"extreme right-wing"* by those opposing, several Commanders commented that this was a ploy to stereotype the EDL and associate them with previous groups. One explained:

> *They are seen that way. But, deep down, those people who are opposing them would know the difference. I'm quite sure they would know the difference. But the people who oppose them use the categorisation of saying they are all the same to rally support for their own ends. Deep down, they know that there are shades of grey within the political spectrum and where people stand, I'm quite sure they do. I don't think many people would be that naive as to not know the difference.*
>
> (Commander O)

Another Commander suggested that local media had influenced perception regarding the EDL's identity:

> *I think our local media here has a complete misunderstanding of what the EDL say they are about. Straight on, as soon as the march is advertised, making links and references back to the previous marches by other groups, neo-Nazi groups, and terrorist groups, which are now banned, in the same article. So, if the media put those three groups in one news article, well the general members of the public probably collate them all into one, you know, "They are all neo-Nazis, and that's what they are." So, disappointment in the local media, definitely, and definitely out trying to stir up a bit of interest and sell a few more papers, by sexing it up a bit more, I think.*
>
> (Commander M)

The EDL were very keen to stress that they were not extremist in their identity. An EDL member outlined the organisational ideology and mission statement and explained how the EDL had worked to rid their ranks of *"far-right"* supporters:

> *Basically, what happened was all those egos and stuff like that, or bullies, people who say, "You do it my way, or it's the highway, or I'll come around and knock on your door," that all got dealt with. And then you had people splintering off and doing their own thing. But not standing by our values. So, we turned round to them and said, "We will never have unity with you lot. As long as you are holding us up, we will never have unity." So, basically, you have people splinter off. We don't get no football firms come along any more. All's it is, is it's women and kids, I mean like youth, and just standing up for the right to demonstrate, the right for freedom of speech, and also highlighting what is going on in England. You know, Jack Straw said, 10 years ago, that there is a problem going on here, when it was first identified in Derby. So, basically, it's us protecting our children. That's how we value ourselves. We are protecting the future of our children, and children's children.*
>
> (EDL A)

Image 6.1 The EDL marching on Lime Street, Liverpool, surrounded by police officers. Used with permission of *Mirrorpix*.

Image 6.2 A member of the EDL within a group marching in Liverpool. Used with permission of *Shutterstock*.

Image 6.3 Counterdemonstrators on the steps outside Lime Street station, Liverpool. Used with permission of *Shutterstock*.

Case study 2 169

Image 6.4 EDL members, flanked by police officers, marching on Lime Street, Liverpool. Used with permission of *Shutterstock*

Image 6.5 Counterdemonstrators on the steps outside Lime Street station, Liverpool opposing the EDL march. Used with permission of *Shutterstock*

170 Case study 2

Image 6.6 Counterdemonstrators outside Lime Street station, Liverpool, wearing face coverings and flying anti-fascism banners and flags. Used with permission of *Shutterstock*

Image 6.7 Opposition against the EDL march in Liverpool. Used with permission of *Mirrorpix*

Those opposing the EDL march were often referred to collectively by participants as the "*left-wing.*" Police participants observed that the same groups had united on several previous events in Liverpool, such as student marches, anti-NHS protests, trade union demonstrations and opposition to "*right-wing*" groups. One Commander suggested the group "*badge themselves differently depending on what event they are attending.*" Another observed the same transience, noting that although there had been three different groups who had

Image 6.8 Police liaison officers deployed at a protest event, wearing light blue tabards. Used with permission of *Shutterstock*

Image 6.9 EDL members marching on Lime Street, Liverpool, marshalled by EDL stewards and surrounded by police officers. Used with permission of *Mirrorpix*

attended Liverpool to march in the past 18 months, "*it's the same left-wing that came out on each occasion.*" Yet another Commander commented:

> *It's quite interesting to see how the different people will turn up to protest often for what they've previously protested against. So, people who previously opposed Mayor Anderson would have effectively sided with him in terms of opposing views against the right-wing on 3rd June.*
>
> (Commander J)

Image 6.10 EDL members escorted by police officers and surrounded by demonstrators on Lime Street, Liverpool. Used with permission of *Shutterstock*

However, all participants identified a diversity within the opposition, and a necessity to understand the identity of diverse groups to identify intentions. Commanders recognised "*a splinter*" in the groups and that "*you can't treat them all the same, because they've all got different perspectives and interests.*" Activists specified their stance in terms of group membership and responsibilities. One commented: "*I wasn't responsible for this demo. I wasn't even responsible for the participants from our branch.*" An Activist defined their level of acceptable activism, and how their identity affected their actions:

> *We are bound by codes of conduct. And, as a full-time officer, when I'm out and representing my union, I could bring my union into disrepute if my conduct … Like in any job. So, you are mindful of what you can and you can't do. I mean, you're not going to resort to doing any criminal damage or physical violence. But you can peacefully protest and demonstrate against, you know, fascists on the streets, in my city, that I love dearly. So, people like that, like-minded people, lots of people come on that basis. There are other people there, I can't speak for them, that may have had a different agenda, which may have been that they would resort to, you know, taking more forceful action is the word I would use. And, obviously, I can't speak for them. But in terms of me and my union, and obviously lots of my other colleagues from the other unions I've named, we would be there to have a peaceful protest, and be compliant in terms of public disorder, et cetera. Because we are representing our union, and we are not there to cause a riot. But we are there to protest.*

(Activist A)

Another Activist observed that most people attending were opposing the EDL for "*a genuine purpose*" but that "*you can see the ones who are there for a different reason, their own motives*" who were identified wearing "*plastic masks*" and "*the scarf around their faces; they are looking like they are wearing combat gear.*" They observed that these smaller groups "*tend to mill or gather sort of separately.*" They described their own stance and how far they would go in opposing the EDL:

> *I try to get as close as I can, and at some stage I was within about five feet of the EDL, although, obviously, I had the police in front, trading banter. But I wouldn't stoop to throw a bottle. I wouldn't stoop to throw these cherry bombs in, or whatever. I wouldn't stoop to pushing a police officer out the way or anything like that. There's a limit. I do my best to protest, but, at some point, this is going to cross the line, and that's when I back away. I'm a shithouse!*
>
> (Activist B)

The EDL also described and identified diverse groups within the left and their perception of the different levels that people would reach in activism:

> *What we would classify as extremist left is Antifa. Black bloc. We call them 'Hate not Hope!' It's 'Hope not Hate', but we call them that. There's Unite Against Fascism, UAF. And the Socialist Workers Party. Let's put it this way, the Socialist Workers Party, they will sit down and try and prevent you from doing the march, as they did in Liverpool. The Antifa, the same as the black bloc. So, we'll classify them as extremists.*
>
> (EDL A)

Activists were, however, very keen to distance themselves from the term "protester." One explained:

> *Activists, rather than protester. Because I may take an action against what I see is, you know, fascist. I feel compelled to go out and as an activist, to say, "Not on my streets. This is my city, and I don't want whatever agenda you are bringing."*
>
> (Activist A)

Another concurred:

> *The definition of the word protester is a bit vague to me. If I go to London, I've been on anti-austerity marches, so I'm protesting against the government. I've been to another one not so long ago where it was a "Save the NHS". So, I'm not protesting against the NHS, I'm a supporter. So, I suppose it depends what the cause is, what you are going there for.*
>
> (Activist B)

It was apparent therefore to all in this case study that recognising the identification of different social actors and groups was important. The term "protester" as identified in the previous case study was again problematic, as it did not reflect the intentions of those in opposition to the march and as a collective noun inaccurately unified those with very diverse responses.

Illegitimacy and lack of trust

A key theme of trust emerged from all those engaged in the events around the EDL march in Liverpool. Gilmore, Jackson and Monk (2016) observed that a lack of trust between protesters and police prevented effective dialogue. This cased study also identified element of a lack of trust between counterdemonstrators and the police, however, a lack of trust was manifested in numerous other settings. Clearly, there was a lack of trust between the EDL and those counterdemonstrating and opposing sides had no intention of engaging in effective dialogue prior to the march. Other areas were also apparent where trust was lacking, owing to perceived illegitimate actions of other groups and this was not only evidenced between out groups: police participants evidenced occasions where trust in colleagues' approaches was questioned.

The EDL had specifically selected the city of Liverpool as the location for their march due to their perception that left-leaning citizens, led by then Mayor Joe Anderson, had previously actively infringed democratic rights to freedom of expression and assembly. There was therefore, at the outset, a sense of perceived illegitimacy in the approach of some of the populous of the city. Similarly, those opposed to the EDL perceived their right to march as illegitimate due to their perception of the organisation being far-right and extremist. Unsurprisingly, therefore, participants from all interested parties in this case study observed a perceived illegitimacy in the actions of outgroups and this led to a lack of trust with external parties.

The EDL perceived the actions of those preventing their march as totally illegitimate:

> *They certainly have the right to freedom of expression. And we have the right to walk in a peaceful and controlled manner, to march in a peaceful and controlled manner, and to our speeches on the day. But the thing is, they weren't respecting our values. And I get sick of ... and I did point it out. When you get people throwing darts, when you get people throwing bottles of urine, when you get people throwing cans of sardines, flowers, broken wood, smoke bombs, used hypodermic needles ... They weren't respecting the fact that we have got the right to democratic speech. At the end of the day, if they had let us do our speech, we wouldn't have been back for about 18 months.*
>
> (EDL A)

Other participants in this case study identified what they saw as illegitimate actions from a small minority within the ranks of those opposing the EDL.

One business participant described witnessing some in opposition throwing "*a lot of missiles*" at the EDL. Several police participants concurred that elements within the counterdemonstration group were illegitimate in their opposition of the EDL. One PLT opined that the police "*need to get to grips with the left-wing*" because "*they are getting away with murder!*" Another stated:

> *To be honest, the EDL had the right to march, and through bullying, intimidation and downright criminality of the left-wing, they were stopped from marching. That's me saying that just as a police officer. It's got nothing to do with having sides. I mean, they have the right to protest. And they were stopped. And not lawfully, in my opinion.*
>
> (PLT M)

Activists saw their whole raison d'être in demonstrating against the EDL as opposing a group whom they believed to have "*vile policies*" which they had a "*right to stop.*" However, even within those opposing there was a sense that some acted in an illegitimate manner. One Activist described a minority who they believed acted in a way not in accordance with their cause:

> *People, and a lot of them I would say, just joined on the day. They had no advanced knowledge of it. So, I would say 90% just your average Joe or trade union. 10%, it's the mindless idiots that I always really hate, because they're the ones that detract from what the issue is. That group, they would act the same way whether you were protesting against the EDL, whether you were protesting against anti-austerity. They are just there, that hard-core, for the mayhem, the mischief, whatever you want to call it. I don't believe they are genuine activists who believe in a cause. I may be doing them a disservice, but I don't believe it for a second. The 10%ers, as I call them.*
>
> (Activist B)

Business participants also described the actions of a minority who were intent on causing disruption and extensive damage. One identified the difference approaches of "*counterdemonstrators that were lawful and were staying in where they were told to go by the police,*" and those that were "*actively moving away*" to "*cause trouble.*"

However, it was not just the EDL or the counterdemonstrators who were scrutinised. Participants from all sides also questioned the legitimacy of some police actions. An EDL member observed that the police were not equitable in implementing public order legislation and stop and search powers. They described how the EDL march was brought to a standstill after activists sat down in the road, preventing the march passage, with some wearing face coverings, contrary to Section 60AA of the Criminal Justice and Public Order Act 1994. They shared the feelings of fellow marchers:

> *They're going, "Oh, these are sitting down now. Why aren't you Section 12-ing them? You can go and get them. You've got your Section 35, you know, power to*

disperse them?" One of my peers was quite irate. They are quite within their rights to get irate as well, because, you know, why aren't they being policed the same way? And this is where we stood up saying this all the time. And you know, like facemasks, Section 60AA. We've always got that on us. And then you see people all scarfed up, with crash helmets on. And the person throwing the smoke bombs, and they use thunder flashes, and they also emit a bright light. The first time it was thrown in, [PLT] shit himself! You could hear them in the city centre 700 yards down the road. And it was a big boom. You know, and our lads, some of my peers were pointing the bloke out. And the police stood there!

(EDL A)

An Activists described a confrontation with a police officer when the officer threatened to arrest their son for "*stepping outside of the cordoning*" when he was "*standing there with two of his friends,*" "*doing nothing*" and only approached because "*he seemed to be an easy target.*" Despite eventually receiving an apology from the officer, the Activist questioned the fairness of the police when there were others within the group acting illegally who were not reprimanded:

Yet there were ones who were covered up, that you couldn't see their faces, who were being allowed to walk around freely. And, that really made me cross. So then ... I think the police officer didn't realise that I was actually the chair of the event, and that's when then afterwards he apologised. He didn't apologise immediately. He apologised once I think he thought ... And I said, "Apology accepted. But you need to be more engaging and a bit more tolerant."

(Activist A)

Furthermore, there were questions raised about police legitimacy and fairness from within. Some police officers questioned the approach taken by commanding officers and believed that the EDL were not treated fairly. In particular, the EDL did not wear face coverings to hide their identity, as they explained that they had been challenged by previous police forces and now self-policed. PLT explained that there was legislation enacted and authorised on the day under Section 60AA (Criminal Justice and Public Order Act, 1994) which gave police officers the power to require any person to remove any item which the officer believes is being worn to conceal identity. However, despite the EDL being subject to the legislation one PLT observed that "*there was Section 60AA in place that was never enforced,*" and that "*little or nothing was done*" in relation to large numbers of opposing group members "*wearing masks*" to the frustration of the EDL.

The perceived lack of internal trust for some police participants expanded to other police officers. One PLT described issues they had encountered with colleagues who "*think that you're not a police officer anymore*" because of performing the role of PLT. Another described how they had been refused a lift back to police headquarters by colleagues after they had tried to diffuse a confrontation, simply because they were PLT officers, which made them feel *"like you were out your own a bit really."* A PLT described how they had challenged a police commander who had directed them to arrests *"as many as they could"* for breaching a Section 14 Public Order Act (1984) order and asked whether other officers could be used instead. They explained the difficult position that they felt placed in:

> *And then, it looks to your colleagues that you may be a coward, or you're unprofessional, or you don't know what you are doing. And it's not that, it's just ... because there was 18 carriers full of police officers who could have arrested those people. So why do the two people who are trying to engage with them, why choose them to go and arrest them? Because that just compromises you. They didn't understand it.*
>
> (PLT K)

Police Commanders described the illegitimacy they perceived in the media reporting prior to and during the march, which they believed had an influence on those attending to counterdemonstrate. Two Commanders described their feelings:

> *The media aren't involved in any planning process. They are not aware of the intel, they're not aware of the issues that we have. And so, if I was going to look at anything here, I'd look at the media. Because how the media framed the February one, the one prior, was that the right-wing were the ones at fault. And they brought weapons, I don't excuse their behaviour. However, the left were using violence that was most likely to result in death. The throwing of the cobbles was by the left. They could have killed somebody. And that never got reported in the media, which then frames how many people that come out for the next one in June. And so, I believe that probably the reporting of the last one had an impact on the left that turned up in this one as well. And then they will praise the left and say that they were great, you know, well-behaved. It's not the case. The left prevented the right doing what they had a lawful right to do.*
>
> (Commander K)

> *Some of the media reporting was very, very unbalanced. You look at the recent history around the EDL. Do they drink? Yes. Can they be disruptive? Yes. And can they use violence? Yes. But actually, it was often the left that are more violent, more disruptive. So, you do question some of the reporting, some of the behaviour.*
>
> (Commander L)

Finally, participants from further afield also experienced unjust responses in the events of 3rd June. Several Business participants described how their staff had been abused with *"colourful language and threatened"* by members of the public who had been disrupted by the march and counterdemonstration. Another described the unfairness for couples who had planned weddings at St George's Hall on the same day:

> *Legally, they can get married. And they've done all the natural thing they can do. They've registered their banns, they've got the registrar, it's all done. It's unfair. What we can't deal with is the unfairness of this. If it's unfair, are you going to stop it? If I want to have my wedding that day, what are you going to do? So, what's the priority? It's quite difficult to get your photos in the garden if there's people legging it around doing whatever they're doing. So, it could have been spoiled to some degree.*
>
> (Business C)

Throughout the case study there was a sense of just cause from different participants: the EDL believed they had the democratic right to march; Activists believed justice was on their side in stopping the EDL marching; and businesses accepted the rights of both to march and demonstrate even to the extent of it affecting their business, however they believed that neither should prevent them from operating. It was apparent that not all causes were achievable and certainly that the EDL and those opposing were not able to both fulfil their objective of marching or preventing a march at the same time. Nor was there any likelihood of both sides coming together for discussions and a compromising approach, due to perceptions of illegitimacy. Police participants therefore saw their role as mediator, attempting to balance the rights of each of the interested parties in a legal framework and under political and media scrutiny, whilst recognising that whatever decisions were made would be criticised to some degree. In addressing this challenge, police commanders selected a dialogical approach, attempting to engage with each of the interested parties and build up a level of trust, allowing each group to understand something of the competing issues and, consistent with procedural justice theory, build trust and confidence in the police decision-making process.

The police therefore sought to police the event by setting a strategy which entailed first identifying interested parties and then entering into dialogue with each. This approach allowed the police to keep all parties abreast of the situation but also assisted the police in understanding the driving force for each group and aided their decision-making in balancing competing rights. It became apparent in the case study that this approach had varying levels of success depending on the groups and the police approach. The next section maps this process.

Mapping the dialogue process

PLT were deployed by police commanders to engage in dialogue with demonstrators pre, during and post the EDL march. Commanders implemented a strategy based on engagement with those wishing to march and counterdemonstrate from the outset. A Bronze PLT was appointed who assessed the intelligence and information and *"pretty much vaguely decided that it was a left versus right protest."* Two teams of PLT were identified: one allocated to the EDL and one to *"the group on the left."* PLT were then tasked simply to engage pre-event with identified groups. A Commander explained the rationale:

> *What we definitely didn't want was having members of staff sent an email from the Force Resourcing Unit and turning up on the day with their refs [refreshments] bag, putting on their blue bibs with absolutely no input at all either on the background of the operation, who the groups are, what they look like, and without having tried some engagement with the group to give them some sort of legitimacy. Because, we didn't want to just have a blue bib meeting someone at Lime Street station as the doors of the train open, and there saying, "Hi! I'm your PLT for the day!" So, it's just not legitimate. It wouldn't be seen as being legitimate by the protest groups or the marching group. Or us as having been sincere at all in any way. So, that's what we really tried to do. Engage with them beforehand.*
>
> (Commander M)

However, the dialogical process exceeded simply engaging with the EDL and Activists: it was *"multifaceted,"* and involved engagement with all the interested parties identified. One of the central lines of communication between the police and key stakeholders was maintained through a series of planning meetings, with attendees from other emergency services, the local authority, Merseytravel, key locations such as St George's Hall and the theatres, and representatives from the Businesses Improvement District (BID). The meetings allowed an assessment of the impact of the march and counterdemonstration on each organisation, providing Commanders with an understanding of their thoughts. One Business participant shared their experiences:

> *We had a series of meetings with the police based on what the expectations were. The police were very thorough in terms of their sharing of intelligence as well. I thought that the social media management was very good. They were able to say, "Well, this is where we are up to." The last thing we went to was trial scenarios. So, if this happens, what is our situation?*
>
> (Business C)

In addition to PLT, other officers were used as conduits in dialogue, often where existing relationships assisted engagement: police commanders; community officers; operational planning officers; and public order tactical advisers. Some further engaged in wider areas, for example, one Commander described how they ran a series of their own *"stakeholder group"* meetings to engage with all businesses linked in to Lime Street train station. There was dialogue at a

180 Case study 2

strategic and chief executive level with key agencies such as emergency services and the local authority. Business stakeholders also described how they further engaged with others in their own organisations and areas of business. However, significantly, all dialogue can be mapped through the Silver (tactical) commander who maintained an overview of the engagement processes, ensured there were "*no mixed messages*" and "*sought the views*" of all those engaged in any way with the events surrounding the march.

An examination of the dialogue between the police and interested parties revealed that this was not simply one of police officers coming along to engage with the EDL and the counterdemonstrators on the day, rather it revealed a more detailed picture of communication undertaken prior to, during and post the EDL march. The complexity of the interaction and dialogue is presented pictorially in a *Dialogical Wheel* (see Figure 6.1). This wheel visually portrays

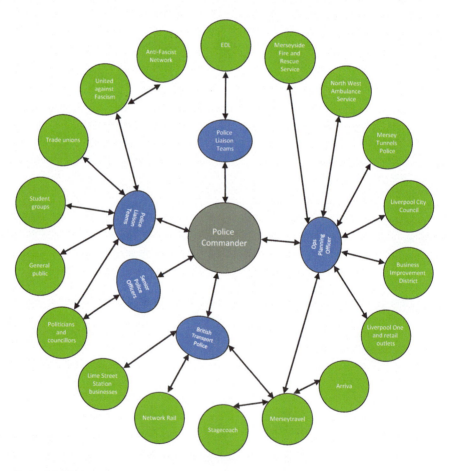

Figure 6.1 The policing of the EDL march dialogical wheel.

the numerous interested parties that were identified as being engaged in dialogue with the police during the research, and the officers who acted as liaisons between the police commander and the groups.

Political pressure

The policing of protests, noted della Porta and Reiter (1998), is heavily influenced by a political response. Wood (2014) observed that police legitimacy is a struggle within the political framework. This case study further evidenced the presence of political pressures in police decision-making. Further, many participants described coercion by local politicians in attempting to sway decision-making in facilitating the EDL march.

Section 6 of the Human Rights Act (1998) that "it is unlawful for a public authority to act in a way which is incompatible with a Convention right." Under the legislation, a public authority is one whose functions are of a public nature and this includes the police, other emergency services and the local authority. The Act places positive and negative obligations on public authorities, and Parliament (2009) provided examples of both for public authorities to secure human right, such as "not placing unnecessary obstacles in the way of individuals wishing to protest" and "facilitating counter protests or protests in the same geographical location."

Police commanders provided numerous examples of how they had worked to balance competing rights to protest and counterdemonstrate throughout the planning and policing of the EDL march. However, many police participants felt that some elected members and representatives of the local authority did not act in a way that complied with the positive and negative obligations, despite the unlawful nature of acting in a way incompatible with the Act. One Commander observed that there were "*some fairly big statements*" being made "*by politicians around their views around the EDL coming to Liverpool.*" Several Commanders described the local authority in Liverpool as "*one of the big players,*" being "*very left-leaning*" and "*very Labour dominated,*" and subsequently there were some "*very strong views from elected members*" voiced, which created "*real challenges.*"

Most participants believed that Liverpool City Mayor Joe Anderson, as the elected leader, created much of the political pressure experienced. Media coverage reported that Mayor Anderson was examining legal challenges to the Home Secretary's position on banning marches, and that he would "not let them march through the city centre ever again" (Thorp, 2017b). Police participants commented on how the mayor "*always has his own say,*" and one Commander opined that the mayor "*actively encouraged*" opposition to the march. Another Commander asserted:

> I think it's been quite public that the mayor, who is historically very well known as a left-wing activist, wanted to ban the march. We looked at the legislation, Section

13, and certainly the criteria weren't met. And, I think he knew that, and probably just wanted to be vocal within his peer group, probably, as far as I'm concerned. It was never achievable, or the grounds, the rationale, certainly weren't there to deliver upon that.

(Commander J)

Yet another Commander shared their views:

The mayor gets really strong left-wing backing, makes his views very clear and is very public about it, which really doesn't help any of our cause. I think, if I'm being honest, it's irresponsible. I don't think it shows him having any understanding of human rights, or the right to protest, or the right to have a view, unless it's his view. So, I have to say I personally, take away the fact that I'm a police officer, I'm not particularly impressed by his stance on all of that. Actually, he could save this city an awful lot of grief by simply giving the instruction, and they would listen to him, giving the instruction, "Allow this to happen, and we'll get rid of them." And then, they won't come back, hopefully. And I think if he took that sort of stance … And he could say, "I disagree with everything that they say." Like we all do. We all disagree with what they say. But there is a human right to this that he completely and utterly ignores, as far as I'm concerned. He probably stands up and says he fully believes in freedom of speech and freedom of expression. But, there's a hypocrisy around how he acts that out.

(Commander N)

Unsurprisingly, those wishing to march, saw opposition led by the mayor, and believed that there was a proactive approach to deliberately prevent their cause:

Liverpool Council, especially Joe Anderson, they didn't want us there, which they always do, they always have. And I will give you a prime example. The route, where we was going, where we was speaking, the pub we was using, the muster point, was put out on the Liverpool Echo. It was put out on the Liverpool Echo on Tuesday, Tuesday or Wednesday. And we don't release that information till late night Wednesday night, before the march. Now, that got put out. So, automatically, the left knew how to stop us. And they was quite well-planned, because they were coming from everywhere.

(EDL A)

Business participants also perceived a political drive to oppose the EDL led by the mayor. One Business participant described how "*the politicians that run the local authority*" provided contradicting views and support for differing marches, that "*the whole thing is much politicised*" and that Mayor Anderson "*doesn't understand the full implications*" in trying to ban the marches of groups who stood "*against the Labour regime.*" A Business participant opined that "*the Mayor of Liverpool was spouting off on Twitter about how he's tried to stop it*" and commented that "*it inflames things for me.*" Another described the "*political calls to put pressure on central government to give local authorities powers to ban such marches.*" Yet another observed:

> *It's fair to say the elected mayor went out to say he wants powers, and still does, powers to ban the marches, which I think is totally dangerous, from a personal point of view. But, yes, he wanted the powers to ban selective … I don't think he realises that if he uses the current legislation as it stands, if you ban a march or a protest, all of the marches and protests have got to be banned. So, I don't think he'd like it if the Santa Dash was caught up in this [laughs]. Well, they probably do understand the full implications, but they want more of their money's worth from the media, than the actual thing itself.*
>
> (Business D)

The political pressure was not limited to the mayor, however, and several participants described wider political pressures. A PLT suggested that the response from Liverpool City Council was different to the EDL march than it might have been for a trade union march: "*I think if Unite or Unison were to go somewhere, and be stopped from marching, there'd be hell to pay.*" A Business participant suggested that "*a lot of politicians*" were "*trigger-happy in sending Tweets out*" and getting "*a lot of mileage*" out of social media and local press, to "*build up their profile*" and "*strengthen their political standing.*" Activists were keen to identify the political support that they received on the day and noted that Liverpool Deputy Mayor Anne O'Byrne gave a speech on the plateau outside Lime Street station. One Activist described the political stance of Liverpool as a city as being significant in providing "*cohesion,*" and its perception as the "*last Bastion in terms of the left*" was what the EDL march sought to challenge.

The political pressure caused issues for Commanders in ongoing relationships with partners from the local authority. One Commander described the local authority as "*very problematic in terms of policing,*" and another described the pressures they felt from a local authority who were "*very keen not to have the event.*" Another Commander agreed and described the strong political view of not wanting the EDL in Liverpool to march and the difficulty they felt in "*trying to bring two political views together.*" The Commander however acknowledged the challenges faced by local authority representatives who liaised with the police:

> *I think they faced that dilemma of, "How do we support the policing as a partner agency, recognising our lawful requirement?" to "How do we not support having the EDL come here?" So, they were really torn between, "We know what we should do, and what's the right thing to do, but we've got a political mandate for a political view of the world which means we should do it that way." And I think that really made it very, very difficult for them. And we had to help them through that journey. And at times, that brought us into conflict.*
>
> (Commander L)

The police as the state?

This case study provided consideration regarding the role of the police as the state in protest events. Mansley (2014) suggested that the police are the embodiment of the state, and this view was supported by an Activist who observed:

> *People's perception are around that the police are the establishment, and they are there really just looking to arrest everyone who are maybe wanting to counter demonstrate.*
>
> (Activist A)

Several Commanders observed that "*the left are anti-establishment,*" and concurred that the police are perceived by some as the establishment: "*we have a crown on our hats, that's what we represent.*" However, despite perceptions, all police participants rebuffed the suggestion that the police represented the state in protest events such as the EDL march, and instead propounded that the police were "*independent.*" One Commander asserted that the police role was to "*protect everyone and allow everyone to have their say.*" Another explained:

> *We are a democracy, we are there to support democracy in this country, and we should allow those that are there their democratic aim to do that.*
>
> (Commander L)

Police liaison

Police liaison and the use of PLT is a relatively new tactic and there is limited research into the use of police officers in this role. The responsibilities of a PLT are clearly defined (College of Policing, 2018), and supported by a national training course (College of Policing, 2013), however, participants provided their own insights into the role. This section provides an evaluation of the tactic through the experiences of PLT and those engaging with them from all interested parties. Examination is provided of the role of PLT and observations regarding their selection and the use of PLT is analysed in their liaison pre, during and post the EDL march.

The role of a PLT and selecting appropriate officers

Despite it being a relatively new tactic, many police officers saw the role as an extension of community engagement, rooted in the tradition of community policing, with the communities being in communion in terms of ideologies rather than geographically based. PLT described how their experiences in community engagement or having a "*background as a neighbourhood officer in local policing*" assisted in them performing the role. Predominantly however those participating described the role of PLT in terms of the qualities they believed were required of an officer to undertake PLT work rather than the responsibilities of the role.

Consistent with Gorringe, Stott and Rosie (2012), good communications skills were identified by many as a key requirement. One Commander suggested that a PLT needed to be someone *"who have just got that knack of being able to engage with people, able to communicate with groups, and having a sensible head on them."* Another Commander offered:

> *I think the type of people that really suit it are people who are generally committed into engagement, who aren't doing PLT role for any other reason, like trying to gather evidence for showing that they are team working or partnership working or anything like that. People who can really understand and accept other people's views. They might not necessarily agree with them, but they are able to overlook that, really, and remain professional.*
>
> (Commander M)

A Commander suggested that PLT needed flexibility in performing a role which did not finish at the end of a shift, rather the *"communication lines"* were needed far beyond that. Other qualities identified were *"negotiation skills"*; *"being calm"*; *"being able to form relationships"*; and patience; *"being able to stand there and get nowhere and not become disheartened."* One Commander asserted that PLT needed to have the confidence to challenge decisions of Commanders, and *"explain why professionally you're unable to take part in a certain piece."* Similarly, a PLT provided an example of when they had *"challenge authority,"* by explaining to a senior officer during the event that *"evidence gathering isn't our role."* Maintaining impartiality was another quality identified by several. One PLT described how Activists had been handing out stickers to *"say no to hate crime,"* and when they refused to wear one was challenged by an *"anarchist."* The PLT recounted how they had explained that wearing one might suggest they were supporting the Activist group rather than the anti-hate crime cause *"and I can't be seen to be taking sides."*

Several Commanders described a specific process which was implemented to select PLT to liaise with right-wing and left-wing groups for *"consistency."* One Commander described how particular officers had been requested to work with the EDL *"because I know how well they can engage with people."* Another described a PLT selected because they had *"quite significant service"* and had *"proved the skills throughout their career, being good at engaging with people."* Aligning PLT to specific groups encouraged the fostering of relationships. It also allowed PLT to *"research"* the groups they were working with *"to get a grounding."* A PLT described how they had *"looked into what the EDL ideology was"* to *"get a background knowledge of what the group was that I was dealing with."*

However, despite Commanders advocating an alignment of PLT with specific groups, two PLT recounted experiences to the contrary. One explained that they had previously policed the *"right-wing"* but for this event liaised with the left, which they believed had the potential to compromise their position and for them to be perceived as an intelligence-gathering officer. Another PLT explained that they had previously liaised with left groups but for this event engaged with the EDL. They recalled recognising several anti-EDL on the day, and even had a confrontation with one of them, which they noted "*might come and bite me on the backside if I'm sent to do a left-wing protest now!*" They concluded:

> *I think if the force wants to develop relationships then we should be aligned to a group and should develop that relationship over time. Because that way, they develop a trust, and they are going to listen to you more.*
>
> (PLT L)

"Stockholm syndrome" and the role of PLT Bronze

PLT exhibited signs of identifying with those with whom they had liaised during this event, although predominately this was displayed through PLT questioning the fair manner in which their group had been treated. The bonds were evident more with those liaising with the EDL, who "*sympathised*" with the EDL, for example, where legislation such as "*Section 14 (of the Public Order Act, 1986) wasn't upheld,*" than with PLT liaising with Activists, who were not exposed to the same prolonged engagement pre-event with specific individuals.

The presence of "Stockholm syndrome" was less of a concern to Commanders for this event than it would have been for a long running police operation. However, it was still recognised as a potential issue. Commanders described how implementing a PLT Bronze addressed concerns regarding potential compromise and bridged the gap between PLT and the command structure (see Figure 6.2). This also advantageously allowed Commanders to have a "*one-step back view,*" prevented them favouring one group over another, and provided "*the wider picture, rather than getting too focussed on the relationship of one person.*" One Commander explained how having a PLT Bronze assisted them in maintaining impartiality in decision-making:

> *At one stage, I wanted to personally go and speak to the EDL, to make sure we weren't getting mixed messages. I was advised against it, around PLT protocols. And in hindsight, it's probably the right thing, because of that danger of becoming compromised.*
>
> (Commander J)

Dialogue pre-event

Most participants concurred with Gorringe, Stott and Rosie (2012) and Watson and Angell (2007) that pre-event dialogue with police and protesters was key in promoting police legitimacy and fairness. Further, consistent

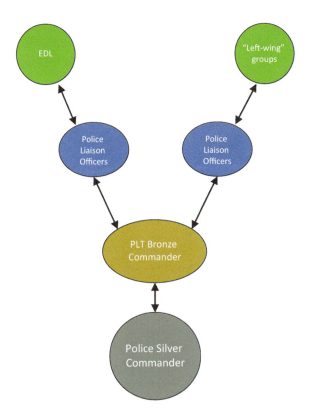

Figure 6.2 Bronze PLT command structure for the policing of the EDL march.

with Smith (2015), pre-event engagement was found to be the most important phase in the use of PLT. This research also extended the use of liaison to other interested parties such as local businesses and travel organisations affected by the EDL march and found that the pre-event engagement was most significant in managing expectations on all sides.

Commanders described their strategic approach based on encouraging pre-event dialogue with all interested parties. PLT described how they were tasked by Commanders to engage with different groups on both sides of the march and protest. Business participants described meetings they attended with the police and other interested parties to plan their own responses on the day of the march. The Activists interviewed in this case study had not engaged with the police pre-event. Nevertheless, when asked, they unanimously saw a benefit for them in engaging in dialogue with the police pre-event.

Dialogue with the EDL was instigated once the police received notification of their intention to march in Liverpool. PLT described how they initiated contact and arranged meetings with the EDL leaders. Police operational planning officers attended initial meetings alongside PLT, to address legal matters regarding advanced notice of a public procession (Section 11, Public Order Act 1986). Thereafter, all engagement with the EDL was undertaken by PLT. Regular dialogue facilitated boundary-setting, managed expectations from both sides, and built relationships. PLT were asked for advice by the march organisers, such as suitable coach parking options and together walked proposed routes. PLT working with the EDL described the pre-event engagement as "*key*," and one observed that the dialogue would not have been anywhere near as successful "*if we'd have turned up on the day and tried to have these relationships.*" The success may also be attributed to the fact that the EDL were also keen to engage pre-event for this march. Waddington (1994) and Joyce and Wain (2014) suggested that there was a focus on organisers "having to negotiate with the police." However, participants in this case study refuted this claim. An EDL member explained how they had provided six weeks' notice for the march, much longer than the legal requirement of six days, "*because the police have to manage those arrangements.*" This allowed the police to implement dialogue with the EDL through the blue tabarded PLT. They expounded:

> *We've worked with liaison now for years, ever since it was first put in place. We call them the Smurf's! The ones in the blue jackets. These days we liaise. So, therefore, we sit down and engage with liaison, and also engage with their silvers and golds controls and commands. So, basically, what's put on the table, it's a clear and precise assessment of what we want to do.*
>
> (EDL A)

Separate PLT were identified to liaise with the "*various left-wing protest groups,*" however, these PLT encountered an initial barrier in identifying the identity of the "*left*" and with whom to engage. Unlike the EDL, whose organisers were legally required to provide notification of a procession, participants explained that there was no requirement for such notification where a counterdemonstration without a procession was planned. This provided a challenge for the police in identifying potential interested parties and individuals willing to engage in dialogue. Commanders did become aware of a "*planning event*" in opposition to the EDL march being advertised on social media as "*an open meeting,*" and PLT were sent along in uniform "*to engage with people at that event if they would allow us in.*" Although the officers managed to have "*general conversations*" with some outside, they were refused entry to the meeting itself. One of the PLT observed that because it was an open meeting, they could easily have gained entry if they attended in "*civvies and not identified what we were there for,*" which would have meant they "*could have found out loads of information.*" However, the PLT opined that this would have prevented future engagement and encouraged mistrust if their identity as a police officer was later established.

Pre-event dialogue was also instigated between the police and interested parties and businesses affected by the planned march. This dialogue was both through formal police-chaired meetings to discuss responses and contingencies and through informal dialogue between Commanders and interested parties, often with the operational planning officer as a conduit. Some participants described this as *"business as usual,"* observing that the EDL march was one of many events in Liverpool where for them pre-engagement with the police was customary.

Dialogue during the event

For those engaging with the EDL, dialogue on the day of the march was an extension of the pre-event engagement. PLT described how they met those marching as agreed at Lime Street station and continued dialogue with both EDL organisers who they had met previously, as well as those attending to march, as the recognised liaison in blue tabards (Waddington, 2013). Participants from both police and EDL described how several issues were addressed through the liaison. A suitable pub was identified for the group, after several other pubs *"shut up shop when they realised it was the EDL."* Alternative car parking was recommended, after parking permission previously granted was removed on the day. Liaison also assisted in addressing opposition seeking to prevent the march. One PLT described how they engaged in dialogue on the day:

> *The EDL I think was starting to react slightly to the left as well, because they were starting to show off a little bit. They would do the usual, you know, the hands out, photograph opportunity, and all that. I think at that point the commander decided that we should start the march. So, I went into the crowd, spoke to [EDL], told them what was expected, that we were going to start the march as planned. As we were starting them, I didn't see it, but I believe some of the left had come in through an alley, through the back. And I don't know if they jeered at them, chanted at them, whatever, but anyway, the EDL had charged down the street in the opposite direction to the march. So, we ran after them, started getting into the crowd, started telling them all to get back. Told [EDL] to tell everyone, to tell the stewards and everything. Unfortunately, because they were riled, it took quite a while to get them all to turn around and come back. I was just trying to say to them, you know, "You want your march, get going!" sort of thing.*
>
> (PLT L)

The PLT described how they continued in dialogue despite growing hostilities, as external factors such as the warm weather and alcohol consumed by the EDL began to exacerbate the situation:

> *They were getting quite angry, to say the least. So, we were having to negotiate with individuals, because you'd have different flashpoints as different individuals were getting at the end of their tether. And, you were just saying, "You are going*

to march, but have just got to be patient." Eventually, the left was moved off, and we did a march out ... From what I remember, we were supposed to turn right, but I think we turned left. And, that part was a contention as well, because they were like, "We can't be moved from the path," in their view. But, again, I just had to negotiate with them, saying, "But, you want to march, and the way you've got to march is now, you know, dictated to how we do it, you know, the best way for your safety." Which, to be honest, they did have as well.

(PLT L)

There was a short period during the day where liaison between the PLT and the EDL was suspended when the PLT were withdrawn by Commanders. PLT explained that they were removed because they were not wearing protective equipment and missiles were being thrown at the EDL, some of which hit the PLT. Dialogue was maintained through mobile phone contact during this time. The withdrawal was not a surprise to the EDL. A PLT described how an EDL organiser had discussed their removal: "*He said that he knows that it's gone wrong when he sees all the blue bibs suddenly disappear.*" However, another PLT regaled that the EDL "*weren't happy the fact that they were basically corralled, people were throwing stuff at them and nothing was getting done about it.*" The PLT were reinstated inside the EDL ranks a short while later and reported that "*going back in didn't appear to change the relationship at all.*" However, the PLT explained that the implication was that it "*took quite a while*" for them to relocate the main event organisers with whom they had spent so much time in dialogue prior to and during the event.

Despite having limited success in liaison with "*left-wing*" groups pre-event, the nominated PLT continued to seek engagement on the day. However, having not had pre-engagement, PLT "*didn't know who to look out for, that familiar face as a PLT that people would be happy to come up to and speak to or be seen being spoken to.*" However, PLT did describe numerous proactive conversations with individuals and leaders of groups within the "*left-wing*" (Drury and Reicher, 2000). An Activist participant also described the positive interaction they had on the day with a PLT, despite not having engaged pre-event.

Dialogue with other interested parties who had engaged pre-event also continued during the event. Some partner agencies, such as BTP and the local authority, were present in the police command centre. Commanders also described how liaison was maintained with the local community through "*neighbourhood Inspectors*" to deliver their "*community confidence plan,*" and interested parties such as St George's Hall were "*kept aware of what was going on*" through liaison via operational planners on behalf of the police Commander.

Dialogue post-event

Authorised Professional Practice advocates maintaining post-event dialogue with protesters though PLT (College of Policing, 2018) and this cyclical nature of dialogue (della Porta and Reiter, 1998) was evident in this study. Commanders described how PLT were tasked "*to go back to the EDL and effectively debrief*" events, even though the EDL had not been allowed to march their planned route. PLT described how they met up with EDL members and that there was a mutual desire to learn from their experiences. An EDL member shared their observations:

> *I had a wash up meeting with [PLT], which I actually thought was very good, because that's the first one I've ever experienced. So that was well taken, actually, because they know what went wrong, and they are turning round to me and saying, "Well, look, you tell us what went wrong in your view."*
>
> (EDL A)

In contrast, no post-event engagement occurred with the "*left.*" Despite limited pre-event engagement, several voiced that failing to engage post-event was an opportunity lost. One Commander explained:

> *If I'm honest, there hasn't been any attempts to go and engage with the left after the event, which could have some worth to it. I mean, those officers, the PLTs, they didn't walk around for a 10-hour day and not speak to anyone. They spoke to people no doubt throughout that day. Are they a leader of the left? Are they an organiser? No, they might not be. But they are still actors within that side of the group. But it is a missed opportunity if we don't go in after events to speak to certain actors and role players within each group.*
>
> (Commander M)

Post-event debriefs were also held with other key groups and agencies that had engaged with the police pre-event. Commanders and Business participants described these as "*really helpful, getting people together,*" which allowed organisations to "*see what we could have done better*" and assisted to "*almost prepare for what would you do differently next time.*"

Human rights

Human rights, and in particular the rights to freedom of expression and the right to freedom of peaceful assembly (Articles 10 and 11 of the Human Rights Act (HRA), 1998) were central to the case study with EDL members wishing to march and those seeking to stop the march equally passionate about exercising their own rights. Within existing literature, the focus is invariably on the police-protester relationship and relates to a balance between the rights of those protesting and the protection of order undertaken by the police (for example, Reiner, 1998; Mansley, 2014). However, an examination of the EDL case study demonstrated that such a view is too simplistic and instead provided evidence that there were many competing rights in play; those wanting to march; those wanting to stop the march; those wanting to carry on with normal life; and numerous organisations, including the police for whom Section 6 of the HRA brought legal obligations as public authorities. The following section examines human rights implications and the challenge of balancing competing rights.

Human rights implications

The events of 3rd June were initiated by the desire for the EDL to march through Liverpool and exercise their rights under Articles 9, 10 and 11 of the HRA in a city where they perceived that this was not accepted. An EDL member explained:

> *We have the right to free speech, in a democratic society. And movement through the city, which is also exercising our right to free speech in a democratic country.*
> (EDL A)

As Neyroud and Beckley (2001) and Mead (2010) identified, the police had a duty to facilitate such political marches, being cognisant of legislation and case law. Police participants in this case study recognised the rights of the EDL to march, having "*given us due notice.*" One Commander explained:

> *Unless the Home Secretary sees fit to ban this march, and then subsequent marches, then the police have got a positive duty to facilitate people wishing to express their views.*
> (Commander O)

However, there was also a recognition of the same qualified human rights being enacted for those opposing the march. One Commander summarised that "*there is the two protest groups, whose rights effectively mirror each other.*" Activists saw these rights as enabling their protest which had the intention of stopping the march. There was therefore immediate conflict as to which side had primacy in their exercising of Articles 9, 10 and 11 (HRA, 1998). One Activist opined that because the intentions of the EDL were "*emotive*" in relation to some of their actions, their right to march should be taken away. They concluded:

> *There's consequences for their actions and what they brought to my city on that day. And part of that consequence was that they were met with a counter demonstration that basically stopped their march.*
> (Activist A)

Another Activist was more accepting of the EDL's right to march, however believed that they held the moral high ground in attempting to stop a group from marching in the city who they believed had an illegitimate cause. They concluded:

> *There's an argument that, whether you like it or not, they have been given permission to demonstrate. So, have we got the right to stop them? Technically, probably not. Have we got the moral obligation to stop them? 100%!*
>
> (Activist B)

However, this event did not solely affect those wishing to march or counterprotest as there were other interested parties who had an opinion on the human rights enacted. Despite the strong feeling of opposition to the EDL march, the business participants in this case study unanimously accepted that the EDL had a right to march in Liverpool, despite potential issues that the march might cause their organisations. Participants explained that marches and processions regularly occurred in the city and all were likely to cause some disruption to businesses. The difference between those marches and the EDL march in 2017 was the strength of the opposition and that there were "*people who want to stop it from even starting.*" A Business participant explained:

> *It's a tricky one, because you always got to the point, 'Oh, why are we putting it on? Why are we doing it in the first place? We know there's going to be issues, we know there's going to be trouble, why are we doing it?' But they are a legitimate organisation. It was done correctly. They asked can they march. And then we couldn't vouch for who's going to turn up on the far left side. But it was a legitimate march, and they've got the right to march.*
>
> (Business C)

Another agreed:

> *The left had thrown the challenge there to some extent by saying, 'We don't want these people in our city.' And yet, ironically, like other protests and marches, the EDL actually followed the procedures. They'd given notice. They'd actually engaged. They'd said they were peaceful. And it was the potential backlash from the anti-protesters that caused the concern, which is ironic really.*
>
> (Business D)

There were also competing human rights alongside Articles 9, 10 and 11 of the HRA 1998 identified by participants that did impact on businesses: the right for people to enjoy their property (Article 1 of Protocol 1, HRA, 1998); and the right to family and private life (Article 8, HRA, 1998). Business participants explained that the planned march and counterprotest had an impact on "*the visitor economy,*" to travellers and to those wanting to shop or attend local museums and theatres. Several also identified the right to marriage (Article 12,

HRA, 1998) as being impacted upon during the event. One Business participant explained:

> We had weddings. St George's Hall does a thousand weddings a year. I think we had eight weddings that day from what I recall. So, if you're getting married it doesn't matter if that march is on, this is the girl's memory for life. So, we had a real duty of care for them.
>
> (Business C)

Police participants also described the human rights pertaining to their decision-making in facilitating an EDL march and simultaneous counterprotest. Despite recognising the rights to march, to oppose and to go about daily business, police officers observed that all were qualified rights. Several Commanders explained that their overarching aim in policing the march was the absolute right to life (Article 2, HRA, 1998) particularly considering violence that had been encountered in previous contentious marches in Liverpool. One summarised:

> *The overarching right for me of course is Article 2, and I will always address that in terms of taking all feasible operational steps to protect life. And, for me, that goes right down to even the steps that we will take that may lead consequentially to a use of force.*
>
> (Commander P)

Business participants concurred and explained that their "*main concern as a business*" was "*the safety of staff and our customers*" and that they did not want "*any of our staff to be concerned or put anyone at risk*," because of the march and counterdemonstration.

Balancing human rights

The balancing of the right to protest with maintaining order has been recognised as a difficult, challenging and unenviable task for the police (della Porta, Peterson and Reiter, 2006; Donald, Gordon, and Leach, 2012; Gravelle and Rogers, 2011). All Commanders in this study assented and described the difficult challenges they encountered in facilitating the EDL march whilst fulfilling their "*positive obligation*" to ensure that "*general members of the public who aren't actively engaged in the protests, are safe*," and "*don't become harmed.*" One Commander explained how they balanced the qualified right to peaceful protest (Articles 9, 10 and 11, HRA, 1998) with the absolute right to life:

> *I am going to facilitate your 9, 10 and 11. They are not absolute. I will balance your 9, 10 and 11 rights but at all times that will be held against the candle of Article 2, and not just your basic the right to life, but those nuanced ones about taking reasonable operational steps to protect life, by planning to minimise recourse to the use of force.*
>
> (Commander P)

However, the most dominant theme in considering human rights in the policing of the EDL march was not a decision between the facilitating protest and maintaining order, rather the challenge of balancing the competing rights of all those affected by the march. The greatest balancing act for the Commanders was to be found in allowing the EDL to peacefully march and protest whilst also allowing the "*left*" to protest in opposition and still allow the general public to go about their daily life with minimum disruption. One Commander observed that although there was guidance in how rights should be balanced, "*it is a challenge in terms of how I should turn that into a practical reality.*" The nub of the challenge was that the EDL wished to march through Liverpool and those opposing fundamentally stated "*they will not march in this city.*" It was therefore impossible for both sides to be appeased and ultimately the EDL march was curtailed on the day. Despite making the decision to direct the EDL march back to Lime Street station, several Commanders "*felt as though we'd failed because we hadn't got that march through.*" One explained that this was not about sides, rather about upholding their right to march. A second said that it was about "*fairness,*" having the same approach for all groups irrespective of their identity. A third observed:

> *I don't think that we were successful at all. Because, we didn't balance the rights of both. Because the rights of the EDL weren't fulfilled. The rights of the left were. Because, they were protesting against, you know, 'That's not going to happen.' And so, their protest in the end outweighed the EDL. And, it's not a case of leaning to one of them over the other. That's not the case at all. We simply couldn't facilitate the right-wing's human rights. Which is disappointing, I think. On two levels for me. One is as a police officer, that's what I signed up to do, to facilitate that sort of stuff. But two, because for Merseyside, they almost are blind to the fact that there is a potential that they may well come back in bigger numbers, they may not, but you will be concerned as to how they would come back.*
> (Commander N)

A further Commander shared their opinions:

> *I feel quite uncomfortable about the march. Let me put it in a different context. Imagine it was the gay community marching for equal marriage, and we didn't let that march finish. How that would be perceived by that community and by a lot of the country? It would be quite uncomfortable, I think, and there would be questions to be answered. In this case though, because they are views that the majority oppose, maybe it feels a bit more easier to justify that this march can't go ahead. But I was still very uncomfortable that we could not facilitate them doing their route.*
> (Commander K)

One Commander explained the challenge was exacerbated when "*some of the left were there just to cause issues.*" Another voiced that although they did not agree with the EDL's principles, they found it "*quite shocking*" that those opposing were "*so unwilling to allow anyone with a different thought to them in this city.*" A further Commander explained that having so many resources drawn into policing the EDL march in the city centre provided a further challenge of maintaining core policing duties with reduced resources across the rest of Merseyside, and further afield where other police forces had provided officers in support of Merseyside Police.

Business participants accepted that there was a balance to be had in allowing everyone to exercise their rights, and many empathised with the police in their role as arbitrators. One accepted that it was "*really hard to get that balance,*" identifying "*where you draw the line,*" and "*what's acceptable or what's not, what would be tolerated, and what wouldn't.*" Another said that they found it "*hard that you hear that there is police shortages,*" particularly considering that the march occurred a short time after the Manchester bombing which required resources to protect and investigate, that so many officers should be needed to police the march and counterdemonstration. One Business participant thought that "*everybody on the day would say their rights were broken in some way.*" Many Business participants not only accepted there needed to be a balance, but actively assisted the police in ensuring the balance was met as far as they could. One Business participant described their role as "*partners in the planning process,*" and once the police decision to facilitate the march and counterdemonstration was made, "*our job was just to try and get the march through and gone, and get it done in as safe a manner as possible.*" Another participant from the travel sector agreed and noted that their customers were treated fairly, irrespective of whether they wanted to march or demonstrate. They observed:

> *To be honest, we will have probably carried people from both sides into town, and we will have probably taken both sides home! And that is our duty as well.*
> (Business H)

However, not all partners were perceived by police Commanders to be as impartial in their approach or supportive of a facilitative approach. Some members of the local authority were actively resistant to the notion of the EDL marching in Liverpool, and these views were voiced in multi-agency planning meetings chaired by police Commanders, despite their positive and negative obligations. Commanders explained:

> *Liverpool City Council saw a view on it, which was an interesting one, as a public organisation. As a public authority, they're there to protect the human rights. Their view was to make it a hostile environment for the right to operate. Which is interesting, because is that really what we want? We don't want to make it difficult for people. That isn't our job. If communities want to make it difficult, then they will do so. But we should be independent, as should the council. Because, there will be many people within the city who hold the same views as the EDL, and maybe they're not marching, but they will hold a view, or a similar view, or a diluted view,*

who would be offended to think that actually the authorities were determining which groups could have a protest. And I don't think it really shows a balancing of 9, 10 and 11 in particular. I wasn't comfortable with that sort of positioning.

(Commander K)

The real challenge for me was this was the first time I had publicly seen, publicly and within partner agencies, publicly seen some of the key stakeholders saying that they didn't want to facilitate the protest. In fact, there was a comment made that "facilitation does not mean making it easy for people to come to the city and protest." And that "we wanted to make it as awkward for them as we could, so they wouldn't come back." I have to tell you from me that fundamentally goes against the planning of this from a human rights perspective.

(Commander P)

Participants from all groups represented in this case study did not see the role of the police as in opposition to either the EDL or the counterprotest group, rather all located the police at the centre of balancing the human rights of *all* interested parties. Participants provided several examples to support the notion of the police being in the middle of facilitating and balancing the rights of everybody. One Activist described how the police tried to intervene when heated exchanges began between the EDL and counterdemonstrators:

It was the police trying to separate the two groups, and that's where it always gets the heated part then, and the police were in the middle, getting it from both sides.

(Activist B)

An Activist described it as "*like a sandwich*" and thought that "*the police are damned if they do and are damned if they don't.*" Another described the scenario as having three elements: "*you've got us as activists, you've got the police, and then you've got the EDL or fascists*" and observed that the "*police are sort of in the middle.*" A Business participant describing their liaison that "*the police were caught in the middle and I think that's kind of key to this.*" A Commander concurred:

I think everybody would say that their rights have been impacted on. Whatever they want to do on that day, they have a problem with. And, we're stuck right in the middle. We are damned if we do, damned if we don't.

(Commander O)

Another Commander explained the precarious nature of the balancing act:

This balancing, this isn't all on one plane. You're trying to balance a plate on top of a spike, and keep it level all the way across. Because it dips at one side, and then it goes up at the other. And then you're all over the place, aren't you?

(Commander K)

One PLT summarised how they perceived the role of the police:

> *Unfortunately, we're ... I was going to say "piggies in the middle" then, but [laughs] not a good example! We are stuck in the middle, aren't we, here. And, while we're doing a job for EDL, or [PLT] was doing it for the left-wing, still our primary focus is we're police officers. And it's doing our job as police officers.*
>
> (PLT M)

A dialogical approach

From the outset, police Commanders sought to utilise a tactical approach centred on dialogue and negotiation with as many interested parties as possible. This following section examines the process that was implemented by Commanders in such approach. Consideration is given to the value of having a designated point of contact within the police with whom to engage, how relationships were developed and an analysis is made of the communication and dialogue. Finally, it is recognised that not all groups and interested parties engaged in dialogue with the police pre and during the event and an examination is made of the reason why some did not or would not engage with the police.

A point of contact

Having access to police decision-makers through officers designated as points of contact was very beneficial for those that engaged with the police. For the EDL, the police point of contact was designated once they provided notice to march, with PLT appointed to facilitate all liaison after an initial meeting. An EDL member described PLT as "*a communication point,*" and explained how this gave them "*100% access.*" They remarked that meeting their PLT beforehand, allowed them to "*put a face to a name,*" and this assisted greatly on the day of the march, as they "*constantly engaged.*"

PLT who had liaised with the EDL also advocated having a point of contact within the EDL. One PLT described how having an "*in*" provided "*group acceptance*" for them in the eyes of the EDL, and this provided evidence of in-group and out-group interaction consistent with the Elaborated Social Identity Model (ESIM) (for example, Drury and Reicher, 2000). They expanded:

> *Because I've got a dialogue with one person, it filters out, and everyone starts approaching me to ask questions, or help with problems or gripes or whatever. So, it was because I'd had dialogue with that one person, who everyone looked to as the lead of that group.*
>
> (PLT L)

An EDL member highly praised the engagement they had received in Merseyside, however commented that they had experienced "*different behaviours from different police in different areas we go to."* They recommended having a *"central point of contact"* to provide a consistent approach and encourage relationship building and trust.

A point of contact was also commended by Business participants, although many observed that there was already regularly liaison in place for normal business, and this was an ongoing process. Several described how they had subsequently become the police point of contact for their own organisations, providing updates internally to staff.

Relationships

Redekop and Paré (2010) advocated relationship building between protesters and police to ensure interests were mutually affected. Hinds and Murphy (2007) observed that relationships assisted in ensuring fair processes were implemented. Similarly, many participants in this case study noted that the development of relationships between the police and interested parties was *"fundamental"* to the dialogical process.

Business participants described their existing relationships with other agencies including the police as maintained through regular communication. One described it as *"a special relationship"* between *"all agencies, but particularly with our roles, between ourselves and the police,"* which was described as different to many other cities in the UK, where the relationship was not as strong. Another Business participant also singled out unique relationships which they suggested had been developing *"in Liverpool from at least 2008, the Capital of Culture year."* A further Business participant described specifically the *"long-standing relationship"* they had professionally with one of the police Commanders, which engendered *"confidence"* as they *"seem to understand the bigger picture."* Business participants described the relationships as *"two-way,"* enabling cooperative working, providing *"reassurance"* within businesses and engendering *"trust"* even when there was disagreement:

> *The communication is very organic, and very two-way. And, because I've worked so many marches and protests, it's quite comfortable as well. Although, I'll be honest with you, there's been occasions where it hasn't been as comfortable as that, because there's been times were some have been at loggerheads.*
>
> (Business D)

PLT described their role as being relationship-based, where early dialogue was essential and post-event engagement further maintained relationships. PLT that had struggled to establish relationships pre-event had still been able to initiate some relationships on the day with individuals who were taking active parts in leading the counterdemonstration. However, there was a feeling that had the PLT been empowered by Commanders to foster future relationships on the day, they would have been able to share contact details and arrange for post-event dialogue, which would have encouraged relationships for future events. There was a strong emphasis by participants on investment and continuity in relationships. Some acknowledging that relationships were made with *"people who are quite difficult to build relationships with"* or someone *"who they might not normally build relationships with in their personal or professional lives."* A Commander saw real value in aligning PLT to *"keep those same relationships with certain groups going."* A PLT shared:

> There is a longevity in this. It's about relationships. I've done it today. I've not spoken to somebody since February, but there's a group now coming to protest at a retail premises, so it's getting back in touch with them. And, I think things probably can then be done a lot smoother and simpler rather than that awkwardness if you've not done that in the first place. So, I think it's broken down a lot of barriers.
> (PLT N)

Communication and dialogue

Waddington, Jones and Critcher (1989) advocated analysis at an interactional level between police and protesters. Bourne (2011) further asserted that the right to peaceful protest was intrinsically communicative. Participants in this case study described how communication and dialogue between the police and interested parties was a significant element of the policing of the EDL march.

The communication between the police and the EDL was described by participants as *"really positive,"* *"of great benefit"* and *"pretty strong."* One Commander suggested that having the dialogue meant that those engaging *"then gave us the consent to be policed even in a public order scenario."* An EDL member explained that the two-way dialogue with the police allowed them to express their views and provided a *"full understanding"* for both parties. Police Commanders described the EDL as being *"really forthcoming"* and *"happy"* to talk *"very openly and candidly"* throughout the whole process, which helped to *"manage their expectations."* One PLT described how when the march was stopped by the opposition, the EDL decided to respond with their own *"sit-down protest."* The EDL were incensed, and were even prepared to be arrested if necessary, however the PLT described how through dialogue with the EDL leaders the situation was averted. Another PLT explained that post-event dialogue was essential for PLT to be effective: *"we need that dialogue after it as well, and to keep it going ... you need that building up between the two parties."*

Despite limited pre-event engagement with Activists, dialogue did occur with police officers on the day of the march. Some of this was varied, and one Activist observed that some of the communication of officers from external police forces with counterdemonstrators *"was quite heavy-handed,"* which exacerbated the situation. Contrastingly, the Activist described another officer who had been present whilst the crowd *"began to push"*:

> This police officer was very engaging, very personable, was making some jokes about the situation, but actually wanted to have some dialogue that wasn't hostile. So,

wasn't like you know being authoritarian and what have you. And there seemed to be a difference. And I think, I don't know whether that's a different in forces, I don't know whether it was because of the brief that some were given different to others. Because there was a collective of police officers there.

(Activist A)

Commanders reiterated that *all* police officers were encouraged to communicate, not just designated PLT in blue tabards. Several Commanders voiced concerns that officers did not readily engage in dialogue at such events as they would in normal policing, concerned that they would "*say the wrong thing.*" One Commander opined:

Culturally, our police officers in those situations will not speak to people. They're frightened to death. The Bobbies are frightened to death. They won't speak to people; they won't challenge people; they won't arrest people; they are terrified. And they won't do their job. And that's our challenge.

(Commander O)

Dialogue was also evident between the police and other interested parties, which Commanders suggested "*helped in people acknowledging the rights of others,*" provided "*assurances*" and allowed others to see "*the benefits for them on the day.*" A Business participant described dialogue with the police as "*very important.*" Another was reassured by knowing that the police were in dialogue with the march organisers:

The advantage for the police was the side that was going to communicate with them and have some dialogue, so that they knew what to expect. And, I thought that was an advantage over previous times when the police have just been reacting spontaneously to things. I think you have got to have more respect for people organising a march that they want to do with the support of the police.

(Business E)

Non-engagement

Those intent on protest do not always engage in effective dialogue with the police pre or during events. Jackson, Gilmore and Monk (2019) argued that the lack of engagement was due to a lack of police commitment to meaningful dialogue, despite the attempts of protesters to negotiate. This case study sought to identify reasons why there were barriers to engagement for some groups.

It was evident from all police participants that there was a universally held belief that "*left-wing*" groups either did not or would not engage with the police. PLT described how they had tried to engage without success pre-event and police officers described how anti-EDL protesters "*turned their backs*" on them, "*ignored them when they speak to them*" and "*did not respond to any kind of engagement*" from PLT.

Commanders identified certain groups they claimed "*would not*" engage, such as the Antifa, and provided varied reasons why. One Commander described non-engagement as "*a historical issue locally.*" Another suggested that this was a global tactic of anti-fascist groups refusing to engage with authority: "*and they'll say, 'I've got nothing to gain from engagement.'*" A Commander suggested that being "*anti-establishment,*" they will not engage with the police who they believe have "*no legitimate purpose.*" A further Commander suggested that having no identified leaders for the left made engagement "*more difficult.*" Another Commander agreed:

> *The left didn't want to engage so as to make it more difficult for us to identify who was involved, or potentially be able to take more proactive action, subsequent reactive action, around incidents arising.*
>
> (Commander J)

A PLT suggested that the left had "*no motive for engaging,*" having no "*natural enemies*" in Merseyside, so knew they would not be outnumbered. A Commander believed that "*there was nothing to gain*" for the left from police engagement as "*they got what they wanted anyway, which was to stop that march.*" Another agreed:

> *Is there a benefit for them to engage with us? I would say at this point in time, there isn't, I guess, because they are winning. So, they could come out in numbers. They can cause us lots of issues. They can disrupt our operation very easily ... Through our dialogue, we set the tone with the right-wing. We've got no dialogue with the left-wing, because they will not talk to us. So, we have to set the tone in a slightly different way, and that is by being proactive on the day.*
>
> (Commander N)

However, several participants, although recognising that the left were "*really difficult*" to engage with pre-event, on reflection believed that the police might have been more successful if they had been more proactive. A PLT suggested that the police may have approached "*some specific groups, such as students, Unison, Unite*" to engage pre-event, which had not occurred. A Commander concurred, suggesting that they police might have "*done more*" in engaging with "*the student population,*" and the "*more general left-leaning population.*" They summarised that even if it was a challenge:

> *I still think you should try, and if you don't get it, you should try again. You shouldn't just give up, because, it also comes back to that "no secrets" approach, which is, telling people what you're going to do, and why you going to do it.*
>
> (Commander L)

Another Commander agreed that more might have been done and opined that it was "*too simple just to say the left*" or categorising them as "*the ones who wear the black colours, cover their faces, and don't want to talk to us*" as this did not recognise the group dynamics. The Commander suggested that some of their attempts to engage with the more difficult to reach groups was "*effectively, just almost like ticking a box*" because it was "*hard work*" engaging with the left with a lot of effort for little reward, unlike the productive engagement that was reaped through dialogue with the EDL. The Commander provided a provided a frank assessment of the police attempts to engage with those opposing:

I think they're suspicious, and they've told us they are suspicious of us. They think we are just there to gather intelligence. And they're probably suspicious of us because they haven't built a relationship as well. You know, they've just had the odd people stood in for operations. They've probably seen those same PLT doing PSU work before, things like that, probably against them, policing them in other ways. And it just doesn't build any legitimacy, really. And we really only want to go and talk to them when it's time for protest, i.e. three days before a protest, "Oh, low and behold, I'm getting a call from a PLT wanting to come and talk to me. Why don't they want to come and talk to me before that?" So, I can totally understand their side of things. I think there's so much benefit in putting a lot of energy into this, particularly with the groups that are difficult to engage with. And, a willingness not to accept that they're not going to engage, and just to keep trying. It's just hard work. And I don't think we just not do something just because it's hard work, which I think is all it is. I think it is possible. There'll always be people or groups that we cannot get through to. But I think we have just got to change the culture of maybe just accepting that some groups are able to engage in this.

(Commander M)

A PLT described not contacting left groups and building relationships through dialogue as a "*missed opportunity*" and observed that those opposed to the EDL would undoubtedly protest against other groups in the future. The PLT observed that building a relationship would "*pay dividends, for themselves for facilitating the protest, and ourselves.*" A Commander agreed that engagement would have benefited the left as well:

We'd potentially been able to, for argument's sake, given them two protest sites along the route, versus one that we ended up enforcing, or trying to enforce.

(Commander J)

However, most telling was the response of Activist participants, none of whom had engaged in dialogue with the police prior to the EDL march. Despite this fact, those that were interviewed in this case study stated that they would have engaged with the police pre-event, had they or their group been approached. Activists were from groups who were actively campaigning as a part of the

UAF network prior to the event and as such, mainstream groups and trade unions were easily identified. The fact that they had not been approached by the police pre-event not only prevented building up a rapport, it provided for them a presumption that the police were only there *"to protect the EDL,"* which *"created bad feeling."* Activist participants stated that establishing engagement required persistence from the police, *"not a tick box to say, 'we went once, and we tried.'"* It needed to be a *"long-term"* and *"sustainable"* process rather than a *"quick fix"* and *"tokenism."* The feeling was that the police had not fully committed to harbouring links through dialogue with the left-leaning groups. Activists voiced a desire to still build a dialogical relationship with the police event at the time of interview, after the event and with no pending protest, and observed that they would be more than happy for the police to contact them and discuss their aims and objectives. Activists recommended that this dialogue should also be through liaison officers, *"not the top brass,"* but someone at the *"grassroots"* who *"through education and awareness,"* can bring groups together and *"build trust."*

It would therefore appear that although steps had been made in building relationships, there is an ongoing process that is required to build trust and facilitate engagement with all parties and the police. Sinek (2009) observed that "Trust is not a checklist. Fulfilling all your responsibilities does not create trust. Trust is a feeling, not a rational experience." Building such trust, Sinek continues, is earned though communication and sharing values. Such trust was clear in some of the relationships fostered between police and interested parties in this case study. Some relationships, such as those with partner agencies, where police and partners regularly meet for a variety of events and scenarios, were honed and based on longevity and consistency. Some, such as with the EDL, were developed over a short period of time prior to the march, since the EDL clearly had need of police support. However, some relationships, and in particular those with the left, were lacking and this was recognised by police and Activist participants alike. Activists observed that they would have been keen to engage with the police if they had been asked. Police participants recognised that this was an area that they could have greatly improved in. This case study identifies an opportunity for the police to engage with groups they traditionally see as hard to reach. However, the police are encumbered with creating long-term relationships with such groups if they wish to engage irrespective of the presence or otherwise of impending protests. Jackson, Gilmore and Monk (2019) argued that protesters were not included as interested parties in delivering a police gold strategy, and therefore not on an equal footing to other groups. It is evident therefore that the police should consider how all interested parties have representation to the police strategic decision-makers. In this case study, neither the EDL nor those opposing had representatives that attended police planning meetings in person. However, access was provided to police commanders through engagement with designated PLT, although notification of the availability of this communication channel varied. It is suggested that, to encourage all to engage, the police need to be clearer as to access through PLT to decision-makers and need to emphasise that liaison does bring voice and ultimately an ability to influence the gold strategy.

As with the badger cull, Commanders in this case study demonstrated the deployment of different approaches to the policing of the EDL march and counterdemonstrations. The use of PLT to engage pre, during and post the march with EDL leaders and with those wishing to engage on the day demonstrated an approach of strategic facilitation (Gorringe et al., 2012). Such an approach was also evident where PLT were deployed during the event to engage with those opposed to the cull. However, there were also strategic incapacitation approaches deployed by police commander, particularly in engaging pre-event with counterdemonstrator groups. In addition, when the march met opposition on Lime Street, the police commanders, it can be argued, used an approach more akin to escalated force, where the potential for police use of force was increased, and a negotiated management approach with EDL leaders where a line in the sand prevented the continuation of the march.

Conclusion

This case study, examining the policing of the EDL march in Liverpool in 2017, provided an insight into the experiences of those who occupied significant roles in event: police commanders; PLT; EDL members; activists involved in counterdemonstrations; local authority members; and those wishing to maintain normality in going about their daily business.

This chapter has provided analysis at the political/ideological, cultural and contextual levels (Flashpoints Model) which provided a grounding for understanding the history of right-wing marches in Liverpool, the prior experiences of participants and their concerns of potential conflict and disorder with the impending EDL march. A structural analysis (Flashpoints Model) of those opposing the EDL revealed that the counterdemonstrators were not a homogeneous group rather consisted of sub-groups (ESIM), depicted pictorially through the production of a Dialogical Wheel. A political analysis also revealed challenges at local and national levels, but also evidenced how ongoing relationships and dialogue with partners diffused potential conflict. Where dialogue was evident, elements of self-policing was identified in protesters and other interested parties.

Trust and relationship building were prominent themes that emerged from the data and this research argues that the findings were consistent with a procedural justice approach. Participants explained how professional relationships developed between the EDL leaders and the police, eliciting trust on both sides, with an investment in pre-event engagement identified as key in the trust-building process. However, lack of engagement was also evident with sparse pre-event dialogue between the police and activists.

Through the evidence presented in this case study, this research argues that a dialogical approach allowed the police to hear the voice of those with whom they engaged, promoting and developing relationship building and trust. Such dialogue allowed the police to remain as *"piggies in the middle"* in balancing the human rights of all those engaged in, opposing or affected by the EDL march. This case study also identified challenges that the police faced in identifying, locating and engaging with counterdemonstrating groups. This research argues however that if the police wish to implement a procedural justice approach to such events, they need to engage with all interested parties and seek to build *"long term"* and *"sustainable"* relationships rather than resorting to *"tokenism."*

This case study has identified clearly that the police can certainly do more in opening and maintain communication channels with all interested parties, particularly those whom the police traditionally hold as *"difficult to engage with."* However, there is recognition also that a dialogical approach is an ongoing process and trust, a key element in implementing a procedurally fair approach, takes time and commitment from all parties for it to develop. Jackson, Gilmore and Monk (2019) argued that police commitment to facilitation and dialogue was not universal, despite contrary assurances in the academic literature. This case study provides further literature that argues not that a dialogical approach is always used as a predominant tactic in protest, rather it provides empirical evidence that the approach does work. This chapter has provided an overview of the experiences of those who were engaged in such dialogue with the police prior to, during and post the EDL march in Liverpool in 2017. The next chapter will further explore the value of this approach and the benefits it brings to all interested parties.

References

Allchorn, W. and Dafnos, A. (2020) *Far-right Mobilisations in Great Britain: 2009–2019*. CARR FRGB Dataset Research Report. London: Centre for Analysis of the Radical Right.

Allen, C. (2011) Opposing Islamification or promoting Islamophobia? Understanding the English Defence League. *Patterns of Prejudice*, 45(4), 279–294.

Atherton, E. (2017) Anti-fascists plan "mass mobilisation" to stop EDL march in Liverpool. *Liverpool Echo* [online], 18 May 2017. Available at: http://www.liverpoolecho.co.uk/news

Bido Lito (2017) *Liverpool: A City of Protest* [online] Available at: https://www.bidolito.co.uk/liverpool-a-city-of-protest

Bourne, K. (2011) Commanding and controlling protest crowds. *Critical Horizons*, 12(2), 189–210.

Burke, D. (2017) Now that's a white supremacist! EDL shows its pasty face as clashes break out and 12 are arrested in scuffles with anti-fascists on the streets of Liverpool. *Mail* [online], 3 June 2017. Available at: http://www.dailymail.co.uk/news

College of Policing (2013) *National Police Public Order Training Curriculum: Police Liaison Team Trainers Guide*. Wyboston: College of Policing.

College of Policing (2018) *Police Liaison Teams* [online] Available at: https://www.app.college.police.uk/app-content/public-order/planning-and-deployment/

Copsey, N. (2010) *The English Defence League: A Challenge to Our Country and Our Values of Social Inclusion, Fairness and Equality*. London: Faith Matters.

Culley, J. (2016) Liverpool riots: Far-right mob clash with anti-fascists in city centre running battles. *Daily Star* [online] 27 February 2016. Available at: http://www.dailystar.co.uk/news

della Porta, D. and Reiter, H. (1998) *Policing Protest: The Control of Mass Demonstrations in Western Democracies*. Minneapolis: University of Minnesota Press.

della Porta, D., Peterson, A. and Reiter, H. (2006) *The Policing of Transnational Protest*. Aldershot: Ashgate.

Dodd, V. and Taylor, M. (2011) Muslims criticise Scotland Yard for telling them to engage with EDL. *The Guardian* [online], 2 September 2011. Available at: https://www.theguardian.com/uk/2011

Donald, A., Gordon, J. and Leach, P. (2012) *The UK and the European Court of Human Rights*. London: Equality and Human Rights Commission.

Drury, J. and Reicher, S. (2000) Collective action and psychological change: The emergence of new social identities. *British Journal of Social Psychology*, 39, 579–604. The British Psychological Society.

Dunn, C. (2017) Dramatic footage of clashes between EDL and anti-fascist protesters as bottles and firecrackers thrown. *Liverpool Echo* [online], 3 June 2017. Available at: http://www.liverpoolecho.co.uk/news

Elgot, J. (2013) Lord Tebbit: 'No evidence' EDL are far-right. *The Huffington Post* [online], 19 August 2013. Available at: http://www.huffingtonpost.co.uk

Elgot, J. (2016) Neo-Nazi group National Action banned by UK home secretary. *The Guardian* [online]. 12 December 2016. Available at: https://www.theguardian.com/world/2016/dec/12/neo-nazi-group

English Defence League (2016) *The English Defence League's Mission Summary* [online]. 3 January 2016. Available at: http://www.englishdefenceleague.org.uk

English Defence League (2017a) *EDL Statement on the Islamic Attack at London Bridge* [online], 3 June 2017. Available at: http://www.englishdefenceleague.org.uk

English Defence League (2017b) *National Demo, Liverpool 3 June 2017: Media Announcement* [online]. Available at: http://www.englishdefenceleague.org.uk

Gilmore, J., Jackson, W. and Monk, H. (2016) *Keep moving! Report on the policing of the Barton Moss community protection camp: November 2013 –April 2014*. Centre for the Study of Crime, Criminalisation and Social Exclusion, Liverpool John Moores University: Centre for Urban Research, University of York.

Gorringe, H., Rosie, M., Waddington, D. and Kominou, M. (2012) Facilitating ineffective protest? The policing of the 2009 Edinburgh NATO protests. *Policing and Society*, 22(2), 115–132.

Gorringe, H., Stott, C and Rosie, M. (2012) Dialogue police, decision-making, and the management of public order during protest crowd events. *Journal of Investigative Psychology and Offender Profiling*, 9, 111–125.

Gravelle, J. and Rogers, C. (2011) Engaging protesters: A smarter way for policing demonstrations. *The Police Journal*, 84, 5–12.

Heneghan, M. (2017) The people of Liverpool send the EDL packing. *Counterfire* [online], 3 June, 2017. Available at: http://www.counterfire.org/news

Hinds, L. and Murphy, K. (2007) Public satisfaction with police: Using procedural justice to improve police legitimacy. *The Australian and New Zealand Journal of Criminology*, 40(1), 27–42.

Hope, C. (2013) 'I am not a Nazi', says EDL leader Tommy Robinson. *The Telegraph* [online]. 16 June 2013. Available at: http://www.telegraph.co.uk/news/politics

Hughes, L. (2017) Faces of hate: 8 Pictures that sum up the EDL. *Liverpool Echo* [online], 3 June 2017. Available at: http://www.liverpoolecho.co.uk/news

Jackson, W., Gilmore, J. and Monk, H. (2019) Policing unacceptable protest in England and Wales: A case study of the policing of anti-fracking protests. *Critical Social Policy*, 39(1), 23–43.

Jenkins, P. (2017) Thousands stop Nazis from marching through Liverpool. *Socialist Worker* [online], 6 June 2017. Available at: https://socialistworker.co.uk/art/44745

Joseph, A. (2015) Six arrests after far-right 'white man march' clashes with anti-fascist demonstrators in Liverpool city centre. *The Mail* [online], 15 August 2015. Available at: http://www.dailymail.co.uk/news

Joyce, P. and Wain, N. (2014) *Palgrave Dictionary of Public Order Policing, Protest and Political Violence*. London: Palgrave Macmillan.

Kassimeris, G. and Jackson, L. (2015) The ideology and discourse of the English Defence League: 'Not racist, not violent, just no longer silent'. *British Journal of Politics and International Relations*, 17(1), 171–188.

Kilgallon, A. (2020) Police interaction and Notting Hill Carnival. *Policing and Society*, 30(1), 28–46.

Mansfield, K. (2017) Riot police surround EDL protest after violent clashes between far-right and anti-fascists. Express [online], 3 June 2017. Available at: http://www.express.co.uk/news

Mansley, D (2014) *Collective Violence, Democracy and Protest Policing*. London and New York: Routledge.

Maxwell, K. (2015) The humiliation of neo-Nazis in Liverpool makes me proud to be a Scouser. *Independent* [online], 16 August 2015 Available at: http://www.independent.co.uk/voices

Mead, D. (2010) *The New Law of Peaceful Protest: Rights and Regulation in the Human Rights Act Era*. Oxford: Hart.

Meleagrou-Hitchens, A. and Brun, H. (2013) *A Neo-nationalist Network: The English Defence League and Europe's Counter-Jihad Movement*. London: International Centre for the Study of Radicalisation and Political Violence.

Morrow, E. and Meadowcroft, J. (2019) The rise and fall of the English Defence League: Self-governance, marginal members and the far right. *Political Studies*, 67(3), 539–556.

Neyroud, P. and Beckley, A. (2001) *Policing, Ethics and Human Rights*. Cullompton: Willan Publishing.

Oaten, A. (2014) The cult of the victim: An analysis of the collective identity of the English Defence League. *Patterns of Prejudice*, 48(4), 331–349.

Parliament (2009) *Demonstrating Respect for Rights? A Human Rights Approach to Policing Protest* [online]. Available at: https://publications.parliament.uk/pa/jt200809/jtselect/jtrights

Pilkington, H. (2016) *Loud and Proud: Passion and Politics in the English Defence League*. Manchester: Manchester University Press.

Pitt, B. (2009) EDL not extreme right wing group, claims Met commissioner. *Islamophobia Watch* [online], 25 September, 2009. Available at: http://www.islamophobiawatch.co.uk

Redekop, V. and Paré, S. (2010) *Beyond control: A mutual respect approach to protest crowd-police relations*. London: Bloomsbury.

Reiner, R. (1998) Policing, protest, and disorder in Britain, in della Porta, D. and Reiter, R. eds., *Policing Protest: The Control of Mass Demonstrations in Western Democracies*, 35–48. Minneapolis: University of Minnesota Press.

RT News (2017) Far-right march in Liverpool blocked by left-wingers, police arrest 12 after clashes. *RT News* [online]. 3 June 2017. Available at: https://www.rt.com/uk/

Sinek, S. (2009) *Start with Why: How Great Leaders Inspire Everyone to Take Action*. London. Penguin.

Smith, M. (2015) *The Use of Police Liaison Teams in the Policing of Events: A Review of Practice*. Ryton: College of Policing. Available at: http://library.college.police.uk

Thomas, J. (2015) Recap: Anti-fascists protest as 'White Man March' in Liverpool is cancelled. *Liverpool Echo* [online], 5 September 2015. Available at: http://www.liverpoolecho.co.uk/news

Thorp, L. (2017a) English Defence League slammed for using Manchester attack to "stir up hatred" in Liverpool. *Liverpool Echo* [online], 1 June 2017. Available at: http://www.liverpoolecho.co.uk/news

Thorp, L. (2017b) Mayor Joe Anderson says he will never allow far-right groups to march through Liverpool City Centre. *Liverpool Echo* [online], 7 June 2017. Available at: http://www.liverpoolecho.co.uk/news

Thorp, L. (2017c) Why you should ignore the EDL march – and attend this amazing event instead. *Liverpool Echo* [online], 1 June 2017. Available at: http://www.liverpoolecho.co.uk/news

Travis, A. (2017) Rudd extends ban to two National Action-related neo-Nazi groups. *The Guardian* [online], 28 September 2017. Available at: https://www.theguardian.com/world

Unite Against Fascism (2017) *Merseyside Defeats Fascist EDL: Victory on the Mersey!* [online], 5 June 2017. Available at: http://uaf.org.uk/2017

Waddington, D. (2013) A 'kinder blue': Analysing the police management of the Sheffield anti-'Lib Dem' protest of March 2011. *Policing and Society*, 23(1), 46–64.

Waddington, D., Jones, K. and Critcher, C. (1989) *Flashpoints: Studies in Public Disorder*. New York: Routledge.

Waddington, P. (1994) *Liberty and Order: Public Order Policing in a Capital City*. London: U.C.L. Press.

Watson, A. and Angell, B. (2007) Applying procedural justice theory to law enforcement's response to persons with mental illness. *Psychiatric Service*, 58(6), 787–792.

Weston, A. (2016a) Far-right group North West Infidels claims it will hold Liverpool rally on Saturday. *Liverpool Echo* [online], 26 February 2016. Available at: http://www.liverpoolecho.co.uk/news

Weston, A. (2016b) Far-right group 'North West Infidels' clash with anti-fascist demonstrators in Liverpool city centre. *Liverpool Echo* [online], 27 February 2016. Available at: http://www.liverpoolecho.co.uk/news

Wheatstone, R. and Weston, A. (2016) Far-right protest in Liverpool turns violent as bricks and fireworks thrown at riot police. *Daily Mirror* [online], 27 February 2016. Available at: http://www.mirror.co.uk

Wood, L. (2014) *Crisis and Control: The Militarization of Protest Policing*. London: Pluto Press.

Chapter 7

The contribution and value of a dialogical approach

The previous two chapters have presented two case studies through which the use of a dialogical approach to the policing of protest has been examined. The chapters have provided insight into how the police firstly identified and sought out a whole range of interested parties and individuals with whom to engage and then selected appropriate officers to create a communication link with the senior police decision-makers, illustrated in a Dialogical Wheel. The chapters have identified the political pressures that have influence on the police in balancing competing rights and have recognised the importance of trust being developed between individuals and police liaison. The barriers to engagement have been documented, however, designating a point of contact has been described as key in fostering strong relationships through dialogue.

This chapter further examines a dialogical approach to the policing of protest and considers the contribution that such an approach made to providing all interested parties a voice and access to the police senior officers enabling them to influence decisions in policing protest events. By returning to both previous case studies simultaneously, an analysis will be enabled through the experiences of those who were involved in the dialogical approach by examining their observations on the value of engaging in dialogue for each individual and the groups they represented.

The value of police and protesters engaging in dialogue has been established (for example, della Porta and Reiter, 1998). Further, the role of Police Liaison Teams (PLT) has been advocated as the conduit between protesters and police commanders, utilising ESIM (for example, Gorringe, Stott and Rosie, 2012) and the Flashpoints Model (Waddington, 2013) as the basis for understanding the dialogical process, and the use of PLT has subsequently been adopted as the national tactic in the UK (College of Policing, 2018), There is limited research into the value of this tactic since its inception. What exists largely extols the use of PLT in de-escalating risk through dialogue and communication (Hoggett and West, 2018) and building a collaborative relationship between the police and event organisers (Kilgallon, 2020), although suspicion has been registered regarding their role as intelligence gathers rather than liaison officers (Jackson, Gilmore and Monk, 2019). This chapter further explores the police–protester

DOI: 10.4324/9781003160533-7

relationship and argues that a dialogical approach to the policing of protest afforded all those engaged in protests a voice with the decision-making police commander for them to best exercise their rights to freedom of expression and assembly.

However, the two case studies examined in this research have evidenced a whole host of individuals and groups affected by or engaged in protest events and highlighted the challenge for the police in balancing the competing human rights of all interested parties. This research extends existing literature to provide evidence that there is value for all interested parties involved in protest events to engage in dialogue. This is important to sociological understanding of policing because, in addition to utilising ESIM and Flashpoints Models, this research proposes that procedural justice theory (for example, Lind and Tyler, 1988; Bradford, 2012) provides a theoretical foundation from which a dialogical approach with both protest groups and other interested parties may be analysed. Such engagement assisted all interested parties in achieving their aims and objectives and assisted the police in their role as "*piggy in the middle*" to balance the competing qualified rights of all those engaged in the event and reduce conflict, by providing a proportionate and procedurally fair policing response.

This chapter therefore analyses the value of a dialogical approach in liaison with protest groups and how this encouraged self-policing and then examines the value of such an approach with other interested groups and similarly the encouragement for them to self-police. The chapter investigates how providing a voice promoted legitimacy and trust with protest groups and others and how this dialogue better equipped police decision-makers to balance competing human rights.

The value of a dialogical approach: Liaison with protest groups

All participants interviewed promoted a dialogical approach to the policing of the badger cull and provided evidence of the value of such an approach to both the police and those opposed to the cull. One Protector described the use of a dialogical approach as "*absolutely fantastic,*" adding "*I couldn't praise the PLT more.*" Another Protector explained how the presence of PLT calmed situations, and described an incident where, "*if it wasn't for the fact that there were liaison officers there, I think it could have possibly got out of hand.*" One Protector admitted that they were "*really surprised how helpful the PLT were in facilitating those protests*" *(Protector A)* and another declared, "*We couldn't have asked for more help, they have been wonderful*" *(Protector C)*. The value of this liaison was not just in the police allowing the actions of Protectors; the relationships also brought further benefits where PLT would assist Protectors in achieving their aims and airing their views with organisations with whom they had experienced difficulty in reaching. Protectors provided examples of incidents where PLT provided mediation with those against whom the Protectors wished to demonstrate. One explained,

> *In fact, if it wasn't for [PLT], we wouldn't have been so successful. Because, what he did, from our behalf, he contacted the NFU and Natural England, and actually got permission for me to go in, and certainly for Natural England, to go in and speak to them. Or to go in and hand them a letter. Or for one of them to come out. So, that was something that I hadn't expected them to actually … I thought they might have been there in the background, but to actually help us to have our peaceful protest, I was surprised, and that was really helpful.*
>
> (Protector A)

Another Protector concurred:

> *The PLTs have given us a point of contact to a lot of these people that we wouldn't have been able to possibly meet with. I think they were more obliging with the police, and we were able to meet with these people. It made us look less threatening, I suppose. It's getting to the right people, you know, so, in that respect, definitely positive.*
>
> (Protector C)

PLT similarly described how they had on occasions "*encouraged*" representatives from organisations to meet with Protectors, and how this had "*upped*" their credibility with Protector groups. PLT described the dialogical process as yielding benefits to the Protectors by providing a contact where they could "*raise issues,*" and "*talk honestly and openly about the good and the bad, the satisfied, the dissatisfaction of the police activity.*" One PLT recalled how several Protectors had recounted that they felt much safer when PLT were deployed. Another described how educating Protectors in what was acceptable assisted the Protectors in achieving their aims of protecting the badger setts without resorting to unlawful tactics. The relationships that were built then allowed PLT to manage situations such as where the behaviour of some Protectors was regarded by the community as anti-social. Several PLT provided examples such as where the community became antagonised by some Protectors leaving gates open or wandering off public footpaths and how these issues were resolved by PLT through dialogue, preventing further conflict, which "*made for an easier life for everybody.*"

The value of a dialogical approach to those engaged in protest and demonstration was also evidenced in the policing of the English Defence League (EDL) march in Liverpool. An EDL member explained the benefits that having PLT engagement made to their planning process. They described being "*quite amazed*" with how the PLT engagement facilitated their march and provided contacts "*with the right people straightaway.*" They described the process as "*sophisticated,*" "*engaged*" and "*not dislocated*" in contrast to their experiences with PLT in other police force areas. They assessed the dialogical process:

> *Totally positive, totally positive. It was totally positive. It's like I said before, both views and expectations, because it's managing expectations, were put on the table. And it was very positive.*
>
> (EDL A)

The approach not only benefited those marching, but also those policing the event. Commanders explained how having open dialogue with EDL leaders provided the police with "*continuous knowledge of their plan*" and "*an ability to respond to it.*" It allowed the police to identify the groups and individuals and their "*feelings*," which in turn allowed the police to react most appropriately and efficiently, inform others of their intentions and amend responses accordingly. One Commander provided an example of the benefits of this dialogue with the EDL pre-event in how they had agreed a meet-and-greet process at Liverpool Lime Street train station for the day of the march. This had allowed the Commander to keep Lime Street open on the day of the march, because they were able to manage the EDL as a group once they arrived, rather than them arriving "*in dribs and drabs at the front of the station into the main city*" which would have caused "*a situation where we would have been having to use force to retrieve the scenario.*" This engagement allowed the police to also address any concerns raised by those demonstrating. One PLT explained how they were able to allay an EDL organiser's fear of police use of force through their conversations:

> *He had a fear that basically we were going to prevent him from doing the march and maybe do some kind of baton charge into them for no reason. I explained to them [laughs] that we weren't likely to do that!*
>
> (PLT L)

PLT explained how their role located them in the centre of negotiations and this allowed "*give and take.*" This was particularly evident where the police were having to manage the aims of the EDL with a left-leaning Liverpool City Council and a vocal Mayor, especially where key locations such as the Liverpool Town Hall were discussed as potential sites for static rallies. One PLT provided an example of how this negotiation worked:

> *Originally, the EDL wanted to tip up, march. They had these mobile speakers and stuff like that, and they were going to go to the Town Hall. So, we put that through to [police commander]. And that was a no-no. He came up with another plan, Derby Square. We went back to them and explained that we didn't want it that way, and why we didn't want it that way. And they were quite receptive. So, it was about ... They would say just what they wanted, us going to*

[police commander] through *[Bronze PLT]*, *"This is what they want."* *[Police commander]* saying, *"Well, they can or they can't have that, and this is why,"* and us explaining to them why they could or they couldn't do something.

(PLT M)

Although there was a clear open dialogue between the police and the EDL, as identified in the last chapter, there was limited engagement between the police and those opposing the EDL march. Many police participants believed that those counterdemonstrating saw no benefit to dialogue with the police, despite some police participants identifying that engagement empowered the groups and afforded them negotiation rights. However, despite having not engaged pre-event, Activists participating in the research did witness advantages in engagement with the police during the event. One described a positive interaction they had with a *"personable"* PLT officer on the day of the march, who diffused a potentially hostile situation thorough dialogue. They believed that the use of PLT *"really helps to break down stereotypical views of the police and what their roles are."* Further, Activists stated that they were not against engagement with the police prior to the event, contrarily they advocated pre-event and post-event engagement, as well as on the day. One explained:

That communication, that dialogue, prevents any misunderstandings or problems that could come, because you haven't had the dialogue. So, I think speaking before, during and after is key in terms of integrating the police as being part of, not on the peripheral, but part of the whole event. Because, I don't see the police to be separate, in my view. They should be integral into both the safety side of it, and keeping the peace, and all the legislation and all that side of it but protecting the activists who are counterdemonstrating.

(Activist A)

Another explained that being interviewed had caused them to further consider the value of engagement with the police:

Do you know, the more I think about it, I think that there needs to be engagement with the police. If I've got to apply for permission to hold a march or demonstration, is there an argument there that to hold a counterdemonstration, that I've equally got to get permission? Because, when you organise a demo, you organise stewards, you organise a lot of other stuff. But, for a counter-demo, there's no stewarding, there's no control, it's just a mob ... I think any relationship that we can build up has always got to be a good and positive thing ... It's been helpful. It's really made me think differently about it all. It's made me see things in a way I haven't looked at it before.

(Activist B)

There is no legislative requirement for those holding protests or counterdemonstrations to notify the police of their intentions, although notification of a procession is required to be given under Section 13 of the Public Order Act 1986. However, despite this fact, Activists in this research, whom traditionally police participants saw as least willing to engage, were keen to promote the value of pre-event engagement which they saw as beneficial for both the police and those who wished to express views and demonstrate.

Therefore, both the police and those marching or demonstrating described the benefits they received from being engaged in dialogue with each other. The approach allowed those wishing to express opinions and views access to a wider audience and, through the liaison with PLT, assisted them in voicing their views and lobbying governmental bodies. The approach also assisted police decision-makers in understanding the viewpoint of different protest groups and aided them in balancing competing rights.

Self-policing in protest groups

HIMIC (2009b) recommended that the police strategic approach to protest events should promote self-policing in the crowds. Sunshine and Tyler (2003) observed that most groups self-regulated when police procedures were seen as legitimate. Further, Gorringe, Stott and Rosie (2012) noted self-regulation in groups, which the police saw as a direct outcome of utilising PLT and provided evidence of self-policing in protest groups facilitated using PLT. Both case studies in this research provided supporting evidence to suggest that a dialogical approach encouraged self-regulation in those engaged in marches and protests.

The EDL demonstrated how being empowered by the police to march had encouraged them to monitor their own group and manage its membership, ejecting those whose views or actions were seen as illegitimate and not adhering to the values and mission statement of the EDL. A member of the EDL marching in Liverpool explained how the group had been "*basically, policing our own people*" and how certain people, such as "*those that hold extremist views, like racists, Nazis*" and the "*football element*" had been excluded from the EDL. This meant that those attending Liverpool were only those "*that stand by our values*" and did not include "*those that just hang on to cause trouble.*" Further, incidents that occurred on the day elicited a self-regulated response. At one point, several marchers indicated their intention to hold a sit-down protest to mirror that of those opposing. The EDL member explained that although there were "*smoke bombs*" being thrown at them, the group did not want to be "*pushed back*" into the train station. They explained how, through dialogue with the police, they were able to agree an alternative route for the EDL to "*march around the corner.*" The EDL member encouraged those intending to sit down to change their plans, and this self-regulation prevented a stand-off and empowered the group to march the group to their final speeches before departure.

Officers policing the badger cull also identified self-regulation within the groups of those opposing the cull. Several participants opined that self-policing was a result of the "*unique relationship*" that PLT had with their communities and described how this "*empowered those groups*" and "*handed over responsibility to them.*" A Commander explained:

> *Nobody wants to be told what to do all the time. They don't want to be told how they are going to manage themselves. But by working with them, and through the liaison process, advising them and saying that they could do that, actually, but just to tweak this little bit here, modify their behaviour, they would find that we wouldn't bother them, we would leave them just to get on with it. We were passing down bits of advice which would allow them to go and make their own decisions. You know, it was just that empowerment that really worked.*
>
> (Commander I)

Being empowered also allowed some Protectors to challenge the behaviours of others within the anti-cull community. One PLT recalled a conversation they had with a Protector:

> *I know this for a fact, because, my liaison point told me this, was that, when they had people coming from all over the country, they spoke to them and said, "You've come in to help us. Thank you very much. But please understand that we have a very good relationship with the police. We don't want that spoiled. So, please abide by the rules that we give you." And, I don't think that you can have better testament to PLT than that. They're almost like taking our job away! You've got a group that's inviting other groups in, and before they come in they're saying, "This is the ground rules. We've got a great relationship with the police. Don't cock it up for us. Otherwise, we'll just get rid of you." And, that worked on so many occasions for us as well.*
>
> (PLT I)

Similarly, a Protector explained how they had been able to manage those who had not been willing to engage with the police:

> *There are some people out there who will take more extreme actions than others. But, you know, sometimes you can get the message off across to them through having liaison with the police. Like, I was able to say to certain people, "Look, this needs to stop, otherwise they're going to come down heavy-handed." And it stopped. And no one came down on us, you know, nothing happened.*
>
> (Protector C)

Further, PLT described incidents where the Protectors they had been liaising with actively supported PLT at meetings and events when they had encountered Protectors who were "*clearly anti-police.*" One PLT recalled:

> *I could probably think of at least three occasions when almost the police were protected by the Protectors saying, "No, we want the police here, they're good, we really like them here."*
>
> (PLT D)

An approach based on dialogue therefore enabled those wishing to express views to set the standards for their groups and determine the membership, empowering them to self-police. Key to this process was the fact that groups felt that the police "*got them*," that through the dialogue and relationships fostered, their PLT understood them and their cause and, even if the PLT did not necessarily agree with their mission statement or stance, their opinions were given legitimacy by the police.

The value of a dialogical approach: Liaison with others

This research contributes to exiguous research into the use of PLT and the value of dialogue between the police and protesters. However, the two case studies further extend this research and evidence the value of liaison between the police and *all* interested parties engaged in protest events. The two case studies provided evidence that the police, businesses, local authorities and other agencies affected by the event all found benefit in engaging in dialogue. Furthermore, this research suggested that the role of the liaison officer, as a key conduit between the decision-making Commander and interested parties, did not always necessitate the deployment of a formal PLT. On occasions other officers were better placed to facilitate dialogue. Such liaison options included senior officers, public order tactical advisers and operational planners, all who had existing relationships and were best placed to engage and continue to build trust.

Business participants who had liaised during the badger cull in Devon and Cornwall described the benefits they experienced in engaging with the police prior to and during the cull period. They explained that having regular dialogue with liaison officers provided them with "*reassurance*" from the police and someone with whom they could "*vent their frustrations.*" It was important that the officer liaising was assigned solely to business individuals, such as farmers whose land was being used for the cull, or cull contractors and not also engaging with anti-cull groups at the same time. This process made an impact on the well-being of those business individuals. One provided an example of where this approach made a difference to them:

> *We had issues of gates left open. At that time, I was able to speak to the protest liaison officer, because at that time we were working with them. I said, "You just need to get a message back to these guys. Leaving gates open is not going to stop the cull. We're going to get animals or someone killed." And, that message was taken back to them. And very quickly, we saw that both sides shut the gates. So, I think it is very positive having police liaison working with both sides, but keeping both sides separate.*
> (Business B)

Business participants also described the benefit of receiving inputs from PLT on how to address confrontational Protectors. They explained that their

PLT attended meetings of local farmer groups and gave them inputs which explained what Protectors were entitled to do by law, but also how the police were approaching the cull and its opposition. These sessions allowed landowners, farmers and cull operators to understand if not agree with the perspectives of those anti-cull as well as allowing them to voice their frustrations and concerns to a police representative who understood their stance and the nuances of their approach to the cull. PLT also provided examples where education in conflict and expectations management had assisted farmers, cull operators, the NFU and the Department for Environment, Food and Rural Affairs (DEFRA) in dealing with Protectors. One PLT recalled an incident in a small village:

> *The Protectors were patrolling outside of a house where the front door literally went on to the road. He was only a young farmer, and he was trying to earn extra money, and he ended up, his wife and two children moved out of the house. They went to live with their parents, because the Protectors were constantly outside of the window, shining their torches in. So, massive trauma. One villager, she put signs up about this individual. Totally divided the village. And for that to happen in [location] is a rarity. Getting the message out to the Protectors and saying, "Look, this is what you're doing. You're destroying this. By all means have your walks, but you're not focussing on that place. It's bordering on harassment, and you've got to calm this down." And it actually worked, again. That was the one I got the vicar involved to get the community back together. So, that actually worked.*
>
> (PLT E)

The approach provided benefit for the local community too. PLT described how they were able to inform police neighbourhood teams about intended Protector activities and this in turn allowed neighbourhood teams to reassure their communities regarding lawful Protector activities along the lanes at night. The police service also benefited from a dialogical approach. Officers described how the approach lessened opportunities for *"bad press,"* *"misunderstandings,"* *"policing it wrong or the police to be portrayed as getting it wrong"* and provided an understanding of police limitations for all. Officers also asserted that early dialogue resulted in a reduction of police staff required for such events. This meant that there were more police resources available to undertake other key aspects of their duties in detecting and preventing harm, protecting the vulnerable, reducing crime and serving the community. Several Commanders commented that they would not now consider ever policing such events without utilising PLT, such was their value in *"facilitating that open dialogue."*

The value of dialogue between the police and all interested parties was also evidenced in the experiences of those affected by the EDL march in Liverpool, such as the local authority, travel organisations and businesses. Officers described the approach as one of *"no surprises"* and one Commander explained how they had used this with *"businesses and stakeholders,"* whereby they had been invited to pre-event meetings where the police explained how they were planning to facilitate the EDL marching through Liverpool:

> *When we first invited them and I gave a bit of an overview, you could just see their faces drop. And then you explained, "Well, look, you need to understand this is the legislation that sits behind it. This is what they are entitled to do, and then we as police, non-judgemental, need to deliver on this. And this is the benefits I see in delivering a safe event." And I was quite open about it, in the hope that if we did deliver a safe event that it may prevent either group coming back to the city for some time in a like capacity. And you could see that talking it through, so having that dialogue with those stakeholders, you could see the uplift, and all of a sudden it encouraged people to work together and to contribute as to how they could assist in delivering.*
>
> (Commander J)

Business participants revealed how attending the police meetings alleviated their fears of disorder, assured them that there were plans in place, gave them an understanding of the intentions of the EDL and the police response, and provided reassurance. The dialogue also allowed them to voice their concerns to the police. One Commander provided an example of where their thinking was influenced on hearing concerns aired by those attending such meetings. They explained:

> *The town hall is a really good one. The local authority believed the town hall was such an iconic site that they could not have that taken over. You know, and that became a real focus for them. And, if we hadn't have had that conversation, I might have just pushed it through. And it might have been the right thing to do ... Anyway, we never got it to the town hall, so it didn't really matter! But it is those kind of things, you know, understanding what people's views are. Understanding the depth of feeling, I think is really key.*
>
> (Commander L)

The process also allowed Business participants to understand the impact the march had on other interested parties. One shared that *"it was good to speak to the other businesses that were affected, and it made us feel more at ease with the plans."* A Business participant summarised that the dialogue ensured *"expectations are managed, no surprises."* Another agreed:

> *We knew that if certain things happened then we would have already planned what response we would have. We had those discussions beforehand, rather than it being a knee jerk reaction on the day.*
>
> (Business E)

The dialogue assisted businesses in coordinating their own responses and appropriately updating their own staff, customers and the public, in a way "*that is not going to set the hares running.*" The process also afforded a voice to interested parties not just with the police but, through the police liaison, with those planning on marching:

> Having that dialogue with the police gives us a chance for the police to go back to the event organisers and say that this is the implications of doing this. Because, we would never have had a dialogue with the EDL, because they would have been elsewhere. So, the police have got those current links. We can put on the table that our concerns are about this, that and the other. They went back. And, once the decision was made, we went with it.
>
> (Business H)

Therefore, the dialogical process provided real benefit for the police and for those businesses and organisations affected by the events and protests for and against. It allowed the police to explain, contrary to media speculation, misinformation and rhetoric concerning public opinion on the validity of protests and marches, what they legally were empowered to do and how the police would be responding. It also allowed businesses and organisations to voice their concerns. Ultimately, it provided clarity for those affected by the protest events and allowed them to plan and address potential issues, and this gave them an element of control and empowered them to self-police.

Self-policing in other groups

This chapter described the presence of self-policing evident in both case studies in those wishing to protest and march. However, the research further extended existing research (Sunshine and Tyler, 2003; Gorringe, Stott and Rosie, 2012) by identifying self-regulation in not just protesters but all interested parties engaged in the events, due to the dialogical approach implemented by the police.

PLT who engaged with the farming community during the badger cull explained how that community "*very much did their own thing,*" "*policed themselves*" and "*sort their own communities out.*" Several participants noted that this was a typical farming approach, where many "*find it very difficult to come together as a team.*" By having dialogue with the police, farmers were able to gain support and address issues, empowered to self-regulate and carry on with business as usual. This was particularly important for Business participants, who revealed that some of their neighbours were not even aware of their involvements with the cull.

Self-policing was most evident in businesses affected by the EDL march in Liverpool. Business participants described how the dialogical approach assisted them in briefing others both within their organisations and partners who had not been involved in police liaison. For many business, facilitating the EDL march and counterdemonstration incurred extra costs at their expense. One participant explained how they had to employ security staff at a time when normally there would be no requirement. Others described extra security measures that were implemented as contingencies to protect their customers and staff, and all described the extra planning and briefings that occurred of staff, contactors and partners. It was clear from the responses of all business participants that the self-regulation was a result of engagement with the police, and acceptance of the balancing of human right and a sense of being empowered by the police to manage their organisational responses. One business participant provided an example of such self-policing and described how they themselves had implemented a dialogical approach in working with their stakeholders to address issues which had arisen due to the impending EDL march. They recounted how they had spoken to a licensee of a business affected by the march and potential counterdemonstration to advise them against using their pavement-based dining area during the march. The licensee was initially reticent, however, they were persuaded to rethink their approach:

> *I just had to go up and say to them, "What's the cost of your front window? Because what we've got to avoid here is any kind of disorder. We want you to operate your business financially, but we want to facilitate the march. But, if things go wrong, yes, and they pick up a stool, or one of your chairs, or one of your tables? It's gone through the window. What's the cost, there?" Because we know the cost of a window is two and a half grand. But people just don't think, it doesn't register. When they think of a march or a demonstration, I think they always think of the Pride march, or the Boys' Brigade, or someone. They don't really look at the possible consequences if something does go wrong. And what we're all trying to avoid and what we're all trying to facilitate safely, they just think in pounds, shillings and pence.*
> (Business F)

The research not only provided evidence of the benefit of a dialogical approach for those groups affected by protests and marches in managing their business and continuing to operate as normally as possible in light of protest activity, it provided insight into how this dialogical approach empowered such interested parties to self-police. This process ensured that all interested parties, those protesting, marching, counterdemonstrating or seeking normality were able to achieve their aims whilst being cognisant and aware of the desires of others and their underlying reasons.

Providing a voice

Both case studies researched provided evidence of the significance and value of providing a voice to all involved in the events. In both cases, there was clear evidence provided demonstrating how a dialogical approach furnished individuals with a voice through the liaison officers, which empowered participants to influence the decision-making police Commanders. The strategy of the police in striving to implement fair procedures entailed them seeking out a voice from every interested party involved and this resulted in allowing each interested party to have their voice heard by the key decision-makers, a key component of a procedural justice framework (Watson and Angell, 2007).

By providing all a voice and a *"place at the table"* of the police decision-makers, participants described how they felt that there was an acceptance by the police of their identity and legitimacy to their aims and objectives. A PLT liaising with Protectors during the badger cull described how dialogue and the affording of a voice assisted Protectors in feeling valued:

> *I think all you need to do is speak to members of the protest community whose biggest frustration I heard was that historically they'd just not had a voice to influence any kind of policing operation. Or if they have had a voice, it's just fallen on deaf ears. So, for individuals within protest communities, Protector communities, to see their opinion and views influence change within a policing plan, is a huge step forward for them.*
>
> (PLT C)

A Protector reiterated:

> *Personally, I felt like there was a voice going through. You know, [PLT] was brilliant. I know he's doing a job and everything, but he made me feel as if I had an opinion, and it mattered.*
>
> (Protector C)

A Commander further reinforces the point, describing how it was key for them to hear such voices:

> *You've got to listen to the community issues. You've got to listen to the Protectors, the anti-cull community. We can't always give them what they want. But actually sometimes, to be heard, it's what they want, the impact on people's lives.*
>
> (Commander I)

An EDL member described the importance of having *"a voice"* through the PLT and further expressed that they felt that their voice was being heard by police decision-makers:

> *There is benefits of having this engagement for me, because this is the first time that our side has been listened to.*
>
> (EDL A)

The dialogical process not only provided a voice for interested parties with the police commanders: it also furnished the police with a voice through liaison officers, with those with whom they ordinarily would not have access, through dialogue and the fostering of relationships and building of trust. One PLT described how the dialogical process provided the police decision-makers with a voice with the EDL, allowing the police commander to *"allay fears"* and *"be able to reassure these people that we would not be tolerating what happened last time"* which *"gave them a voice."*

Despite the evident benefits of the process, several PLT observed that it was key that not only was a voice provided but that it was heard by police decision-makers, and this required investment from Commanders. One PLT opined:

> *I think that the dialogue method does work, but I think more time needs to be given to it. Before and after, if you want that relationship to be built. And they want us to go into groups and ... not be accepted but listened to.*
>
> (PLT L)

The benefit of this approach based on dialogue, therefore, afforded everyone with a voice, should they be willing to engage. This allowed the building of bridges between diverse groups, through the police as a central conduit, and this in turn nurtured the building of trust, which will be explored in the following section.

Legitimacy and trust with protest groups

Across both case studies, there was clear evidence that a dialogical approach had encouraged the development of trust between the police and protest groups and this created a sense of understanding of the actions of out-groups and an acceptance that although they did not hold to the same values of other parties, their actions and approach were nonetheless legitimate. For all participants, engaging in dialogue culminated in the building of trust between the police and those seeking to protest, march or demonstrate, and this resulted in a perception of legitimacy in the actions of other groups. Legitimacy, trust and relationship building were intrinsically linked in the descriptions provided by participants, echoing established research in the fields of ESIM (for example, Reicher, 1996) and the Flashpoints Model (for example, King and Waddington, 2005). However, the building of trust has also been established as a key component in applying an approach based on procedural justice theory (for example, Sunshine and Tyler, 2003). This research provided evidence in support of utilising all three theoretical approaches to examine a dialogical approach to policing protest events.

Participants from the police, Protector groups and the EDL across both case studies described the process of building relationships and trust as cyclical in nature. Relationships were often built on trust, and as the trust developed, so the relationships deepened. One PLT summarised:

> *As soon as you build up that trust with someone, you will form that relationship and you will make progress.*
>
> (PLT A)

Participants also described how an empathetic approach engendered trust, when each individual tried to see the situation through the eyes of those with whom they were engaging, showing an acceptance of the rights of out-groups to freedom of thought and to express their beliefs even where these were antipathetic to their own. PLT described how they empathised with those with whom they were engaging, and Protectors and Business participants voiced their understanding of the role of PLT and that the "*police had a job to do.*"

Luft and Ingham (1961) argued that trust was developed when individuals shared their open self with others, and this approach of transparency was also identified in both case studies, as participants showed their human side and were received as individuals. One PLT described how they would share stories about their personal life with Protectors to expose their human side, reveal an openness with them and develop trust. This trust was clearly reciprocated, as one Protector shared:

> *The PLTs realised we were just ordinary people doing what we believed was right. And none of us were up to anything untoward, as well, so I think that made it easier for all people concerned.*
>
> (Protector C)

A Commander shared the feedback they had received:

> *From the protector movement we've had very positive emails at the end of the cull saying, "Well done. It was an excellent relationship. So, we trust the police a lot more now."*
>
> (Commander H)

Trust and transparency therefore required a two-way approach within existing relationships. One Commander commented:

> *It's having that transparency. You've got to build up that level of trust with that group. When you build that trust, people will talk to you and will trust you. You build it up, you understand what they're doing, they give you that level of trust, but you've got to give some back.*
>
> (Commander E)

A Protector explained how trust might be extended to those traditionally less engaging, such as hunt saboteurs, who have historically come into conflict with the police rather than engaged with them:

> *I think trust is key, because you build up a relationship with the police. It makes us, possibly even sabs further down the line, the ones that are less trusting, if there is someone that you can come to and know that they can be trusted,*

you're likely to go to them, whereas if you're talking to a blank face, it can be rather daunting.

(Protector C)

Tyler and Lind (1992) suggested that legitimacy was dictated by the fairness of the procedures implemented, and this approach further promoted relationships built on trust between police authorities and the public and encouraged a dialogical approach (Bottoms and Tankebe, 2012). Police participants in both case studies also described how trust was built on fairness and impartiality, consistent with procedural justice theory. It was recognised that building this trust was intrinsically linked to selecting the right police officers to engage with each group, and that there needed to be a transparent and consistent approach with clearly defined lines of communication. This approach, although time-consuming and more resource-intensive in terms of using dedicating PLT to work with specific groups and individuals, rather than using whichever PLT was available, provided dividends in encouraging the building of relationships and, though longevity, fostering trust. One Commander from the badger cull case study observed:

The minute you lose your impartiality, you've lost it. The minute your PLT is talking to the contractors and is engaging with the protesters, you've lost it. You know, in my view, you have to keep that separate.

(Commander E)

The responses of Protectors also supported the observation that relationship building between named PLT developed trust over time. One Protector described a relationship built on trust with a PLT, "*because he was true to his word.*" Another described their PLT as "*a pretty fair guy,*" and described how the dialogical approach they had experienced was very different from the policing response to the opposition to badger cull in "*the old days.*" They summarised:

This cull is completely different. The police are acting completely different to what they've done in the past, which I found to be quite refreshing.

(Protector B)

This sense of shared experiences in building trust over time was reflected in the observations of many participants. A PLT explained how they had started with "*groups of people who absolutely just didn't trust us whatsoever,*" but because they had "*valued them as a community*" had witnessed a "*massive turnaround*" in the dialogue engaged. A Commander noted:

We've managed to build up a relationship over a number of years with Protectors, and we've also learned the lessons together ... So, you're constantly building up an element of trust in relation to that relationship going forward.

(Commander B)

Trust, through dialogue, was for many participants a key ingredient in resolving potential conflict. One PLT recounted how they had built up a relationship with a Protector and through shared experiences, fostered a trust which enabled the PLT to go to decision-makers in support of their cause. They explained:

> *The trust and rapport was very much two-way. I'll use [Protector] as the example. I'm then able to trust them an awful lot more, because I know that they've told me that something is going to happen or something is not going to happen. For example, the protest at the NFU office. They are saying, "This is what I want to do. We are going to have plenty of people here, but we will respect the NFU's right to go about their daily business." They did that. So, the next time we have the next protest, at Natural England, for instance, we'll have the similar sort of conversations, and I can reassure Natural England that this is what they will do, they will stick to their word. And that did bear fruit, and it helps us again to reassure those other agencies. But again, that's two-way. We will say to [Protector], "These are going to be the ground rules here." But they are happy with that and will trust us with that.*
>
> (PLT A)

By implementing this process and keeping a consistent dialogue ongoing between identified representatives, further trust was generated, and this became cyclical in nature. This trust extended to addressing challenging situations where it allowed an understanding and compliance based on a strengthening relationship. One Protector provided an example:

> *I did have accusations made against me of assault ... To be honest with you, [PLT] was fair. He could have, you know, basically, the police could have just nicked me. But he did ring me up and say, "Look, we've had accusations made against you, and we really need to talk to you." To which I said, "Well, I'm really busy, as you know. What happens if I don't come in with this?" "Well, we'll have to arrest you. We'd far prefer it if you come in voluntarily," which I then did. Which was a nice way of doing it, because it didn't disrupt the timetable of what we were doing.*
>
> (Protector B)

PLT liaising with EDL members also talked of a trust that was built on "*explanations*," "*reasoned arguments*" and negotiation. Consistent with Watson and Angell (2007) an early engagement was identified by police participants as being essential in building trust. However, all PLT observed that continuity was key in eliciting trust. PLT cautioned against Commanders aligning them "*one day with the right-wing and the next week with the left-wing*," which provoked "*scepticism*" and mistrust. One Commander explained how from the outset their strategy was one of building trust with all parties including the EDL, which required legitimacy in setting boundaries:

> *For us to be legitimate, the EDL had to have the confidence. For them to have the confidence in us, we needed to be honest and forthright in our communication, and*

that's why from the word go I set out for them what we could and couldn't do, and what would and wouldn't be tolerated.

(Commander P)

Another Commander observed that because the PLT had built relationships with EDL members, the PLT were better able to explain on the day why the Commander had decided to "*turn the march around.*" The Commander explained:

I think that the dialogue that we'd previously had, the relationship that we'd previously built, did assist us with the acceptance of what we were telling them. They knew throughout my tipping points, my expectations. It was explained to them that we needed to do it, and why, i.e. for their safety, and they effectively trusted us, and got on with it.

(Commander J)

A Commander summarised how fairness impacted upon their decision-making:

When people believe that it is procedurally fair, and they are treated in a fair and equitable manner, they will consent to be policed. And that was what the dialogue was primarily about. Because, without that procedural fairness, you get people coming back the following week and the following month. And it's not about supporting one group or the other. It's about what is the greater good.

(Commander P)

Despite the limited engagement with Activists, PLT still identified elements of trust playing a significant part. One PLT further described an encounter they had with one Activist with whom they had previously engaged. The Activist approached the PLT for them to be their "*alibi for her not breaching her bail conditions*" because there was "*that trust*" because of previous engagement. The PLT described how the trust was reciprocated and how the Activist left the area before the march began. Furthermore, Activists also described how through liaison on the day, there was "*understanding*" regarding police decisions and "*compliance*" despite not always agreeing with the decision because of the explanations. One Activist concluded:

Trust. It's a trust thing, that's what you're looking to get. It's trust. So, say for example an Activist had a named person that he knew, and he's dealt with, because he organises demonstrations. He would immediately know Joe Bloggs to go to. And Joe Bloggs know somebody else, and there's that relationship, a rapport, and there's a trust. And okay, sometimes you may disagree and there may be a "Why?" But at least you've got that understanding and that trust.

(Activist A)

Therefore, across both case studies, it was evident that a dialogical process encouraged the development of relationships and this led to trust. This meant that the police, through PLT, were able to understand not only what those protesting wanted to do, but also why they sought certain actions. It also provided those protesting with an understanding of the legal and political framework in which the police needed to operate, and furthermore an appreciation of how their actions were perceived and accepted by out-groups.

Jackson, Gilmore and Monk (2019) observed that protesters perceived to be PLT primarily involved in intelligence gathering, and that this reinforced suspicion and intensified the lack of trust between protesters and the police. However, this research found the polar opposite in that those protesting and marching not only actively sought to provide information to the police, the way in which this process continued and how the police used and responded to the information provided actually aided the relationship-building and created a deeper trust between protesters and the police.

Moreover, there was a sense from participants that those protesting and marching sought to provide not just information but intelligence to the police. This required an understanding of the difference between the two terms. Intelligence is defined as "information that has been analysed to assess its relevance and reliability" (National Crime Agency, 2022) and "information that has undergone an evaluation process to assess its worth" (National Anti Fraud Network, 2019). Participants described how they provided information to PLT regarding their intentions and trusted the PLT to not only share the information with police decision-makers but also vouch for their integrity and honesty, in effect turning the information into intelligence by assessing its worth. PLT explained how they would then furnish the police commanders with the information but would also provide details of how those with whom they had liaised had been "*true to their word*" and their actions could be trusted, providing a further assessment of the reliability of those with whom they liaised. This assessment not only informed police commanders in their decision-making, but it also created further trust between the police and out-groups when those liaising saw that their voice was being listened too and valued.

Legitimacy and trust with other groups

It was not just between the police and protest groups that legitimacy and trust was evidenced in both case studies through a dialogical approach, the research also unveiled that a strategy centred on liaison encouraged and developed trust between the police and all interested parties, including other emergency services, local authorities, businesses and residents. This further evidenced that an approach consistent with procedural justice theory underpinned the dialogical process between the police and all interested parties.

Participants from both sides of the police–businesses relationship in the EDL case study described an ongoing relationship built on trust, which in many cases had survived the test of time. One Business participant explained that a key element was having "*confidence in what Merseyside Police were telling us*" which meant that they were "*happy to go with*" the Commander's decision. Another observed that "*trust does play a part,*" built on "*relationships*" where both parties are "*always fair.*" A further Business participant concurred, and described how their relationship with the police decision-makers was based on trust and this empowered them to support sometimes challenging situations:

> *I say this hand on heart, I don't ever feel that it's a chore, like I'm being asked for something that's unnecessary or anything like that. I know that if [police commander] comes and says to you, "Can you help me, can you do this for me?" I know the reason, and why they need it. It's not just something that's pie in the sky or something and they want it, there's a real reason why. And I really feel that I need to respond to that, and make that happen for them, because I know that they've got my back just as much as I've got theirs.*
> (Business G)

Police Commanders similarly described how trust had been a major factor when operating in both established relationships and in new relationships that were forged in the planning processes. One described how they had built relationships "*with people that I wouldn't have done historically,*" and that this had led to "*trust, even with those that wouldn't naturally engage with what we are trying to do.*" Another described how that had given and received reassurances through openness and transparency in liaison, cultivating further trust.

Building and developing relationships based on trust was also evidenced in examples provided by cull liaison officers and business participants who engaged during the badger cull. One described how liaising only with the pro-cull community had assisted in building trust with them:

> *We had this clear corridor policy that we don't talk to either side of the fence. And, it definitely worked, because the trust that I have now got from the farmers, because they know I do not talk to the protest side. They do know there are policemen talking to them, but the trust that I have built up now has gone tenfold from that time.*
> (PLT E)

A Business participant reaffirmed the significance of having a trusting relationship in engaging with the police:

> *Our big issue really about working with the police to start with, was around about trust, because we've always had to try and keep everyone's identity as secure as we possibly can. We know that even within our local area, there'd be members of the police who would be opposed to the badger culls, and we can't guarantee they're not going to feed information back. So, it's a case of really getting the right person and developing that confidence to work with that person, knowing they're there for you.*
> (Business B)

A dialogical approach therefore encouraged relationship building between all interested groups and the police, allowing each side to understand the rationale behind decisions made and provide a voice in the process. This approach furthered trust between groups and allowed an understanding of the legitimate aims of out-groups even where the views were polarised. For the process to be effective, selecting the right PLT in liaison was fundamental.

Using dialogue to balance human rights

It has been recognised (for example, Starmer, 1999; Mead, 2010) that the police performed a balancing act in facilitating peaceful protests and managing the human rights of all affected by an event. HMIC (2009a) described the role of the police in such events as "arbiter," although Gilmore (2013) questioned the neutrality of the police in this role. Neyroud and Beckley (2001) further recognised the complexity of the police dilemma in balancing competing rights. Both case studies examined in this research provided evidence that supported the position of the police at the centre of "*the real fine balancing act*," and participants from all interested parties opined that the police needed to "*sit on the fence*," were "*piggies in the middle*" and "*damned if they do and damned if they don't*."

However, despite identifying the police role as one of arbiter, there is a lacuna of research into how the police might undertake this balancing role. This research provided evidence, through two contrasting case studies with diverse demographics in terms of location, duration and participants, that by locating themselves in the centre of the balancing act and utilising a dialogical approach, Commanders were aided greatly in balancing the rights of all interested parties. Further, implementing a dialogical approach provided a fair process and a voice for all affected by the policing of the protest event. Participants in both case studies from every group of interested parties: the police; businesses; and both sides of the disputed cause provided evidence of how the dialogical process assisted in balancing the competing human rights of everyone.

In addition to balancing competing human rights, participants in this research provided examples of how implementing a dialogical approach had reduced conflict. A dialogical framework where those engaging believed that the police treated each party with fairness and were concerned about their welfare and views provided all parties with an understanding of the issues of others. The process not only assisted in balancing human rights, but reduced conflict and the threat of disorder and subsequently the police recourse to the use of force.

PLT engaged in the badger cull explained how a dialogical approach allowed them to explain to those with whom they engaged the implications for the police in balancing human rights and allowed them to give practical advice and guidance on what was acceptable. PLT described how they reassured Protectors that the police were happy for them to walk the byways and pathways but were able to outline boundaries and the implications of their walks on the privacy of residents. One PLT explained how the dialogue enabled groups who wanted to make their point to "*have that maximum impact, respecting obviously, the human rights articles, but at the same time reassuring the community who were all impacted that there is not going to be a mass riot.*" Another explained that they also took the opportunity to explain to Protectors the necessity for them to observe the rights of farmers and those working on the cull. Yet another talked of how the engagement allowed an education of all that "*trespass is okay as long as you're not intending to commit a crime,*" and an explanation that there were human rights at play as well as criminal offences. A further PLT provided an insight into how they had been able to educate the farming community about the balancing act in play:

I think that the farmers did not know about peaceful protest whatsoever. So, in my educational speeches and my expectation and conflict management talks that I give them, they really do shuffle their feet a lot. Because one of the scenarios I give is that they're coming out of their private "drove," what we call down here a "drove," which is a sort of grass patch between fields. And there's a protester blocking their path on the main road. And I say to them, "Peaceful protest?" "No! Get out of my way! You shouldn't be allowed to do this. We'll get the police, and they'll get rid of you!" And I'll say, "Well, it is!" And, they don't like it at all. And I said, "We'll come along, and we'll negotiate how long they can be there, so we'll facilitate that peaceful protest, and then they'll go on their way." And they say, "Well, this isn't right." "It's not right," say the farmers. And then, I'll refer to the milk protests that we had in Devon, where there is a massive dairy, where tractors went up there and blocked the path of vehicles. I said, "Are you happy with that?" "Ah, okay then." And, they all look down at the floor and shuffle their feet, and that's a great one, as they laugh. And they love it!

(PLT E)

A Commander described how the relationship that a PLT had built allowed the Commander to address an issue of balancing the rights of Protectors with those of the landowner. They described the issue that the landowners faced with civil trespass and described an incident when an elderly couple who repeatedly refused the polite requests of the police to stick to the paths. The Commander explained:

It's a civil offence, so there wasn't a great deal we could do in that situation. Through the PLTs, we spoke with [PLT]. A couple of phone calls later, yes, they still trespassed, but when they were politely asked to get back onto the paths, they did. So, it was a simple situation. And that was repeated any number of times.

(Commander I)

Various PLT recounted conversations where they were able to discuss the human rights concerns of different groups but were also able to explain the rights of others and ask them to respect their rights as well. One PLT commented, "*Getting them to understand that balance was, I think, a great success.*" There was evidence from all areas of an acceptance of the rights of others, gained through the dialogical work that was undertaken. Some PLT described their groups "*begrudgingly acknowledging that they too have to respect those rights,*" and acknowledging that "*there is a massive grey area in the middle,*" in relation to balancing rights.

Significantly, Business and Protector participants spoke of their acceptance that outsider parties also had rights that were in competition, which they had gleaned from dialogue with their respective police liaisons. It was evident that even though participants did not agree with the stance of outsider parties, they accepted that there was a conflict over which the police had an arbitrating role and engaging with the police allowed their rights and arguments to be considered. Examples provided and the language used illustrated that Business and Protector participants had taken on board what PLT had shared with them. One Business participant described the "competing human right" and their acceptance that "people have a right to protest," however they explained that there was a complexity when the protest involved trespass:

> *When it's civil trespass it's governed how people's rights to invade people's private property. And that is where it becomes an issue. Policing wise, I think a mistake we made initially was that we didn't really engage the police to explain to landowners in particular, really, what the police could and couldn't do. On the side of it, there's a comparison to, like a protest, I always say, in all these meetings now, you know, if someone is by your entrance and blocking it for a while, then technically, that's not very different from what farmers have done when they've been blockading supermarkets. So, again, there is that line between what you have a right to do and what you do not have a right to do. We have seen, well, I would say, certain situations from the protesters side, where they really pushed those limits.*
>
> (Business B)

One Protector observed that they acknowledged the rights of the "*shooters*" and realised that they had a job to do. Another Protector commented that they were "*well aware of the rights of the farming community.*" A Protector observed that the media painted the situation as two-sided between Protectors and the farming community, however this was not reflective of how they felt:

> *Everyone's got a right to think and say what they want, as long as it's done in an orderly manner. On all sides. It's not just my opinion that counts. Everyone's does. And I'm quite sure, from what I've seen, from the interaction that I've had, the farmers are being ignored. I certainly wouldn't see it as a "them and us."*
>
> (Protector C)

Examples were also provided by participants in the EDL march case study of how those engaging with the police altered their plans and working practices in cognisance of the human rights of other groups, because of the dialogue effectuated. A PLT explained that "*the EDL did modify what they wanted to do and recognised other people's rights.*" Commanders described how their liaison with businesses pre-event allowed an understanding of the balancing act that was required in facilitating a march, counterdemonstration and enabling the public to go about their business. Business participants described how understanding competing human rights through police liaison meant that they implemented "*contingency plans,*" including extra fencing and additional security, to facilitate the rights of others. On the day, PLT described how they had spoken to members of both sides during the stand-off and how explaining the rights of opposing groups assisted in diffusing some tensions.

One example cited by many participants which highlighted how police dialogue aided the balancing of human rights concerned several weddings planned for the EDL march day at St George's Hall. Business participants explained their concerns and the concerns of brides, families and staff that the EDL march would "*destroy*" wedding days and entail serous disorder on the steps of the Hall. Commanders explained how they utilised PLT to discuss the concerns with the EDL. A PLT recalled how having explained to EDL organisers that there were weddings due to take place on the same day, some of which had been planned for a long time, the EDL changed their plans as "*they didn't want to impact on anybody's day like that.*" Another PLT recounted their conversation:

> *We told them about the weddings in St George's Hall and that obviously we didn't want people there at St George's Hall, demonstrating. And [EDL] was quite happy about that. They said, "Well, we're not going to do that." They changed the route a number of times to accommodate ourselves and to accommodate hotspots.*
> (PLT M)

An EDL member corroborated the conversation and explained that they only became aware of the weddings once they had spoken to the PLT. However, they expounded that through the liaison they had "*taken into consideration everyone else's human rights,*" and assured the PLT that their march would not impact on the planned weddings at the Hall. Commanders explained how they were then able to further reassure the affected businesses and ultimately, despite contingencies being in place, balanced the right of those getting wed with the rights of the EDL wishing to march. A Business participant explained how understanding the rights of those wishing to march and counterdemonstrate, through the police dialogue, assisted them in both warning and informing wedding parties of possible disruption and allowed them to implement contingency plans, such as sourcing alternative ingress and egress points. Further, there was a compromise made in having police resources visible:

> *We didn't want it like that on the front of the Hall. We didn't necessarily want the image of 100 vans outside the Hall, or whatever it was, 80-odd vans. We gave*

that up. Because of the dialogue, we were able to do options, like reinforcing the fence line. We probably didn't need to do it, but we did as an extra precaution.

(Business C)

Every participating Commander who had policed the badger cull in Devon and Cornwall provided several examples of situations where dialogue had significantly assisted them in balancing competing human rights and in doing so had reduced conflict, the potential for disorder, improved public confidence in the police and ultimately reduced resources. Commanders provided an insight into how they utilised relationships forged to aid their decision-making. One Commander explained how having different liaison officers working under them had aided their decision-making in balancing the rights of government agencies with those wishing to protest against the cull. The Commander described how PLT would identify a location outside a government facility where a proposed public demonstration would be, and how they would then negotiate with the government department to facilitate a gathering or the handing in of a letter. The Commander described the initial reticence that had been encountered in negotiating with those wishing to protest outside the government building, but explained that, through PLT dialogue, a set of guidelines which were eventually agreed between both parties. The Commander explained:

We would agree where people would stand, it wouldn't be stopping people coming to work, that their workers wouldn't be seen by individuals and things like that. And also, facilitate a private meeting between the protest representative and a representative at the government agency, whereby privately there would be a letter handed over and they would have a very short discussion and an acceptance of the letter, and then protesters would leave. They would then agree to that and then we'd go back to the PLT and say, "They've agreed. Is your side happy with that?" "Yes." And then, the event. So, that was something that we did regularly. And all the events went without a hitch. And we had positive feedback from the protesters and the government departments, saying, "Do you know what, we didn't have anything to worry about there. And in fact, it was really good that we met people, and actually had a really good conversation over our differing views." So, that was a real positive.

(Commander H)

Another Commander provided examples of how the approach allowed the police to challenge and change inappropriate behaviour. The Commander described how police officers had identified cull contractors who had been concealing their vehicle registration marks and their own face. Through dialogue, it was ascertained that the cull contractors were doing so because they feared being identified and targeted by those opposed to the cull. The Commander described how explaining how the wearing of face coverings was perceived by the Protectors as intimidation and this resulted in the contractors changing their approach. This approach was applied to both sides equally, and the Commander further described where those opposed to the cull were challenged:

> *In one of the areas the anti-cull groups besieged a farmhouse and they also surrounded the car and intimidated a farmer's daughter. We were able to go back to them and say, "This is completely unacceptable. Is this the kind of fear that you want to be known for in terms of how you carry out your tactics?" And as a consequence of that feedback, that open dialogue, they modified the proceedings, and we didn't see any besieging of farms, and we didn't see any face coverings being used to intimidate people on that side of the fence. So, the open dialogue, the understanding of the impact of behaviour and the wider picture has really influenced two groupings about the same issue in different places.*
>
> (Commander B)

Another Commander detailed where dialogue had resolved potential conflict and facilitated a proportionate response:

> *On one particular night, it seemed to be a concerted protection effort night involving those that we had initially sought to engage with as the Protectors, as opposed to those who might employ different tactics. They were in radio comms with a group where there was some culling going on in a field. And basically, the ability of the PLTs there to defuse the situation ... They actually got the protesters who were in the field with cull operatives to come out of the field. They were hiding in trees, flashing torches, you know, the normal tactics. But, through the personal relationship that they had with the Protectors, the PLT were able to ... It was almost a negotiation process to get them to get the others who they were in contact with to come out of the trees and onto the road, the far side. Because there was a real risk of them in the field with firearms. Now, I took the opinion at the time, that because we had that good engagement with them, that actually a Section 35 I didn't think was proportionate at the time, because we had such a good interaction with the protectors, and they'd, you know, reciprocity. They'd done something for us, so we'll do something for them. We'll look after them and the other Protectors on the other side.*
>
> (Commander F)

Previous chapters have explored a range of approaches to the policing of protests: escalated force; negotiated management; strategic incapacitation; and strategic facilitation. It has been argued that the different approaches identified are not sequenced historical developments but provide a tool kit of strategic options for the police commander to utilise. Both case studies support this argument and have provided evidence of where different police approaches have been utilised, often simultaneously. Both case studies have consistently demonstrated that a predominant approach of strategic facilitation using PLT was implemented, however conscious decisions were made by Commanders to employ other approaches with different groups at different times. For example, a negotiated management approach was evidenced with certain anti-cull groups during the badger cull and strategic incapacitation with those opposing the EDL march pre-event. Furthermore, the police commander chose to remove PLT from engaging with EDL leaders when tensions were high and missiles were being thrown which, it is argued, can be described as a choice by the police commander to move from an approach of strategic facilitation to one of escalated force. However, throughout, a dialogical approach was consistently aspired to by Commanders, to ensure that the voice of those engaging was heard and a fair process was promoted. Therefore, the research evidences that police commanders have a range of approaches to utilise in protest events; however, the decision to use one approach over another should be informed by implementing a dialogical approach throughout.

Both case studies therefore provide supporting evidence of the benefits to both police and those wishing to march and protest in engaging in dialogue pre, during and post events. Further, this research extends the engagement to all interested parties, and evidences self-regulation in all parties due to a dialogical approach. Furthermore, both case studies provide evidence that a dialogical approach assists the police as arbiter in providing a procedurally fair process to balance the competing qualified rights, by providing a voice, through liaison officers, for all interested parties with the decision-making police Commander.

Conclusion

Both case studies that have been presented in this chapter provide analysis of the contribution that a dialogical approach made to the relationship building between police and protesters pre, during and post events, extending limited existing research and extolling the value of the approach for police and protesters alike. The contribution of a dialogical approach can be analysed through the application of both ESIM (for example, Drury and Reicher, 2000) and the Flashpoints Model (for example, King and Waddington, 2005) and that both models can be blended to provide a solid theoretical framework for understanding a dialogical approach to policing protest events. Both case studies identified at an interactional level that because the police dissolved those opposing or protesting into smaller, identifiable groups, rather than considering them a homogenous group, the police were able to engage with each one in turn and identify their aims and objectives. The research further observed the presence of self-policing as identified in both ESIM and Flashpoints Models and argues that this was a by-product of police dialogue and empowerment.

This research extends exiting literature by arguing that dialogue was not limited to police–protester liaison but included dialogue between the police and interested parties with a diverse involvement in the protest event, and analysis of such engagement can be conducted through the application of both ESIM and Flashpoints Model. Further, the value of a dialogical approach can be observed through the implementation of a procedurally fair approach and analysis suggests that procedural justice theory is compatible with and complementary to both ESIM and the Flashpoints Model. Implementing a dialogical approach provided a voice with the police decision-making commander to all interested parties and, by using designated officers as liaison, relationships were encouraged, developing trust. This allowed not only fair decisions to be made but ensured that the rationale was communicated to engaging parties, encouraging legitimacy.

This research provided evidence that a dialogical approach provided benefit to those wishing to march or protest and allowed them to achieve their aims through negotiation with the police, even at times when these aims pushed boundaries of legality. Further, the approach benefited police commanders as they tried to undertake the "unenviable task" (Gravelle and Rogers, 2011) of balancing the competing human rights of so many different interest parties and allowed the commander to remain, as far as possible, the "*piggy in the middle.*"

It is recognised that this research is based on two case studies where a dialogical approach was implemented and where this was a strategic driver in the police response and that not all police responses have utilised such an approach in the same manner. The case studies may not be reflective of all police approaches to protest events. However, the two cases do demonstrate that an equilibrium can be achieved if all parties are willing to engage in dialogue. The research contends that interested parties entering into dialogue may need to be prepared to give and take and find a common ground or at least are willing to seek one. It is acknowledged that some parties are not prepared to alter their stance and compromise; however, even in these cases, it is argued that there is value in them getting their point across and having their voice heard.

The police ultimately need to make a decision in balancing competing rights based on current legislation. However, such legislation can be and is challenged in a democracy and history is full of those whose actions have changed law and policies and resisted injustice (Knowles, 2016). The police must ensure that where groups choose not to engage that they do not make the presumption that this automatically implies that groups are non-compliant. Rather, the police should actively seek to understand why and consider where trust might be built. The building of trust with communities is a long-term process, requiring investment by the police to invest in a procedurally fair process with reconciliatory gestures to demonstrate an intent to increase trust (O'Brien and Tyler, 2019). Through the two case studies examined, this research proposes that the police must view those engaged in protest in the same light, as a community that is not geographically based, but rather transient and built on common beliefs and values. Having recognised such groups as a community in their own right, the police should then seek to build community cohesion and invest in the process all year round rather than simply appointing an available liaison officer a week before a protest event. In this way, the police continue to build trust with each group and the dialogue becomes a meaningful process based on two-way communication, providing a voice, encouraging self-policing and ultimately reducing the necessity for the police to intervene.

References

Bottoms, A. and Tankebe, J. (2012) Beyond procedural justice: A dialogic approach to legitimacy in criminal justice. *Journal of Criminal Law and Criminology*, 102(1), 119–170.

Bradford, B. (2012) Policing and social identity: Procedural justice, inclusion, and cooperation between police and public. *Legal Research Paper Series Paper 06(2012)*. New York: University of Oxford.

College of Policing (2018) *Police Liaison Teams* [online] Available at: https://www.app.college.police.uk/app-content/

della Porta, D. and Reiter, H. (1998) *Policing Protest: The Control of Mass Demonstrations in Western Democracies*. Minneapolis: University of Minnesota Press.

Drury, J. and Reicher, S. (2000) Collective action and psychological change: The emergence of new social identities. *British Journal of Social Psychology*, 39, 579–604.

Gilmore, J. (2013) 'This is not a riot!': Regulation of public protest and the impact of the Human Rights Act 1998. Ph.D. thesis. The University of Manchester.

Gorringe, H., Stott, C and Rosie, M. (2012) Dialogue police, decision-making, and the management of public order during protest crowd events. *Journal of Investigative Psychology and Offender Profiling*, 9, 111–125.

Gravelle, J. and Rogers, C. (2011) Engaging protesters: A smarter way for policing demonstrations. *The Police Journal*, 84, 5–12.

Her Majesty's Inspectorate of Constabulary. (2009a) *Adapting to Protest*. London: HMIC.

Her Majesty's Inspectorate of Constabulary (2009b) *Adapting to Protest: Nurturing the British Model of Policing*. London: HMIC.

Hoggett, J. and West, O. (2018) Police Liaison Officers at football: Challenging orthodoxy through communication and engagement *Policing: A Journal of Policy and Practice*, 14(4), 945–961.

Jackson, W., Gilmore, J. and Monk, H. (2019) Policing unacceptable protest in England and Wales: A case study of the policing of anti-fracking protests. *Critical Social Policy*, 39(1), 23–43.

Kilgallon, A. (2020) Police interaction and Notting Hill Carnival. *Policing and Society*, 30(1), 28–46.

King, M. and Waddington, D. (2005) Flashpoints revisited: A critical application to the policing of anti-globalization. *Protest, Policing and Society*, 15(3), 255–282.

Knowles, K. (2016) *A Brief History of Social Movements in the UK* [online] Available at: https://theculturetrip.com/europe/united-kingdom/articles

Lind, E. and Tyler, T. (1988) *The Social Psychology of Procedural Justice*. New York: Plenum Press

Luft, J. and Ingham, H. (1961) The Johari window: A graphic model of awareness in interpersonal relations *Human Relations Training News*, 5(9), 6–7.

Mead, D. (2010) *The New Law of Peaceful Protest: Rights and Regulation in the Human Rights Act Era*. Oxford: Hart.

National Anti Fraud Network (2019) *Intelligence Management Training* [online] Available at: https://www.local.gov.uk/sites/default/files/documents/Intelligence%20Management%20Training

National Crime Agency (2022) *Intelligence: Enhancing the Picture of Serious Organised Crime Affecting the UK* [online] Available at: https://www.nationalcrimeagency.gov.uk/what-we-do/how-we-work/

Neyroud, P. and Beckley, A. (2001) *Policing, Ethics and Human Rights*. Cullompton: Willan Publishing.

O'Brien, T. and Tyler, T. (2019) Rebuilding trust between police and communities through procedural justice and reconciliation. *Behavioral Science and Policy* 5(1), 34–50.

Reicher, S. (1996) The battle of westminster: Developing the social identity model of crowd behaviour in order to explain the initiation and development of collective conflict. *European Journal of Social Psychology*, 26, 115–134.

Starmer, K. (1999) *European Human Rights Law: The Human Rights Act 1998 and the European Convention on Human Rights*. London: Legal Action Group.

Sunshine, J. and Tyler, T (2003) The role of procedural justice and legitimacy in shaping public support for policing. *Law and Society Review*, 37(3), 513–547.

Tyler, T. and Lind, E. (1992) A relational model of authority in groups. *Advances in Experimental Social Psychology*, 25, 115–191.

Waddington, D. (2013) A 'kinder blue': Analysing the police management of the Sheffield anti-'Lib Dem' protest of March 2011. *Policing and Society*, 23(1), 46–64.

Watson, A. and Angell, B. (2007) Applying procedural justice theory to law enforcement's response to persons with mental illness. *Psychiatric Service*, 58(6), 787–792.

Chapter 8

Conclusion and recommendations

This book has examined the policing of protest and examined some of the challenges facing the police service in facilitating peaceful protest. The book has identified a variety of methods that the police have implemented in policing protest events and suggested that the different approaches may be viewed as a tool kit of possible responses available to police commanders and that police commanders utilise the approaches most applicable to achieve their strategies in policing the event in question. The book has examined the legislative framework within which the police must operate and particularly focused on the challenges of balancing competing qualified human rights. An examination of the author's journey as both insider and outsider researcher has provided insight into not only police research but considerations for all those conducting research within areas where they have extensive experience or expertise.

The main body of this book has examined a dialogical approach to the policing of protest events and has considered the contribution that the approach has made to the balancing of competing human rights. Through the conducting of semi-structured interviews, the voice of those engaged in or affected by protest events has been heard: protesters and counterdemonstrators; business representatives the subject of protest; police commanders as decision-makers; police liaison officers; local authority members; and members of businesses and organisations who are in some way affected by the event. Two diverse and contrasting case studies provided empirical data by which to examine the policing of protest events: the badger cull in South West England and an English Defence League (EDL) march in Liverpool. The events contrasted rural and inner-city settings; south and north of England locations; environmental and political protests; and an extended protest and a one-day event.

The data from the two case studies examined provided evidence that there is value for both the police and protesters in engaging in dialogue together pre, during and post events, to build relationships and engender trust. This research provided the first empirical research into the use of Police Liaison Teams (PLT) since the tactic became a national option and further evidences the contribution that the use of such officers has made to the dialogical process. The research explored in this book draws the conclusion that engaging in a

DOI: 10.4324/9781003160533-8

dialogical process with the police was of benefit not just to police and protesters, but to all interested parties involved in the protest event. Furthermore, this research argues that by engaging in dialogue, the police encourages an approach consistent with procedural justice theory which builds trust and confidence, provides a voice for interested groups and better equips police commanders to proportionately balance the competing human rights of all parties.

The research in this book has sought to address the identified lacuna in the literature by examining the role and identity of a range of groups and interested parties affected by a protest event and considering their interaction with the police and the balancing of their human rights. This research has considered the research questions identified at the end of Chapter 3: the value of a dialogical approach to the policing of protest events; the extension of a dialogical approach to include all interested parties; and the contribution made by the approach to the balancing of competing human rights. This final chapter will address the research questions, provide recommendations for the development of a dialogical approach to the policing of protest and detail further research opportunities that this empirical research has identified.

Addressing the research questions

The examination of protest policing made through the analysis of two case studies firstly provided further evidence of *the value of implementing a dialogical approach to the policing of protest events in the UK*. This book has augmented research into the use of PLT (for example, Waddington, 2013; Stott, Scothern and Gorringe, 2013) and provided primary data since the inclusion of PLT as a national tactic in Authorised Professional Practice (College of Policing, 2018). This research has concluded that both the Elaborated Social Identity Model (ESIM) (Gorringe, Stott and Rosie, 2012) and the Flashpoints Model (Waddington, 2013) provided a strong theoretical framework for examining a dialogical approach and argues that both models can be blended. For example, analysing at a structural level of the divergence in ideologies between the numerous groups opposing the EDL march (Flashpoints Model) allowed identification of groups within groups so they might be policed individually rather than as a homogeneous unit (ESIM). Further, this research purports that procedural justice theory (Bradford, 2012) provided an academic basis for examining the interaction. For example, trust and legitimacy, key components of a procedural justice approach, were identified as significant impact factors in the police response to the EDL march. Furthermore, this research argues that ESIM, the Flashpoints Model and procedural justice theory were mutually compatible and may be blended to provide a sound theoretical framework for examining a dialogical approach to the policing of protest. This was evidenced for example by analysing at an interactional level the intergroup encounters between the police and protest groups and examining the relationships and social interaction.

This research concluded that using a dialogical approach assisted both members of protest groups and the police in building relationships and that PLT provided a key link between the police decision-making commander and representatives of diverse protesting groups. This research evidenced numerous advantages for the police in engaging in dialogue with protest groups: promoting self-policing within protest groups; reducing conflict and disorder; enhancing public confidence in the police; and reducing police resources. This research also evidenced advantages for protesters in engaging in dialogue: mediation; representation; and a voice with the police decision-makers. Even those that had not engaged pre-event, who some police officers described as "*hard to reach*," advocated a dialogical approach and saw advantages in building relationships with the police. Contrary to Waddington's (1994) observations that police negotiation involved officers who were spuriously friendly in their engagement, this research evidenced the development of two-way relationships with give and take on both sides that was not limited to organisers (Joyce and Wain, 2014) but accessible to all involved in the protest across a wide continuum of protest intentions and responses. Instead, this research supports Waddington's observations (2016) that the police demonstrated a commitment to facilitating the rights and goals of peaceful protesters using PLT and that describing the liaison as a "sham" (Baker, 2014), implying that the police intended to coerce compliance, was a cynical misrepresentation of the police strategy and implementation of a dialogical approach. Examples were provided by police commanders and PLT of their desire for impartiality in policing protest events. Police commanders described how they sought to hear the voice of all those engaged in protest and even at times within both case studies, accepted protest actions that bordered on criminality. The research identified the importance of pre-event engagement between PLT and protesters, which provided points of contact and allowed relationships to be built on mutual trust. The engagement proved beneficial to both sides during the event and post-event and encouraged self-policing within protest groups, where protest groups changed their plans to accommodate out-groups.

Peterson (2006) argued that the police needed good knowledge of protest cultures and networks to be effective in policing protesters and that this knowledge was most effectively gathered over a period through direct contact with those organising protests. This research provided supporting evidence for Peterson's argument and identified that PLT were most effective when best placed to build knowledge of group cultures through relationship building. The research identified barriers and negative connotations perceived when the police utilised the collective noun of "protester" and identified numerous other terms that were favoured by participants, for example, protector, activist and demonstrator. Further, considerations were established for the police commanders to ponder in selecting the most appropriate officers to perform the role of PLT. The research concludes that police commanders should align PLT to specific groups and organisations and cautions against using PLT haphazardly or with opposing groups. In conclusion, the research provides evidence that the officer conducting dialogue should be specifically selected as the most appropriate to build open lines of communication between group members and police commanders. Further, by allowing the dialogue to be a continuing process, the building of relationships is encouraged, promoting trust between the police and the groups and assisting in ensuring a fair process is encouraged.

Secondly, the research examined in this book concludes that *a dialogical approach should be extended to include all interested parties affected by a protest event*. An examination of human rights legislation and case law within the *Policing and Protest* chapter established competing qualified rights that are engaged during protest events. Empirical research from both case studies identified numerous interested parties that were affected by the protest events whose human rights were engaged during the event. This research identified such interested groups, including businesses that were the subject of protest; landowners; business members; local authorities; emergency services; travel companies and organisations; the local community; politicians and councillors; and other interested parties. The research contends that there are clear advantages for all interested parties in engaging in dialogue with the police. A dialogical approach allowed the police to inform other parties of police decisions and rationale. It also afforded interested parties a voice with the police and provided an opportunity for them to inform police decisions.

The research examined in this book concludes that the role of the police officer acting as a liaison between police commanders and interested parties was significant in maintaining dialogue and encouraging relationship building and trust. Akin to the role of PLT with protest groups, the liaison officer engaged pre, during and post events and maintained a two-way dialogical link. The research identified several different officers performing the role of liaison between the police commander and the parties: PLT; operational planners; public order tactical advisors; cull liaison officers; chief officers; community officers; and public order commanders. The research discovered that, comparable to the conclusion with choosing PLT, selecting the most appropriate liaison officer to perform the role of dialogical conduit was of primary importance. Many liaison officers were selected due to their existing relationships with interested groups rather than whether they were trained as PLT and where appropriate the selected officers received training to further equip them in the role. Utilising diverse liaison officers also entailed diversity in dress codes, from the recognisable PLT light blue bib to regular police uniform through to attire more suitable for liaison with the farming community to protect the anonymity of individuals who were liaising with the police. Despite the diversity, a clear command structure was described in both case studies and this research contends that by having such clarity, the integrity of the liaison role was maintained irrespective of the rank of the officer performing the role.

Finally, this research concludes that *applying a dialogical approach assisted police commanders to proportionally balance the competing human rights of all those engaged in the event*. Further, it reveals that a dialogical approach encouraged an approach based on procedural justice, which promoted transparency, fairness, impartiality and a voice for all parties (Blader and Tyler, 2003). The dialogue allowed police commanders to understand and consider the views, opinions, aims and objectives of each group, which better equipped commanders to balance competing rights. Where police commanders sought to restrict or prevent groups from certain actions, such as a desired march route, the research evidenced occasions where the police decisions were communicated to groups through liaison officers and where subsequently the groups modified their behaviours and accepted the rights of others. Where the outcomes were not favourable for groups, the research provided evidence of acceptance of the decisions by the groups because individuals felt that their voice had been heard and considered by the police in the decision-making process and that they had a right to reply. Furthermore, this research concludes that the dialogue also impacted on police decisions and examples were provided where the police, rather than maintain control, on occasions facilitated actions that were not always lawful.

The research presented in this book concludes that the role of the police commander was not one of balancing peaceful protest with maintaining order (for example, Peterson, 2006; Mansley, 2014) rather was more nuanced with the commander located as *"piggy in the middle"* of numerous interested groups and individuals needing to balance competing qualified rights in their decision-making. The research identified numerous parties who had a vested interest in protest events and described how the police sought to engage all groups in dialogue pre, during and post event. This research argues that the police were independent and unbiased in their decision-making, even where political pressure was exerted. Contrary to Mansley (2014) who proposed that the police were the embodiment of the state at political demonstrations, the two case studies provided examples where the police negotiated with politicians and councillors and balanced their wishes with those of protest groups and marchers. Rather than supporting the "state" in seeking to "stamp down on any action outside of the usual channels" (Mobbs, 2009: 19), this research evidenced how the police made decisions independent to and at times contrary to the perceived "state" (for example, DEFRA; local politicians; and the Mayor of Liverpool). The research concludes that by engaging all parties in dialogue, including political groups and individuals, police commanders were better placed to balance competing rights and, through dialogue via liaison officers, keep all parties abreast of the decisions made and the supporting rationale dialogue. Furthermore, this research contends the approaches to policing protest, namely escalated force, negotiated management, strategic incapacitation and strategic facilitation, traditionally viewed as a sequenced historical development, are rather strategic options available in the tool kit of the police commander. The research provides evidence that by applying a dialogical approach the police commander is best placed to select the most appropriate policing response to the individuals and groups engaged in the protest event.

Gilmore, Jackson and Monk (2016) suggested that effective dialogue was repressed by a lack of trust between protesters and police. However, this research evidenced a clear trust reciprocated between police and protesters which became the foundation for relationship building. Moreover, this research evidenced trust-based relationships between the police and all interested parties engaged in the protest events. Some relationships were long-standing, for example, between the police and partner agencies such as other emergency services and the local authority. Others were formed due to the uniqueness of the events, for example with cull operators and businesses subject to or affect by the protests. However, this research found that at the heart was open dialogue which encouraged the building of relationships and provided a voice to those engaging with the police decision-makers, allowing an open, transparent and fair process (Tyler and Lind, 1992) to be observed by all interested parties. This in turn propagated trust, which further deepened the professional relationships and the research evidenced in-group (Drury and Reicher, 2000) acceptance of the police liaison officers within the communities with which they engage.

Recommendations

The research in this book has engendered three key recommendations which are offered to aid police commanders, liaison officers, members of protest groups and all those affected by protest events in the UK. The below provides practical recommendations which might be considered in planning the policing of events. This research advocates that all affected by protest events should engage in dialogue with the police and that the police should seek to build and maintain relationships with each group based on trust. Further, the recommendations made should be considered when preparing national policy on the policing of protests and the use of PLT as a tactical option.

1. The police should identify all interested parties and map the dialogue between them and the police.

This research recommends that when planning a dialogical approach to the policing of protest events, police commanders should identify all interested parties that are involved in or affected by the protest, including groups within groups, and seek to establish lines of dialogue between the police commanders and representatives from all interested parties. The badger cull was perceived by outsiders as entailing groups who were anti-cull protesting against the farmers who were carrying out the cull (for example, Morris, 2016). However, this research identified numerous interested parties affected by the cull who might not be considered as social actors with a vested interest in the policing of the cull, including schools, feed merchants and hunt saboteurs, with whom the police engaged.

In identifying groups within groups, it is recommended that the police avoid contentious nomenclature, such as the term "protester," and through liaison officers determine preferred collective nouns for each group, utilising terminology that will assist in providing identity to each key group and promoting relationship building. It is recommended that the dialogue is mapped to detail all interested parties, establish existing lines of dialogue and identify gaps so that the commander may seek to foster new relationships and ensure that all parties maintain dialogue and have a voice with the police decision-makers. A Dialogical Wheel template is provided to assist in mapping the dialogue (see Figure 8.1). The wheel is constructed with the police commander at the centre to represent the role of the commander as arbiter (HMIC, 2009) in balancing competing right, not being drawn onto one side or another. Each interested party is positioned on an outer circle, all equidistant from the police commander, to represent the impartial and fair approach required of the police commander in their decision-making. The police liaison officers are located as conduits, providing a dialogical link between the police commander and the interested parties, whilst the spokes denote the two-way flow of dialogue.

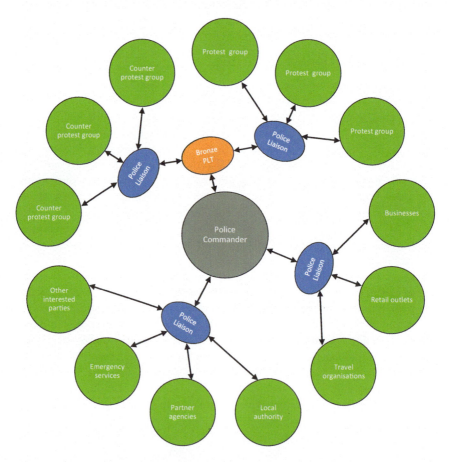

Figure 8.1 The Dialogical Wheel template.

In identifying liaison officers, it is recommended that police commanders select the most appropriate officers and, if necessary, provide them with suitable training, rather than utilising trained PLT on a random basis. Police commanders should determine which officers are best placed to undertake the role of liaison officer to foster new and build on existing relationships. Although PLT ordinarily fulfil the liaison role, commanders may consider other options where existing relationships may be utilised in the dialogical process, for example where senior officers, community officers or operational planners have established relationships and lines of communication. It is also recommended that where there are opposing parties engaged in protest, police commanders appoint a Bronze PLT to assist in guarding against potential Stockholm Syndrome, to ensure that PLT maintain their impartiality as police officers and to mediate between opposing PLT and liaison officers and ensure that commanders "*reset the compass to true north.*"

2. *Everyone affected by the protest event should consider the values of engaging in dialogue with the police.*

UK legislation places an onus on march organisers to provide the police with written notification (Section 11, Public Order Act 1986) and therefore there exists an open channel for potential dialogue, although some (for example, McCarthy and McPhail, 1998; Waddington, 1994) have suggested that on occasions "negotiated management" has witness organisers being coerced by the police into negotiating. In contrast to marches or processions, static protests, demonstrations and counterdemonstrations require no prior notification to the police under UK law and therefore protests may appear spontaneously without any prior engagement with the police. This research argues that there is benefit both to the police and those intending to protest to engage in dialogue prior to events irrespective of legal requirements.

It is therefore recommended that those intent on peacefully protesting or counterdemonstrating consider seeking to engage with the police prior to events. This research has evidenced barriers to engagement; protesters expressing a lack of trust and a concern that the police are interested solely in gathering intelligence; and police officers presuming that those not engaging are intent on criminality or disorder. For dialogue to be considered between the police and protesters, the police must accept that some individuals and groups do not wish to engage, but should still not presume, as identified by Gilmore, Jackson and Monk (2016) that groups not engaging do so because they are intent on disorder. In return, those engaging in protest must embrace the potential for open and honest engagement with the police and believe that there are advantages in them liaising with the police that outweigh non-engagement.

This research further recommends that all interested parties should consider engagement with the police prior to, during and post protest events. This research concludes that there is benefit to all parties in engaging in dialogue: businesses that are the subject of protest; those affected by the protest, such as the local authority and other agencies; and the local community. This research has similarly evidenced barriers to dialogue where businesses have not wished to engage for fear of being identified and becoming the focus of direct action. This research contends that to address barriers identified and promote engagement, trust between the police and all interested parties is key, as identified in the final recommendation.

3. A procedural justice approach should be sought with all those affected by the protest event to facilitate a dialogical approach.
It is recommended that the police advocate a procedurally just approach to encourage dialogue, the building of relationships and trust with all those affected by the protest event. Both case studies evidence that by encouraging lines of dialogue through police liaisons with all interested parties as identified through the mapping of a Dialogical Wheel, the police commander provided a voice for all parties, was better positioned to balance conflicting rights and was equipped to provide information and rationale to all affected by the decisions made. The research argues that doing so encouraged an approach based on procedural justice theory (for example, Bradford, 2012) where interested parties were less concerned by the results of the decisions made but more minded that a fair process had been implemented and their voice had been heard.

At the heart of implementing a fair process in decision-making is the use of information and intelligence, the starting point for police commanders in following a decision-making process (College of Policing, 2014). Those engaging with the police should understand how information becomes intelligence and how PLT will "*go in to bat*" for those with whom they have engaged over a period of time. However, police commanders must ensure that PLT "are not deployed to gather intelligence" (College of Policing, 2018). This book has evidenced a potential for the police to misuse the relationship forged with those engaging and seek intelligence from sources not deployed for this reason. Police commanders must seek to preserve long-term relationships rather than have a short-term "*not on my watch*" mentality to the policing of protest events.

It is therefore recommended that the police seek to build relationships and trust with *all* interested parties. Police commanders should consider how best to implement a procedurally fair approach, hear the voice of all interested parties and maintain open lines of communication. This research found that selecting the most appropriate liaison officers encouraged relationship building and that time spent in pre-event engagement was most important in fostering such relationships. It is recommended that police commanders should invest in liaison officers and allow them time to build rapport and trust. Police commanders should consider aligning liaison officers to specific groups and not appoint PLT randomly to groups, which may both compromise the officers and create suspicion with those with whom they wish to engage. Applying such an approach will assist commanders in selecting the most appropriate police approach to employ with individuals and groups pre, during and post protest event.

Particularly for groups not engaging, or groups that the police perceive to be "*hard to reach,*" for example activists counterdemonstrating against the EDL march and hunt saboteurs active during the badger cull, this book has evidenced a willingness on behalf of such groups to engage, if approached. The research has identified that those who protest spontaneously may be more difficult to identify and engage with pre-event, but also identified that at times such groups are themselves event organisers and therefore more willing to engage. For example, those groups that opposed the EDL march in Liverpool (Unite Against Fascism, 2017) had a long history of previous marches within the city (for example, Houston, 2011; Bartlett, 2014; James, 2013; Unison, 2014) and had previously engaged with the police to some extent. This research argues that the police must be more proactive in approaching groups perceived as being harder to reach and invest time in the groups rather than expect the groups to suddenly engage immediately prior to or during a protest event. It is therefore recommended that the police commander should consider how to nurture relationships with such groups whether they are event organisers or counterdemonstrators, to maintain relationships and build trust. The police must seek to invest in "*sustainable*" relationships rather than engage in "*tokenism*" and regard each group as a community in its own right, discerned not by geographically but through holding a common belief and set of values that unites the community. The police must ensure that dialogue is two-way and must be prepared to foster long-term relationships on the terms of the protest groups and not the police. This research provides evidence that by investing in a procedurally just approach and continuing to attempt to engage with all groups, self-policing will be promoted. Further, the building of trust will lessen the suspicion, in those who do not wish to engage, that the police are merely seeking to gather intelligence and will encourage groups to consider benefits to them from entering into dialogue with the police.

Reflective limitations and further research

In reflecting on the research presented in this book, it is acknowledged that selecting two case studies on which to provide recommendations has limitations when drawing conclusions to inform national policy. Although rich in depth, the data for the case studies provide a small snapshot of the UK policing response to deploying a dialogical approach to protest events and it is recognised that those interviewed may not represent all voices or opinions from their respective groups. This research does, however, provide initial analysis of the use of PLT in the UK after their inclusion as a national tactic. Further, the research allowed inaugural analysis of police dialogue with all interested parties and not solely with protesters.

It is recognised that this research is limited in examining those that had not engaged in dialogue and why there might have been a reluctance. Although two participating Activists who demonstrated against the EDL march had not engaged pre-event and provided some insight into their reasons, access to further participants was restricted to those that responded and were willing to be interviewed. However, the main focus of this research was to concentrate on the contribution that a dialogical approach made to policing protest events and therefore gathered data primarily from those police officers, protesters and interested parties who had engaged in dialogue with each other in order to evaluate this contribution.

Whilst conducting this research, other academic fields were considered and although not fully explored, it is suggested that further investigation would provide another level of research in examining a dialogical approach to the policing of protest. It was particularly identified that a relational sociological approach (for example, Tilly, 1978; White, 1992; Donati, 2010; Mische, 2011; Crossley, 2010) might provide a complimentary theoretical framework in which to examine dialogical interaction.

Crossley (2015: 66) described his approach to relational sociology as one which "affords primacy, both ontological and methodological, to interactions, social ties ('relations') and networks" and concluded that people's lives, thoughts, actions and desires were always interwoven with those of other people and as such affected each other within society. Donati (2010) analysed the component social spheres that comprised society and identified the different levels at which they exist: the micro (for example, at family level); the meso (for example, at a local community level); and the macro (for example, at a national, international or global level) of society. Both Crossley (2010) and Donati (2010) suggested that relational sociology gave the potential to analyse interactions on both micro and macro levels and argued that relationships and interactions can exist between human beings, organisations, multinational organisations and nation states. As such individuals, organisations, governments and multinational corporations do not exist in isolation but are the consequences of interaction and various kinds of networks.

Understanding a society from a relational approach entails seeing it as reducible to the relationships within it, with the social being the patterned networks of connection between social actors (Crossley, 2010). Applying such an approach to this research would entail considering the interested parties identified in the Dialogical Wheel as social actors involved in protest events at micro, meso and macro levels. It is suggested that further research may be embarked upon to consider whether a relational sociological approach might be epistemologically compatible with and complementary to the theoretical framework established in this research and provide a deeper sociological analysis of a dialogical approach to the policing of protest.

Summary

This book has examined a dialogical approach to the policing of protest and the balancing of human rights. The word "dialogical" has been designated throughout as the collective term to describe the interaction between the police and interested parties and encompasses all the terms identified throughout this book, including liaison, engagement, dialogue, negotiation and communication. Significance has not been placed on the term used, rather the extent to which the police and interested parties entered into dialogue throughout the policing period and the value of this dialogue pre, during and post events. Further, the research extends a dialogical approach and argues that this approach was not limited to police–protester interaction but encompassed a whole spectrum of engagement and dialogue, including partnership meetings, formal police-led coordination group meetings, one-to-one liaison with operational planners and continuing the established relationships with partners.

This book has provided further research into the use of PLT and provides inaugural data since the inclusion of PLT as a national tactical option. This research reaffirms the argument (for example, Gorringe, Stott and Rosie, 2012; Waddington, 2013) that using a liaison-based approach brought benefit to both the police and protesters. This research extends the existing literature and contends that engaging in a dialogical approach is beneficial to all those affected by a protest event and that there is value for all parties in liaison pre, during and post the event. Furthermore, this research has examined the balancing act that the police must perform in facilitating the human rights of all parties. This research argues that the role of the police in balancing competing rights is one of "*piggy in the middle.*" It contends that by mapping out all interested parties and seeking a point of dialogue between each identified interested group and the police commander through the conduit of an appropriate liaison officer, the police can employ a procedurally fair approach in attempting to balance competing qualified human rights. Furthermore, this research concludes that trust will develop through ongoing relationships between the liaison officers and interested parties, empowering all groups to self-police and allowing all groups to make concessions based on an understanding of decisions and rationale.

References

Baker, D. (2014) Police and protester dialog: Safeguarding the peace or ritualistic sham? *International Journal of Comparative and Applied Criminal Justice*, 38(1), 83–104.

Bartlett, N. (2014) Unions gearing up for Thursday's strike against 'poverty pay'. *Liverpool Echo* [online], 8 July 2014. Available at: https://www.liverpoolecho.co.uk/news/unions-liverpool-gearing-up

Blader, S. and Tyler, T. (2003) A four-component model of procedural justice: Defining the meaning of a "fair" process. *Personality and Social Psychology Bulletin*, 29(6).

Bradford, B. (2012) Policing and social identity: Procedural justice, inclusion, and cooperation between police and public. *Legal Research Paper Series Paper 06(2012).* New York: University of Oxford.

College of Policing (2014) *National Decision Model* [online] Available at: https://www.app.college.police.uk/app-content/national-decision-model/

College of Policing (2018) *Police Liaison Teams* [online] Available at: https://www.app.college.police.uk/app-content/public-order/planning-and-deployment/

Crossley, N. (2015) Relational sociology and culture: A preliminary framework. *International Review of Sociology*, 25(1), 65–85.

Crossley, N. (2010) *Towards Relational Sociology.* Abbingdon: Routledge.

Donati, P. (2010) *Relational Sociology: A New Paradigm for the Social Sciences.* London and New York: Routledge.

Drury, J. and Reicher, S. (2000) Collective action and psychological change: The emergence of new social identities. *British Journal of Social Psychology*, 39, 579–604.

Gilmore, J., Jackson, W. and Monk, H. (2016) *Keep moving! Report on the policing of the Barton Moss community protection camp: November 2013 –April 2014.* Centre for the Study of Crime, Criminalisation and Social Exclusion, Liverpool John Moores University: Centre for Urban Research, University of York.

Gorringe, H., Stott, C and Rosie, M. (2012) Dialogue police, decision-making, and the management of public order during protest crowd events. *Journal of Investigative Psychology and Offender Profiling*, 9, 111–125.

Her Majesty's Inspectorate of Constabulary (2009a) *Adapting to Protest.* [pdf] London: HMIC. Available at: http://www.justiceinspectorates.gov.uk/hmic

Houston, J. (2011) Liverpool strikers march from Pier Head. *BBC News* [online], 30 November 2011. Available at: https://www.bbc.co.uk/news/uk-england-merseyside-15938902

James, R. (2013) March against fascism demo Liverpool. *Unite the Union* [online], 12 October 2013. Available at: https://unitetheunion.org/what-we-do

Joyce, P. and Wain, N. (2014) *Palgrave Dictionary of Public Order Policing, Protest and Political Violence.* London: Palgrave Macmillan.

Mansley, D (2014) *Collective Violence, Democracy and Protest Policing.* London and New York: Routledge.

McCarthy, J. and McPhail, C. (1998) The institutionalization of protest in the United States, in Meyer, D. and Tarrow, S. eds., *The Social Movement Society: Contentious Politics for a New Century*, 83–110. New York: Rowman and Littlefield.

Mische, A. (2011) Relational sociology, culture, and agency, in Scott, J. and Carrington, P. eds., *Sage Handbook of Social Network Analysis*, 80–98. London. Sage.

Mobbs, P. (2009) NETCU, WECTU and NPOIU: Britain's secretive police force: politicising the policing of public expression in an era of economic change. *The Free Range Electrohippies Project.* Available at: http://www.fraw.org.uk/fraw_admin

Morris, S. (2016) Badger cull: Animal rights group publishes names of farmers. *The Guardian* [online], 23 March 2016. Available at: https://www.theguardian.com/environment/2016

Peterson, A. (2006) Policing contentious politics at transnational summits: Darth Vader or the Keystone Cops? in della Porta, D., Peterson, A. and Reiter, H. eds., *The Policing of Transnational Protest*, 33–74. Aldershot: Ashgate.

Stott, C., Scothern, M., and Gorringe, H. (2013) Advances in Liaison based public order policing in England: Human Rights and Negotiating the Management of Protest? *Policing*, 7(2), 212–226.

Tilly, C. (1978) *From Mobilization to Revolution*. Reading: Addison-Wesley.
Tyler, T. and Lind, E. (1992) A relational model of authority in groups. *Advances in Experimental Social Psychology*, 25, 115–191.
Unison (2014) Thousands March in Liverpool for fair funding for public services. *Unison* [online], 17 March 2014. Available at: http://www.unisonnw.org/
Unite Against Fascism (2017) *Merseyside Defeats Fascist EDL: Victory on the Mersey!* [online], 5 June 2017. Available at: http://uaf.org.uk/2017
Waddington, D. (2013) A 'kinder blue': Analysing the police management of the Sheffield anti-'Lib Dem' protest of March 2011. *Policing and Society*, 23(1), 46–64.
Waddington, D. (2016) From 'iron fists' to 'bunches of fives': A critical reflection on dialogue (or liaison) approaches to policing political protest. *European Police Science and Research Bulletin*, 1, 30–43.
Waddington, P. (1994) *Liberty and Order: Public Order Policing in a Capital City*. London: U.C.L. Press.
White, H. (1992) *Identity and Control: A Structural Theory of Social Action*. Princeton: Princeton University Press.

Index

activism 172; far-right 158–159, 166–167, 171; "left-wing" 162–163, 170, 171; *see also* English Defence League (EDL) march
Adang, O. 4, 5
Allen, C. 159, 166
Al-Makhamreh, S. 79
Alvesson, M. 78
Anderson, J. 156, 181
Angell, B. 58, 134, 186, 226
Animal Plant Health Agency (APHA) 110–111
Anti-Fascist Network 155
Association of Chief Police Officers (ACPO), Tactical Tasking and Co-ordination Group (TTCG) 8
Atak, K. 42
Atkinson, P. 87, 154

badger cull 2, 11, 74, 82, 101, 149, 150, 222, 225, 229–231, 234, 240; Animal Plant Health Agency (APHA) 110–111; background 102–105; bovine tuberculosis (bTB) 102–105, 115; Camp Badger 109–110; cull liaison officers (CLOs) 123–124; dialogue during the event 135–136; dialogue post-event 136–137; dialogue process 121–125; fairness of policing 127–129; farming community 111–112; human rights implications 137–139; hunt saboteurs 108–109; identifying interested parties 106–112; illegitimacy 118–121; interested parties 106; interview locations 93–95; interviews 91–92; licenses 103–104; "Middle England" group 107–108; negotiated management 125; opposition 104–105, 107–111, 115; Police Liaison Teams (PLT) 111–112, 114–115, 119–120; political pressure 125–127; pre-event engagement 133–135; relationship building 143–145; self-policing 215–216, 220; stakeholders, identity and nomenclature 112–115; strategic facilitation 124–125; value of a dialogical approach 211–212, 217–218
Baker, D. 41
balance 32
Barton Moss environmental protest 9
Bartos, O. 31
Baxter, N. 17
BBC News 5
Beckley, A. 39, 40, 192, 230
Benedictus, L. 38
bias 83
Black Lives Matter 28
Blader, S. 58, 59
Blair, T. 3
Bottoms, A. 58
Bourne, K. 200
bovine tuberculosis (bTB) 102–105, 111, 115
Bradford, B. 57, 58
Brannick, T. 78–79, 85
Brearley, N. 17, 25, 113
Breen, L. 79
British Transport Police (BTP) 164, 165
"broken windows" theory 25
Brown, G. 5
Brun, H. 158–159, 166
Buckle, J. 79
Bunce, A. 83
Burgess, R. 79, 81, 84, 86
Bush, G. W. 2
Button, M. 25, 26, 33, 106, 113

Camp Badger 109–110
Canada 24
Cardiff City Football Club 59
carrot and stick approach 20–21
case studies, identifying 81–83
cases: *Appleby and Others v The United Kingdom [2001] ECHR 6* 39; *Percy v Director of Public Prosecutions [2001] ADMN 21* 39; *Plattform Ärzte Für das Leben v Austria [1988] EHRR 204* 39; *R (McClure & Moos) v Commissioner of Police of the Metropolis* 40; *R (on the application of Hicks and Others) v Commissioner of Police of the Metropolis [2017] UKSC 9* 40; *R (on the application of Laporte) v Chief Constable of Gloucestershire Constabulary [2006] UKHL 55* 39–40; *Redmond-Bate v Director of Public Prosecutions [1999] ADMN 23* 40; *Regina (Brehony) v Chief Constable of Manchester Police [2005] QBD 23* 39
citizen journalist 32
Clapham, A. 40
coercive strategies 23
Coffey, A. 87, 89
Coghlan, D. 78–79, 85
Coleman, R. 31
College of Policing 8–10, 56, 67, 78, 82, 86
command and control 25
conflict theory 31
containment 7, 26, 53
Copsey, N. 166
Corporate Social Responsibility (CSR) 26–27
counterdemonstrations, English Defence League (EDL) march 163–164, 174
Covid-19 pandemic 28, 31
Crabtree, B. 87
Creswell, J. 74–75
criminal justice, legitimacy 57
Critcher, C. 54, 55, 200
Crossley, N. 250
crowd psychology 7, 50; classic theory 51; Elaborated Social Identity Model (ESIM) 3, 7, 51–53; escalated force 19; Flashpoints Model of Public Disorder 54–56; legitimacy 53; Social Identity Model (SIM) 51–52; training 51; *see also* Elaborated Social Identity Model (ESIM); Flashpoints Model of Public Disorder

Dahlsrud, A. 33
Dawson, P. 76
de Lint, W. 24, 41, 42, 145
decision-making 244, 248; fairness 227; impartiality 127–129, 140–141; intelligence gathering 228; political pressure 125–127, 181–183; *see also* fairness
della Porta, D. 18, 20, 22, 23, 30, 32, 41, 42, 55, 125, 136, 181
demonstrations: counter 161–163, 174; "Smash NATO" 27
deterrence policy 57
Deutsch, M. 58
Devon and Cornwall Police 91, 104, 105, 107–108, 112, 128, 136, 217, 234
dialogical approach 1–2, 4, 7, 11, 50, 58, 63, 67, 68, 77, 82, 83, 106, 107, 206, 210, 237, 241, 242, 251; badger cull protests 121–125, 135–136; balancing human rights 230–236, 243–244; communication between police and protesters 41–42, 200–201; Elaborated Social Identity Model (ESIM) 3, 7, 36, 51–53, 56; English Defence League (EDL) march 178–180, 189–190; Flashpoints Model of Public Disorder 54–56; non-engagement 147–149, 201–205; point of contact 142, 198–199; Police Liaison Teams (PLT) 1–2, 9–11, 28, 36, 50, 53, 63–67; post-event dialogue 136–137, 190–191; pre-emptive 133–135, 186–189; providing a voice 221–223; relationship building 142–145, 199–200; stakeholder group meetings 179–180; trust with all interested parties 228–230, 243; trust with protest groups 223–228; two-way communication 145–147; value of 211–215; *see also* negotiated management; Police Liaison Teams (PLT)
Dialogical Wheel 12, 123, 149, 180, 246
dialogue officer 4
DiCicco-Bloom, B. 87
disorder 54; *see also* Flashpoints Model of Public Disorder
Donati, P. 250
Drury, J. 51–53
Dwyer, S. 79

Easton, K. 77
EcoStream 37–38
EDL march: face coverings 176–177; minorities 175
Elaborated Social Identity Model (ESIM) 3, 7, 36, 51, 53, 56, 61–64, 106, 124,

210, 241; concept 52; conditions 52; dynamics 52
Elam, G. 83
Elwood, S. 88
empathy 224
English Defence League (EDL) march 2, 11, 74, 206, 222–223, 228–229, 233, 240; background 154–160; business participants, self-policing 220–221; communication between police and EDL 200–201; counterdemonstrations 155, 161–163; dialogue during the march 189–191; dialogue process 178–181; far-right supporters 158–159, 166–167; human rights implications 191–198; identifying interested parties 160–165; illegitimacy 174–175; interview locations 93–95; interviews 92–93; key stakeholders 163–164; lack of trust between parties 174; "left-wing" opposition 170, 171; non-engagement between police and participants 204–205; opposition 157–158, 163; organisers 160–161; point of contact 198–199; police participants 165–166; policing 164–165, 176–178; political influences on policing 181–183; pre-event engagement 186–189; role of PLT 184–185; selection of PLT officers 185–186; self-policing 215; unions 172; unjust responses 177–178; value of a dialogical approach 212–215, 218–220
environmental activism 25, 33; *see also* badger cull
escalated force 18–19, 41
European Court of Human Rights (ECHR) 34
European Union 2, 5
Evidence Gathering Teams 9
evidence-based policing (EBP) 74, 75; experience versus 76–77; knowledge and 76
experience 79; versus evidence-based policing 76–77; insider research 79–80
Extinction Rebellion (XR) 66
extremism 166–167

face coverings, EDL march 176–177
facilitators 27–28
fairness 62, 195, 227; of badger cull policing 127–129; of EDL march policing 176–177; legitimacy and 57–60
Family Liaison Officer 8

farming community, self-policing 220
far-right groups 158–159, 166–167, 171
Farsides, T. 52
Fitwatch 10
fixed speed cameras 60
Flashpoints Model of Public Disorder 50, 53, 54, 56, 61, 62, 64, 241; criticisms 55
Fleming, J. 76
Flick, U. 77
Flyvbjerg, B. 81
Forward Intelligence Teams (FIT) 9, 10
freedom of assembly 138, 191
full-time protesters 25, 113

G8 summit protests 24, 30
gatekeepers, recruiting 84–86
Gillham, P. 22–23, 30
Gilmore, J. 29, 33, 38, 40, 42, 66, 147, 201, 204, 206, 228, 230, 245, 246
Gordon, J. 37
Gorringe, H. 2, 21, 22, 24, 27, 32–33, 51, 55, 63–65, 119, 121, 130, 185, 186, 215
Gothenburg Committee 3–4
Grace, J. 33
Grahame, K., *The Wind in the Willows* 102
Gravelle, J. 26–27
Greenberg, R. 77
group engagement model 58
Group of Twenty (G20) 1, 5
Guest, G. 83

Hall, L. 17
hard policing 26
Hedkvist, T. 3
Her Majesty's Inspectorate of Constabulary (HMIC) 1, 26, 38, 53, 63, 215, 230
Her Majesty's Inspectorate of Constabulary and Fire and Rescue Services (HMICFRS) 33–34
Hermanns, H. 87
Herzog, H. 87–88
Hinds, L. 59
Hoggett, J. 51, 59–60, 75
Holgersson, S. 3
Horn, R. 77, 80
Hough, M. 57–58
House of Commons Home Affairs Committee 6
human rights 6, 10, 11, 16, 74, 86, 158; absolute 36; badger cull, implications 137–139; balancing 32–35, 37, 139–141, 181, 194–198, 230–237, 243–244; EDL march, implications 191–198; legislation

35–38; limited 36; negative obligations 35–36; positive obligations 35–36; public order training 7–8; qualified 36–38; qualified, balancing 38–40
Human Rights Act (UK, 1998): Article 5 40; Article 9 192–194; Article 10 40, 192–194; Article 11 36, 39, 192–194; Article 17 37–38; balancing qualified rights 38–40; Section 6 181
Hutchinson, P. 52

incapacitation 23; *see also* strategic incapacitation
information strategies 23–24
Ingham, H. 224
in-groups 56, 245
insider research 78–80, 83; recruiting gatekeepers 85–86
intelligence gathering 53, 66, 120, 228
interview/s 81; badger cull 91–92; coding 96; dress code 89; EDL march 92–93; ethical considerations 89–91; locations 87–88, 93–95; preparation 86–87; presenting findings 95–96; selecting participants 83–84
Islamophobia 158, 159

Jackson, W. 29, 33, 42, 57, 66, 147, 159, 201, 204, 206, 228, 245, 246
John, T. 25, 26, 33, 106, 113
Johnson, L. 31, 83
Jonathan-Zamir, T. 76
Jones, K. 54, 55, 200
Joyce, P. 18, 20, 41, 188
justice 57, 178; *see also* fairness; procedural justice theory

Kassimeris, G. 159
Kennedy, J. 156
Kilgallon, A. 32, 66–67
King, M. 17, 21, 30, 55, 125
King, M. L. 17
Kirby, S. 76
knowledge: evidence-based policing and 76; insider 83, 242
Koper, C. 75

law enforcement 18
Le Bon, G. 19, 51
leadership, protester 21–22
"left-wing" 162–163, 170, 171
legitimacy 18, 50, 52, 53, 56, 59, 61, 62, 64, 66, 134, 223, 225, 227, 241; badger cull 118–121; EDL march 174–178; fairness and 57–60; of media reporting 177; power and 57–58
Lewis, P. 83
liaison officer 10, 63–64, 66, 92, 130, 133, 145, 149–150, 204, 217, 243, 244; *see also* Police Liaison Teams (PLT)
liaison-based approach 50, 53
liberty 32–33
limited rights 36
Lind, E. 58, 225
Liverpool 154; *see also* English Defence League (EDL) march
Liverpool Echo, "Faces of hate: 8 pictures that sum up the EDL" 157
Louis, M. 79
Luft, J. 224
Lum, C. 75
Lydon, D. 60
Mansley, D. 16, 19, 26, 30, 33, 127, 138, 244

Martin, D. 58, 88
May, T. 29
McCarthy, J. 19, 20, 41
McComish, J. 77
McPhail, C. 19, 20, 41
Mead, D. 31, 192
Meadowcroft, J. 158
media 31–32, 54, 163, 166–167; legitimacy 177; *see also* social media
Meleagrou-Hitchens, A. 158–159, 166
Merkens, H. 85
Merseyside Police, 85
Metropolitan Police Service (MPS) 82, 92, 155, 156–157, 160, 164,–165, 196, 229
"Middle England" group 107–108
Milani, J. 57
militarised police 28–29
Mills, G. 33
Mobbs, P. 30, 33, 138
Monk, H. 29, 33, 42, 66, 147, 201, 204, 206, 228, 245, 246
Moran, M. 55
Morrow, E. 158
Mullings, B. 80
Murphy, K. 59
Myers-Montgomery, J. 28–29
Myhill, A. 56, 60

National Action 155, 157; *see also* English Defence League (EDL) march
National Policing Improvement Agency (NPIA) 7–8, 78

negotiated management 19–22, 24, 41, 53, 67, 125, 236, 246; communication between police and protesters 41–42; Police Liaison Teams (PLT) 213–214
neighborhood policing 27, 56
NetPol 9–10
New York Police Department (NYPD) 25, 30
Newburn, T. 55–56
Neyroud, P. 39, 40, 192, 230
Nind, M. 84
no surprises approach 7
Noakes, J. 22–23, 30
non-engagement 147–149, 201–205
North West Infidels 155, 157; *see also* English Defence League (EDL) march
Northern Ireland 31

Oaten, A. 159
O'Byrne, A. 183
Operation Obelisk 8
Oskarsson, M. 41–42
out-groups 52, 56, 61

Palmer, I. 76
Paré, S. 42, 68
Paternoster, R. 57
Patton, M. 83
Pauwels, L. 59
peaceful protest 2, 32–33
Pearson, G. 59–60
persuasive strategies 23–24
Peterson, A. 22, 23, 32, 42, 242
Phythian, R. 76
Pilkington, H. 159, 166
plural policing 26
police and policing 1, 16, 228–230; balancing human rights 32–35, 37, 139–141, 194–198, 230–236; balancing qualified rights 38–40; "broken windows" theory 25; carrot and stick approach 20–21; coercive strategies 23; command and control 25; communication with protesters 41–42; Corporate Social Responsibility (CSR) 26–27; deterrence policy 57; EDL march 164–165, 174–178; *see also* English Defence League (EDL) march; escalated force 18–19, 41; evidence-based 74–77; Family Liaison Officer 8; Forward Intelligence Teams (FIT) 10; hard 26; impartiality 127–129, 196–197; information strategies 23–24;

intelligence gathering 53, 66, 120; legitimacy 53, 60–61, 181; liaison with others 217–220; liaison with protest groups 211–215; liaison-based approach 53; militarised 28–29; negotiated management 19–22, 24, 41, 53, 125; neighborhood 27, 56; no surprises approach 7; persuasive strategies 23–24; plural 26; political influences 30–32, 125–127, 181–183; professionalism 26; Protestor Liaison Officers (PLO) 8; public order training 7–8; recommendations 245–249; response to the EDL march 161–163; self- 61, 64, 66, 215–217; state power 127–129, 184; strategic facilitation 27–28, 62, 124–125; strategic incapacitation 22–27, 61; style 18; trust with all interested parties 228–230; trust with protest groups 223–228; *see also* Devon and Cornwall Police; dialogical approach; Merseyside Police
Police Liaison Teams (PLT) 1–2, 11, 28, 36, 50, 53, 63–68, 82, 107, 109, 210–211, 240, 251; badger cull protest 111, 112, 114–115, 119–120, 123–125; Bronze 133, 186; criticisms 9–10; dialogue during the cull 135–136; EDL march 160–161, 176–178, 184; EDL march, dialogue process 178–180, 189–191; non-engagement 147–149, 201–205; officer selection 130–132, 242–243; point of contact 198–199; post-cull dialogue 136–137; pre-emptive dialogue 133–135, 186–189; relationship building 143–145, 199–200; role of 129–130, 184–185; selection 130–132, 184–185; Stockholm syndrome 132–133, 186; two-way communication 145–147
policy: deterrence 57; notifiable association 89; *see also* badger cull
political influences on policing 30–32; badger cull 125–127; English Defence League (EDL) march 181–183
positive obligations 39
Posner, P. 78
post-event dialogue 136–137, 190–191
Potter, B., *The Tale of Mr. Tod* 102
Poulton, E. 89
power 20, 30, 94, 95; imbalances 39, 74, 96; legitimacy and 57–58; state 31, 127–129, 184

pre-emptive dialogue 133–135, 186–189
procedural justice theory 50, 56–57, 62, 132, 210, 225, 237, 241, 248–249; group engagement 58–59; legitimacy 60–61; social engagement 60
professionalism, police 26
protesters 17–18; communication with police 41–42; English Defence League (EDL) march 173–174; full-time 25, 113; leadership 21–22; nomenclature 114–115; transgressive 22–23, 27
Protestor Liaison Officers (PLO) 8–9
protest/s 1, 32, 50; balancing human rights 32–35; Barton Moss 9; Black Lives Matter 28; definitions 16–17; EcoStream 37–38; environmental 25, 33; G8 summit 24; G20 London summit 5–6; legitimacy 18, 56, 66; peaceful 2; single-issue 22; *see also* badger cull; English Defence League (EDL) march
Public Order Management System (POMS) 19–20
public order training 7–8, 26
qualified rights 36–37; balancing 38–40
qualitative research 77

Quinton, P. 56, 60

Raab, D. 34
Radburn, M. 66
Ratliff, T. 17
Reclaim the Streets 25
red zones 23–24
Redekop, V. 42, 68
Reform Section 5 17
Reicher, S. 51–53, 61
Reiner, R. 22
Reiter, R. 18, 20, 22, 23, 30, 32, 41, 42, 55, 125, 136, 181
relational sociological approach 250
relationship building 142–145, 199–200, 206, 242, 248; trust and 223–230
research: ethical considerations 89–91; identifying case studies 81–83; insider 78–80, 83; interviews 81; qualitative 75–77; recruiting gatekeepers 84–86; selecting participants 83–84; self-ethnographic study 78–79; *see also* evidence-based policing (EBP); interviews
Rhodes, R. 76
Ribbens, J. 87

right to assembly 20, 181; lockdowns 31; *see also* human rights
riots 55; Scarman report 19
Ritchie, J. 83
Roadnight, J. 9, 66
Robinson, T. 158
Rogers, C. 26–27
Rosie, M. 2, 22, 24, 32–33, 51, 55, 63, 64, 130, 185, 186, 215
Rudd, A. 155

Sarah Everard vigil 9
Scarman report 19
Schweingruber, D. 19, 20, 41
Scothern, M. 65, 119, 121
Scotland 24
Scottish Dawn 155; *see also* English Defence League (EDL) march
Seidman, I. 81
self-ethnographic study 78–79
self-policing 61, 64, 66, 217; badger cull protest 215–216; EDL march 215; EDL march, business participants 220–221; farming community 220
Sherman, L. 75, 76
Shively, G. 83
Sinek, S. 204
single-issue protest 22
"Smash NATO" demonstrations 27
Smith, J. 105, 187
Smith M. 10, 81
social engagement, procedural justice theory 60
social identity theory 51–52, 59
social media 32
South Yorkshire Police (SYP): Police Liaison Teams (PLT) 63–64
Spelman, C. 103
Stake, R. 81
stakeholder group meetings 179–180
Stanko, E. 76
state power 31; police and 127–129, 184
Steinke, I. 77
Stephenson, P. 6, 158
Stockholm syndrome 132–133, 150, 186
Stott, C. 2, 7, 51–53, 59–60, 63–66, 75, 119, 121, 130, 185, 186, 215
strategic facilitation 27–28, 62; badger cull 124–125
strategic incapacitation 22–27, 61
student demonstrations 52
style, policing 18

Sunshine, J. 57, 59, 215
surveillance 24
Sweden 41; dialogue officer 4; Gothenburg Committee 3–4; US-EU Summit of leaders of the United States and European Union 2–3

Tactical Tasking and Co-ordination Group (TTCG) 8
Tajfel, H. 51
Tankebe, J. 58
training 26, 50, 78; crowd psychology 51; police 7; Police Liaison Team (PLT) 9, 66; Protestor Liaison Officer (PLO) 8–9; public order 7–8, 26
transgressive protesters 22–23, 27
transnational protests 22
transparency 224–225
trust 42, 50, 58, 67, 81, 84, 101, 119, 121, 178, 204, 205, 241, 245, 248; empathy and 224; between police and all interested parties 228–230; between police and protest groups 223–228; transparency and 224–225
Turner, R. 16–17
two-way communication 145–147
Tyler, T. 57–59, 215, 225
unions 172

Unite Against Fascism (UAF) 155–157, 161–162; *see also* English Defence League (EDL) march
United Kingdom: 1980 Green Paper 19; Badgers Act (1973) 103; Criminal Justice and Public Order Act (1994) 175–176; Department for Environment, Food and Rural Affairs (DEFRA) 102, 103, 105; Family Liaison Officer 8; Forward Intelligence Teams (FIT) 10; G20 London summit protests 5–6; Her Majesty's Inspectorate of Constabulary (HMIC) 1, 26; *see also* Her Majesty's Inspectorate of Constabulary (HMIC); Her Majesty's Inspectorate of Constabulary and Fire and Rescue Services (HMICFRS) 33–34; House of Commons Home Affairs Committee 6; Human Rights Act (1998) 1, 16, 34–36, 68, 138, 155; *see also* Human Rights Act (UK, 1998); National Policing Improvement Agency (NPIA) 7–8; Police, Crime, Sentencing and Courts Act (2022) 34; Police Liaison Teams (PLT) 9; Police Order Act (1986) 39; Protection of Badgers Act (1992) 103; Protestor Liaison Officers (PLO) 8–9; Public Order Act (1986) 17, 19–21, 177, 215; Reform Section 5 17; Scarman report 19; Terrorism Act (2000) 155; Wildlife and Countryside Act (1981) 103; *see also* badger cull; College of Policing; English Defence League (EDL) march; Police Liaison Teams (PLT)
United States 28
Universal Declaration of Human Rights 35
US-EU Summit of leaders of the United States and European Union 2–3

value of a dialogical approach: badger cull 211–212, 217–218; EDL march 212–215, 218–220; liaison with others 217–220; liaison with protest groups 211–215
Van Damme, A. 59
Villiers, P. 17, 18, 22
Vitale, A. 24–25, 33
von Kardorff, E. 77

Waddington, D. 2, 27, 28, 41, 42, 53, 55, 64–65, 121, 125, 132, 135, 144, 242
Waddington, P. 18, 20, 21, 30, 32, 41, 50, 54–55, 125, 188, 242
Wahlström, M. 3, 4, 41–42
Wain, N. 20, 41, 188
Wanat, C. 85
water cannon 29
Watson, A. 58, 134, 186, 226
Wegener, C. 80
Weitzer, R. 31
Wells, H. 60
Werren, C. 24
West, O. 66
Willis, A. 18, 22, 35
Wood, L. 28, 30, 33, 42, 181
Woodward, K. 79

Yates, J. 89

zero-tolerance 25